Mindful
Body
Calisthenics

The Ultimate
Bodyweight Training
Guide To Build Muscle,
Lose Weight, and
Increase Flexibility
3 Books In 1

Daily Jay

any losses, direct or indirect, that are incurred as a result of the use of the information contained within this document, including, but not limited to, errors, omissions, or inaccuracies.

Table of Contents

Book 1

Book 2

Book 3

BEFORE YOU START READING! I have this special bonus that I am going to reveal to you:

https://bit.ly/DailyJayyy

Up there is a link that will direct you to a website where you can get a fitness calculator. I actually used this exact same calculator to get an estimate and track how many calories I needed to eat in a day to achieve the body of my dreams when I was just getting started in my journey.

Just insert your name and email and it will be sent straight to your email.

Book 1

Calisthenics for Beginners

Get in Shape and Stay in Shape for the Rest of your Life without Going to the Gym

Introduction

"Taking care of your body, no matter what your age, is an investment."

-Oprah Winfrey

These simple words, spoken by Oprah Winfrey, are profound and wise. It is never too late to start taking care of your body. Whatever effort you put in is a huge investment with incredible returns. You improve your overall looks, your health, your quality of life, and your relationships with everyone you interact with. Maintaining your body completely changes how you look at the world. Your mindset changes, and you see the positive in situations where before you saw only the negative.

The goal of this book is to provide you with the necessary tools to begin calisthenics with confidence, backed up by facts and not people's opinions. This book will show you that you can have the body you have always wanted, without spending hours in the gym each day, nor spending a fortune on exercise machines and equipment.

The world is currently experiencing a pandemic that impacts every human on the planet. If we learn only one thing from this, it is that we must face the critical importance of taking care of our bodies even when we are unable to go to the gym or participate in the sports we love. This is the goal of this book, to show you that it can be done, and how to do it.

Why Specifically Calisthenics

Calisthenics is not only for super fit athletes who wish to maintain their ripped looks and fitness levels. It is accessible to the majority of people of different ages, fitness levels, and different states of health. Today there are specially developed calisthenics routines for seniors as well as school-going children, and it places no limitations on gender.

In 2017, the Sport and Exercise Sciences Research Unit at the University of Palermo, Italy published the results of a study called 'The effects of a calisthenics training intervention on posture, strength, and body composition." The study concluded that calisthenics training is a "feasible and effective training solution to improve posture, strength, and body composition without the use of any major training equipment".

Calisthenics differs from other forms of exercise and appeals to people for many reasons, such as the following:

- Anyone who is out of shape and wants to change how they feel and look can do calisthenics.
- You can do this form of exercise literally anywhere and at any time. You are not bound to a specific place or time frame.
- People who experience health problems and want to change to a healthier lifestyle can do calisthenics.
- Anyone who does not like going to gyms and working out on all the machines available there will enjoy calisthenics.
- Every person who prefers their workout routines to be natural and free, and not dependent on any specific piece of equipment, without which they would be unable to exercise, will prefer calisthenics.
- People who want to use their own body weight to increase their strength, muscle tone, and development can use calisthenics.
- Anyone who has fallen into a rut with their current training program of monotonous exercise workouts will like calisthenics.

What Do You Stand to Gain?

Calisthenics brings literally endless gains into your life, and we will go into detail about the specific benefits in Chapter 5. The gains calisthenics will bring you fall into four broad categories that each cover a very wide range of benefits.

Endurance

Consistently practicing calisthenics routines builds your muscular endurance, and over time will build up your body's resistance to muscular fatigue. As you progress with calisthenics, you will keep challenging your body until you involve the muscles throughout your entire body in building endurance. The muscular endurance of your cardiovascular system also builds through calisthenics routines, which is a huge health benefit for anyone.

Strength

Calisthenics is associated with building muscle strength, which it does incredibly well. Often, however, people do not realize how much calisthenics also strengthens your joints and contributes to bone health. This is exactly why the US Military uses calisthenics in their basic training for the building of strength, and also to help prevent injuries. Using calisthenics for building muscular strength is much gentler than, for instance, weight lifting, which takes a toll on the body with greater wear and tear.

Flexibility

When you start out with calisthenics, you become acutely aware of stiffness and tightness in body parts you always considered to be very flexible. This is where the benefits of calisthenics workouts really kick in, as these exercises have the full range of movements that your body should be capable of. The longer you do calisthenics, the more flexible your entire body becomes as your strength increases and your body adapts.

Changes to the Metabolic Rate

Calisthenics strength training builds muscle mass, and at the same time tones every part of your body. This means that your resting metabolic rate will be higher than before. Thus, your body continues to burn more calories during the resting phase and throughout your entire day. The second way your metabolic rate changes is that when you consistently do calisthenics workouts, your heart rate rises. This represents aerobic exercises. Aerobics is recognized by doctors worldwide as one of the most effective ways for the human body to burn calories. Calisthenics, therefore, addresses the problem of burning excess fat and calories from two directions, by changing your metabolic rate to work more effectively.

Questions All Beginners Have

It is natural for beginners to have questions and uncertainties when they are about to embark not only on a new exercise regime, but in reality, on a major change in lifestyle and mindset.

This book tackles the important questions and provides insightful answers and guidance for questions such as the following:

- Is there a greater risk of injuries without gym staff to assist and guide me?

- Will calisthenics definitely be able to address my personal goal or issue?

- Will I be able to see results quickly?

- How will I stay motivated in the long term?

- Does science back up the principles of calisthenics?

- What equipment will I need to buy?

- Will I keep on seeing results after the initial changes?

- What benefits will I gain from doing calisthenics?

- What are the dos and don'ts of calisthenics training?

- Is there an average amount of weight that can be lost through practicing calisthenics?

- What are the common mistakes people make?

Chapter 1

Mindset

Who Is This Book for?

What is Calisthenics?

Calisthenics is a type of exercise that uses the body's own weight to gain strength. It improves your muscular volume and shapes your body for proper athletic form, depending on your own natural features and tendencies. Calisthenics is a fitness form that uses body weight and gravity to build strength and promote health. The term originated from the Greek words "Kalos" and "Stenos", the first word meaning beauty, and the second meaning strength

(Thomas et. al., 2017). Aside from bodybuilding, it's commonly used with school children, in gymnastics, and in outdoor practicing.

One of the famous calisthenics exercisers is Hannibal Lanham (Hannibal for King), who attracted the attention of millions to this discipline by showing his skills in parks in Queens, New York.

Kenneth Gallarzo, the co-founder of the World Calisthenics Organization (WCO), started off as a fitness trainer. He became interested in calisthenics after seeing another person in the gym doing a fascinating exercise he had never seen before. After researching calisthenics, Gallarzo came to understand that this form of exercise is a great foundation for other strength-gaining disciplines.

However, calisthenics is more than just another commercial exercise program that promises a lot and delivers little. Studies showed that calisthenics effectively improves body composition, strength, and posture (Thomas et. al., 2017). The recorded benefits of calisthenics are numerous, and will be explained in more detail as we go.

How You Benefit from Calisthenics

Your body isn't made to only move forwards and backwards. Calisthenics adds rotations, twists, pushes, pulls, squats, and jumps to your movement.

Calisthenics exercises require more muscle use for you to build muscle when done at a moderate and slow rate, and more calorie burning when done at a slower rate with more cardio training. This is because higher muscle engagement also increases fat burning. Practicing calisthenics will help you become stronger, fitter, and slimmer. Aside from this, there are more proven benefits of these exercises:

- **Flexibility.** As you don't need equipment for calisthenics, you can exercise anywhere and anytime. You don't have to commit to a certain schedule or make the time to go to the gym, which is great if you're busy, or if having a constant schedule (although recommended) is challenging for you. Instead, you should dedicate a space for freestyle training, like a functional frame or Swedish ladders. As you can see, the only commitment with calisthenics is to plan well and actually do the exercises with discipline the right way.

- **Naturally toned shape.** Calisthenics will help you burn fat, increase your power and strength, and strengthen your entire body. It will boost the secretion of endorphins and help you feel more energized. Calisthenics trains multiple groups of muscles at the same time. For example, push-ups train the spine, abdominal muscles, chest, and arms. This way, your body will look more proportionate, and you won't worry about balancing your exercises. Your body will shape and sculpt in a natural way that fits your shape and body type, with muscles being toned to their optimum level.

- **Mindset change.** Calisthenics helps you connect with your body and improve physical awareness. Repetitive workouts can become boring, so exercisers lose motivation. However, calisthenics, while including repetitions, changes its types of exercises and exercise routines. Once you master one skill level, you will move on to the next one. Your challenges increase as your body shapes up.

- Last, but not least, calisthenics prevents physical injury while exercising. This is because the exercises don't allow you to overstrain a certain muscle type.

Calisthenics sound much more appealing with the idea of not having to pay for a gym membership, pump iron, and schedule around your weekly workouts. At the same time, doing exercises that shape your body naturally is healthier and has greater psychological and health benefits than pumping iron.

How to Start with Calisthenics

So, how should you begin? The following sections will discuss some of the basic principles of calisthenics and the bare essentials you need for a successful body transformation.

Calisthenics is all about exploring your natural potential and pushing boundaries further and further, in a way suitable to your individual body type and shape. Surpassing one level after the other will eventually give you superb strength, and will become a fun way to exercise. Bodyweight training with calisthenics is often difficult to start. Not knowing things like where and how to exercise and how to get going can be frustrating, but a proper mindset and knowledge of exercise routines should help you start.

As you decide to start with calisthenics, you'll probably be confused about how to start correctly. Should you simply do more planks and pushups? Or is there a bit more to organizing your workouts for the best result? The rule of thumb is that most beginners make some mistakes, but they are easy to correct. Exercises are learned with practice, and results become more visible the more you exercise. To start, focus on building a proper mindset for learning and practicing calisthenics.

Build Foundations: Earn Your Right to Progress

Earning your right to progress means first building foundations for long-term exercise. Most people who are just starting with calisthenics get addicted to the initial progress. You're trying new routines and getting better by the day. Your brain and body are being stimulated, and you naturally want to go further and further. Still, it is important to stay focused on your body and have a clear direction to follow. Upscaling will start to become challenging at one point or another, and unless you're ready to confront these roadblocks, your motivation might suffer.

So, how do you start with calisthenics? Although you probably got to know this concept by seeing exercisers doing advanced movements, as a beginner, you'll have to start slowly, for the sake of both your health and safety. Ideally, you'll start with basic exercises like:

- **Press-up.** This exercise can be adjusted for beginners. To do a beginner press-up, do pressups with your hands on a bench and feet on the ground. Once you master this exercise, you can move on to regular press-ups. For starters, do up to 20 repetitions.

- **Dips.** After you're able to do 20 press-ups, you can start exercising with dips. To perform a dip, pull yourself up on a bar and bend your elbows to dip down, then straighten back up.

- Squats, lunges, and planks.

- **Rows.** This is an interesting exercise where you hold onto a bar, facing toward your chest, and lean backward, with feet firmly on the ground. You should make sure that your back is as parallel with the floor as possible.

Don't Compare Yourself to Others

The second rule is to never compare yourself with others. Comparing yourself to those who started before you and have a long background with calisthenics can ruin your motivation. Every person progresses at their own pace and in their own time. On top of that, everyone's body is different. Your age, health, training history, and how athletic you are now will determine your beginner stage and your direction with exercise. Instead of comparing other people's journey's with your own, be inspired by them and use their progress as motivation for where you want to be.

Combine Strength with Movement

The balance between strength and movement is the key to building natural, lasting strength and vitality. Most people focus only on strength, as it is the most popular goal to pursue. However, as you'll learn, the manifestation of your strength and what you're able to do with it doesn't only rely on your muscles. Instead, balance, flexibility, coordination, and mental clarity gained through balanced exercise will improve both your looks and physical performance. The balance between movement and strength gives you flexibility and mobility in your joints. For starters, if you're having problems with range of motion, which is often the case with those who live a sedentary lifestyle, the following overhead positions will help you improve:

- **Handstands.** Handstands are an exercise that increases body control and strength. Unless you have a background in fitness, you'll only be able to do them once you've set a basis with regular beginner exercises. Notably, risk from injury while attempting handstands as a beginner is low, and your hands won't be able to support your body unless your current physical ability allows it. There are many variations of this exercise, and beginners are best off with the so called "line handstand", in which you keep your body in a straight line. This position will open your shoulders, strengthen and tighten your core, and protect your back. Long-term, this exercise will help you build skills that are beneficial for other exercises.

- **Human flags.** Feel like turning yourself into a human flag? The good news is that you'll have a fun time doing it, even if you fail. While this exercise also isn't the most beginner-friendly, attempting a beginner version is sure to get your blood running, which is always a good thing. Before you start training to perform a human flag, you will have to be able to hold a single arm hang for 30 seconds, do four sets of 10 pull-ups, and hold a side plank for 45 seconds. This is the very basis of the training, after which you'll train by doing elbow side planks, reach side planks, inclined side planks (five sets of 45 seconds on each side), hanging hip hikers, and pike shoulder push-ups (15-20 repetitions for a half-minute).

Trust Your Body

Given that calisthenics exercises use only the strength and movement of your body, your brain will prevent you from injuring yourself by limiting the movements that are overstraining. You won't be able to use the muscles that are too tight, nor make movements that are too much for your joints to handle, helping you prevent injury and learn how to listen to your body. Moving according to your own body characteristics and possibilities helps you create a more beautiful shape and use your strength, instead of restricting it.

Working with your bodyweight is both one of the biggest advantages and one of the greatest challenges of calisthenics. However, it takes some time to understand how the body adapts and grows from creating resistance on its own. With calisthenics, your body becomes its own weight. As it grows and increases in weight, so does the resistance. As you can see, this is a never-ending process with endless possibilities to advance.

Developing calisthenics skills will require taking good care of your joints. They will be more strained as you exercise harder. Range of motion and the strain put on your connective tissues will increase as you start developing your calisthenics skills. For example, when you do pushups with your initial weight, you'll be working with an easier load, compared to increased body weight after some time spent growing your muscles. This will put extra strain on your joints, but they'll take longer to adapt to this change. This is because your ligaments and tendons don't get the same amount of blood flow as your muscles.

Focus on Core Alignment

Traditional workouts use machines and other equipment, but calisthenics requires proper body alignment to support your body weight, and for the biggest benefits. Focusing on body alignment requires working your core every time you exercise. To use your core correctly, you should follow the rules that will be explained further in the book to control your body alignment.

Your shoulders give the biggest motion range and allow different movements. However, their stability needs improvement through consistent exercise. Shoulder exercises should be one of your biggest priorities. Shoulder setting and pushing, as well as pulling will be important. Practicing opposing motions helps stabilize your motions.

Balancing your hands is another important aspect of calisthenics. For this, you should practice frog stands in the beginning, and then move on to tiger bends, handstands, elbow levers, and other more challenging exercises.

At the end of the day, your journey should be fun and inspiring. Boredom is a sign that you should switch routines and include new, more challenging exercises. You've now learned what calisthenics is all about, and what you need to do before you start training. But wait! It's not yet time to start doing any exercises. There's still a lot for you to learn for a well-planned, methodical exercise regimen and diet that will produce healthy, visible results. The next chapter will shed more light on calisthenics principles to follow for healthy and safe exercise.

Chapter 2

Calisthenics Principles

Now that you know what calisthenics is and the advantages over weight lifting, we will discuss calisthenics principles in more detail. Principles in calisthenics show you how to arrange your workouts and specific exercises to get to the best result, and also how to overcome some of the challenges of this training concept. There are numerous exercise programs out there, each designed to produce maximum results for different groups and types of exercisers. However, for any training program to work, one must acknowledge the individual characteristics of each person. Your exercise program will depend on your individual goals and body characteristics. For example, if you want to increase strength, you'll have a different exercise program than if you worked to increase muscle definition. All of this is also affected by your health and previous experience with training, and also by how much time you can devote to exercise. Following general principles when exercising will help you design a more effective exercise program and achieve better results.

When you embrace calisthenics, your whole lifestyle changes. As with any changes, you need to build on strong foundations for success and sustainability in the long run. Calisthenics is not just exercising; it becomes a way of life.

In this chapter, we will go through the key or foundational principles of calisthenics. We will define the most common terminology, specific problems everyone who practices calisthenics faces, and how to resolve it. We will also work through the basic rules and focal points each beginner needs to know and understand. The three basic principles of exercise that apply to anyone, regardless of their skill level, include:

Overload

This principle states that adaptation will happen when your body is exposed to more strain or stress than normal. When you overload your body with higher performance and increased physical strain, it will improve its performance to meet these demands. In this sense, overload is a stimulus, and a much-needed one to see results when exercising. Without it, you'd only see mild to moderate improvements.

Your body will adapt to stresses put upon it to handle it better every time, meaning it will make your muscles bigger and bigger. These changes are even visible on a cellular level, with improved cardiovascular performance in those who exercise frequently and intensely. This is how your levels of physical fitness increase, which manifests in faster and better physical performance, and bigger, stronger, better-defined muscles. Below is how you can manipulate overload to generate desired results.

How often do you exercise? Frequency introduces regularity to your exercise program. The rule of thumb is that periods of exercise are followed by periods of recovery. It balances the stress out, and allows your body to heal from the strain and adapt to the new circumstances, which is vital if you want to see any results. Periods of training should be followed by periods of recovery for you to see results, and both of these are essential. Both training and recovery require adequate nutrition and quality sleep. While a proper diet supplies enough fuel for exercise, quality sleep helps your body heal and recover.

The intensity of exercise is also important. You will need an optimum balance in the intensity of exercise to generate enough stress and achieve results, but not too much to burn out or injure yourself. The rule is that the intensity increases by either increasing resistance, or increasing the number of repetitions. However, keep in mind that too many repetitions may get in the way of building strength. Instead, you can add exercises, shuffle exercise modes, or change the tempo to increase the intensity of your workouts.

Exercise duration depends on exercise intensity. It's recommended for more intense exercises to be performed for shorter amounts of time, and less intense ones for longer. This will give you enough intensity without overload.

SAID Principle

The SAID principle stands for Specific Adaptation to Imposed Demands. This principle dictates targeting specific goals or activities to improve skills. This principle states that the type of adaptation that will occur from the exercise depends on the type of stress placed upon a particular part of the body, a muscle, or a muscle group. To achieve your goals with exercise, you'll choose the kind of exercises you do based on the result you're trying to achieve. One example of differing results is wanting to become a fast runner, versus wanting to lose weight and improve health. The first goal will be best achieved with outdoor sprinting, while the second will need a focus on cardio exercise, body strength, and lifestyle changes. Simply put, your training sessions should align with your goals.

SAID also means that the human body has the ability to adapt when neurological and biomechanical demands are imposed on it. Thus, you need to work smarter instead of working harder blindly. The SAID principle is your guideline.

- **Specific:** Do not choose your activities randomly. Choose science-based activities that have been proven to work.

- **Adaptation to**: Be very clear about what adaptation you want to happen during this phase of training.

- **Imposed:** Activities must be performed consistently over a specific time frame.

- **Demands:** Perform your chosen activity(s) with sufficient intensity to cause the adaptation you desire, while performing the activity correctly and safely.

Progressive Overload

The principle of progressive overload means that you gradually and continuously increase the demands that you place on your entire musculoskeletal system. Doing this helps you to gain strength, endurance, and muscle size. So, in order to gain strength and develop muscles, you have to keep making your muscles work harder than they did before. So, once your muscles get used to, for example, lifting a specific weight or doing a specific exercise, you will then increase the weight or increase the reps and sets to make your muscles work harder again.

Your exercise will have to become progressively more difficult to achieve harder performance levels. Unless you increase the intensity of exercise progressively, you will reach a plateau. Good results will require progressive overload, and a significant transformation will require long, dedicated work. The basic resistance exercises can be broken down into:

- **Multi-joint exercises**, also known as core exercises, like squats. These exercises will require stabilizing your torso to keep your spine in a neutral position. They are also called structural exercises. A squat, for example, includes stress placed on the spine, and requires engaging core muscles to keep it stabilized. It also engages ankle, hip, and knee joints and puts a strain on the gluteus maximus, quadriceps, and hamstring muscles.

- Core exercises can be further broken down by increasing movement speed. The so-called explosive, or power exercises are done at higher speeds.

- **Single-joint exercises**, or assistance exercises. These exercises engage only one primary joint and recruit either one small or one large muscle group.

Leverage Training: Body vs. Machines

Using your own bodyweight to exercise, instead of machines, is the most natural and practical way to exercise. Body leverage training has become extremely popular because it is so functional, and because you can do it anywhere, at any time, and alone or in a group.

Reps and Sets

Below are the number of reps and sets you need to do during leverage training to fit your specific goals.

- Strength: 5-8 reps

- Power: 2-4 reps

- Endurance: 15-20 reps

- Hypertrophy: 8-12 reps

Resistance

Resistance exercises mean that you use an external form of resistance to contract your muscles for toning, strengthening, building mass, and endurance training. The great part is that you do not need gym machines to achieve this with calisthenics. You can use your own body weight or a set of resistance bands, or even grab a few tins of food off the pantry shelf. Basically, anything that is handy to make your muscles contract will work.

Good examples of calisthenics resistance training tools are:

- **Resistance bands.** These provide great resistance when stretched, for example, around arms or legs.

- **Any form of suspension equipment.**

Suspension bars and rings, or even a sturdy tree branch will do. The suspension uses your own body weight and gravity to perform the exercises.

- **Free weights**, with the classical equipment for strength training being kettlebells, dumbbells, and barbells, but a couple of sandbags work just as well.

- **Medicine balls** are used to great effect for resistance training and are suitable for all ages and levels of fitness.

- **Bodyweight only**. Getting into shape and building a great physique does not depend on a gym and all the machines lined up there. All it really takes is you using your own body weight and perseverance. You can do chin-ups, squats, and push-ups anywhere and anytime, and you don't need a gym membership for this. Bodyweight resistance training works great when you travel, whether for work or for fun, and you don't need to drag bags full of bulky equipment around with you.

Top Three Problems and How to Resolve Them

All beginners face three problems, or drawbacks, when they start their calisthenics journey. That said, it is not the end of the world, as the answer is to take the problems on board, then find the solution and implement it.

Freedom

Yes, it does sound strange, but the freedom that calisthenics gives people is also a drawback. You are not bound to be at the gym and you can do your workout anywhere. You are also not bound by a time schedule and you are not booking time on equipment. For some people, this is not good because they struggle without a specific routine. This could lead to inconsistency in doing their workouts regularly. The other end of the scale is also a possibility, as you can work out literally anywhere and anytime, so you might fall into the trap of doing too much, too often.

Variety

The saying that variety is the spice of life is truly correct. For example, there are 21 different ways to do push-ups, and if you are only familiar with two or three ways to do them, your workout routines will become boring. It is important to bring variety into your workouts because once boredom sets in, it could lead to demotivation.

Here again, you could be at the other end of the scale, where you want to try every possible variation of each exercise. This means you are not focusing on any single type of exercise, but randomly working out. This will negatively impact the path you wish your progression to follow. Yes, it can be confusing for beginners, but as with everything in life, you must find a good balance to keep you motivated and on the path you chose.

Simplicity

The very simplicity of calisthenics can be a drawback for some people. They find it difficult to deal with plateaus that might last for a long while, or they become bored with following a set workout plan. Others feel that, unless they use tools and equipment, they are not making noticeable progress. Should you find that you are getting bored, it is time to make some changes to your workout plan.

The Solutions to These Problems

To resolve the above problems, you need to come up with a disciplined and strict workout plan to keep you focused and always pushing forward.

Create a workout routine from where you are now, with the focus on where you want to be.

Work out a plan on paper or on your computer, and print it out. It is important to have a visual reminder of what your goals are and which exercise routines will push you to achieve those goals.

Make sure that you include your workout session in your daily calendar, at a convenient time for you.

These actions will sharpen your focus and also prevent you from doing too much or too little.

Key Rules and Focal Points

Throughout this book, we will repeat this: calisthenics is more than just physical exercises. It is a mind and body experience. As you master your own body, your mind plays a very large part in this for you, in order to reap all the benefits of calisthenics. It is therefore very important to bring your mind and body into balance when you start out with calisthenics.

Patience and Consistency

Most people do not have an overabundance of patience in whatever they do. They want to get it done and see the results ASAP. Two words each beginner must keep in mind at all times are patience and consistency. Without cultivating patience in your workouts and working hard, you will not achieve the results you strive for. Your workouts will become inconsistent when you want instant results, as you will become despondent. The key is patience and keeping at it.

No Cheating

There are no quick fixes and shortcuts when you do your workouts. Your body is an incredible biological machine designed to do an amazing range of different forms of motion. To achieve your goals and reap the lifelong benefits of calisthenics, you need to focus on doing the full range of motion that your body is capable of. Cheating and trying to take shortcuts is futile; you are only cheating yourself. Focus on doing each exercise to perfection, and do this every time you do a workout. Don't cheat yourself. You are worth putting in the full effort every time.

Set Realistic Goals

When you start out with calisthenics, everything is new, and you see improvements with every workout. This is a very exciting time, and you have all the right to enjoy this. Over time, though, as your body becomes fitter and stronger, your rate of improvement will slow down. This is natural, and to avoid disappointment you need to set realistic goals of what you want to achieve in a logically achievable workout plan.

Stop Comparing Yourself to Others

As a beginner, you will be doing generalized workouts. This is how it should be. Through generalization, you learn and find out whether you want to progress to be a specialist. For example, you might pick a focus and specialize in handstand routines. Do not compare yourself to anyone, especially not anyone who has been doing calisthenics for a long time and who specializes in it, because you put undue pressure on yourself. As a generalist, you'll do a large variety of workouts, whereas a specialist only focuses on his or her specialty. Your progress will be slower because your focus is much wider, and this is normal and nothing to worry about.

Use social media logically to get more information and ideas. Do not compare yourself to the celebrities posting and boasting about their progress and their achievements. Yes, acknowledge that these people work hard to achieve their personal goals, because that is true, but do not use them as the yardstick for your own progress. Social media often does much more harm to beginners, and even to more experienced practitioners of calisthenics. The whole celebrity hype can erode people's self-worth. Your goal with calisthenics is to be the best you possible, not strive to be a copy of anyone else.

Maintain Diet and Lean Muscle Weight

Your diet plays a huge role in your progress with calisthenics. You cannot bulk up through eating junk food, or just enormous quantities of food. It simply does not work this way. You have to strive to achieve and maintain lean muscle weight through a good training program and a balanced diet. Fat body weight cannot replace lean muscle weight. Your food intake and your training program must be in line with the specific objectives you want to achieve.

Proper Training Plan

You must have a properly set up training program worked out for your specific needs and goals. You cannot just stumble along doing random exercises and expect to gain any benefits. Without a training program, you will fall into the trap of just doing what is easiest to do and what comes to mind. You will then do whatever you feel like doing in your daily workout sessions, instead of what you need to do to achieve your goal. Grabbing random exercises for your training will lead to random progress that takes you nowhere.

Create a training program and stick with it for a minimum of 6 weeks before reevaluating your goals. You can then decide whether you wish to continue longer with this specific training program, or move on to another one.

Stomp Your Ego Down

Ego has no place in any form of physical training, and this definitely is the case with calisthenics. This goes for men and women. You cannot allow your ego to rule you. All you will achieve is getting injured. This will set your training back and make it more difficult to achieve your goals. Learn from the countless people who have allowed their egos to short circuit their logic. Stomp your ego flat into the dust and do calisthenics the right way, without overreaching yourself.

Chapter 3

Flexibility and Mobility

Flexibility and mobility are often overlooked in fitness. Diet, muscle strength, definition, weight loss, and other training aspects tend to prevail over paying attention to the mobility of your joints and tendons. However, flexibility and mobility have far greater importance than most people realize. They reduce pain during daily activities, and are important for cardiovascular health. Many suffer from chronic lower back pain, which is caused by the lack of flexibility and mobility in the body, as well as tight hamstrings.

A sedentary lifestyle causes the lower back to become rounded, which affects body weight pressure on the lower back and causes pain. The lack of mobility in your lower back links with reduced productivity and diminished work performance as well.

Studies also found that flexibility is linked to mortality. The less flexible people are, the higher the chance of cardiovascular disease. Both flexibility and mobility refer to the ability of your joints to move through a range of motion. Mobility can also reduce due to tightness in muscles, which doesn't allow proper physical activity and increases the risk of injury. Studies also found that flexibility and mobility exercises should be used as a preventive measure against injury, and not only when the injury occurs.

Flexibility and Mobility Exercises

Working on your mobility will help prevent injuries and increase strength. As a beginner in calisthenics, you're most likely focused on the number of exercises you can do and the repetitions that will create the desired result. While this is understandable, long-term strength and balance require exercising mobility and flexibility. Mobility includes two different aspects of flexibility:

- **Passive flexibility**: Low-stress muscle, tendon, and ligament flexibility, like doing splits on the ground.

- **Dynamic flexibility**: high-stress flexibility in your ligaments, tendons, and muscles. Exercising dynamic flexibility is important to improve fitness ability levels and maintain flexibility under high stress. This requires a high level of strength, as well as exercising ligament and tendon flexibility. Simply put, muscles shouldn't be your only point of focus when exercising. Your tendons and ligaments require the same amount of attention, as they suffer an equal amount of stress when you're exercising, but take longer to recover and adapt.

Regardless of your muscle strength, you can get injured doing mundane daily tasks if your ligaments aren't flexible enough. Poor motility can be corrected with certain stretching exercises designed to improve your flexibility. Although they might appear boring because they don't improve strength and grow muscles, they're necessary for you to stay healthy in the long run. Working with your bodyweight helps this, because your body has an instinct to balance itself and, as said earlier, won't allow you to make movements that will injure it. But what can you do to improve mobility? There are a couple of types of exercises that you can do:

- **Passive stretching**. Shoulder extension exercises include back levers, V sits, and skin the cats. They stretch tight muscles in your shoulders and hands, particularly in your biceps, that get in the way of extending shoulders properly. They will help extend muscles in the backs of your arms and help exercises using weights.

- **Passive shoulder stretches**. Doing exercises with tight shoulders can not only reduce their efficiency, but also lead to tearing muscles and rupturing tendons. Exercises like V sits and German hangs, particularly their advanced versions, will require a lot of shoulder flexibility.

What should your stretches look like? You should start slowly with three sets of one-minute holds, three times each week. After you gain more experience and mobility, you should focus on doing more German hangs (skinning the cat), starting with up to five sets of half minute holds. Once you've mastered beginner stretches, you can move on to do more demanding warm-up exercises, such as:

- **Motion range exercises**. These exercises take joints through full-range motions. The tension doesn't have to be high with these exercises, but they're still essential. These exercises include mobility exercises for shoulders, including the one described below.

- **Shoulder dislocates**. These exercises are simple, and can greatly improve the mobility of your shoulders. To do them, you'll need a wide grip on a light bar or a dowel rod. With arms raised in front of you and extended elbows, maneuver the bar as high and behind your head as possible. The rod should weigh between five and ten pounds. If lighter, the exercise becomes about passive flexibility. Here, you want to engage muscles as well, not just joints and ligaments. As a beginner, you should start with a wider grip and bring your hands closer together as you progress. When you're able to do the exercise with hands only slightly apart from shoulders, you can increase the weight of the rod and go back to exercising the wide grip again. Your mobility will increase as you increase the challenge, and progression will always be done by increasing weight and starting over.

The main focus of this exercise is for you to achieve a full shoulder blade, or scapula, range of motion. Your scapula should protract with your arms extended outwards, and your shoulder blades should stretch. Then, they should retract as you lift your hands and pull them behind your head. Shoulder dislocates aren't speed exercises, and should be done slowly and patiently.

- **Skinning the cats.** Not literally, of course. This exercise mimics the position of the animal in said situation, and it's far less grueling and difficult than it sounds. It's done by hanging from a pull-up bar and raising the body up and in front of you. You should practice doing the movement as far out as possible, then slowly getting back to the start position. The first couple of repetitions might be slow and difficult if you're a beginner, but that's not a problem.

This exercise engages both a lot of strength and a lot of flexibility, and you should be patient with yourself before you're able to produce Instagram-worthy repetitions. Your ability will improve as you repeat the exercise. To practice safely, your shoulder blades should be slightly retracted when you're hanging from the bar, and before you've started the movement. Doing so will help you lift your body more easily to start the movement.

- **Shoulder distractions.** This exercise doesn't bring your shoulders to their full motion range. It stretches ligaments, as it distracts your upper arm bone from your joint capsule. The exercise feels pleasant even with an injury. To do it, you should use a five-to-ten-pound weight and bend over. Rest the non-swinging hand on a chair, and then relax and swing the other arm in a circular motion, both clockwise and counterclockwise. When you do this exercise, synovial fluid lubricates the joint and helps it become more flexible. However, it should be done slowly and patiently. Don't rush to speed or to use a full motion range. The purpose of the exercise is to distract the humerus, improving ligament mobility in your shoulders as a result. There's never too much of this exercise. Ideally, you'll do it every day, and as often as you like.

Mobility exercises are a great warm-up before doing handstands, and should be done in two-minute intervals.

Lacking flexibility can not only limit your movement, but also make you feel stiff and slow. Regardless of strength, a lack of flexibility can become limiting to your performance and even everyday activities. Once you've set a strong foundation with push-ups, pull-ups, and dips, more progression will require more flexibility and mobility. Harder exercises, like the back lever, muscle-up, and L-sits will require adding flexibility exercises to your daily routine. These stretching exercises will make it much easier to practice more advanced moves, for example:

- **Better Front Fold exercises.** These stretches help make handstands, hanging leg raises, Vsits, and L-sits easier. These exercises might look as if they only engage the core, but that's not true at all. They also require posterior chain mobility. Foot folds allow you to fight gravity without adding resistance to your muscles. Tight feet and hamstrings are typically present in beginners, and straightening legs during an Lsit appears impossible, regardless of strength. Muscle strength alone won't secure proper V- and L-sits without flexibility exercises. However, once you focus on exercising your hamstrings and the flexibility of your front fold, the resistance in these areas will reduce. To do these exercises correctly, you should try straightening your legs in a comfortable pike position on the floor. For starters, you can do them with your back rounded, and then flatten the back as you progress with exercises. However, exercises will also require a long warm-up.

Overhead Mobility

Overhead mobility exercises relax the muscles in the back of your arms, your upper back, and your shoulders. Passive stretching exercises will improve your overhead mobility, which will help with upper body exercises like handstands. For this, practice these two exercises:

- **Chin-up dead hang,** which stretches your shoulders with external rotation. A basic dead hang has numerous benefits, from decompressing the spine to stretching arm, back, and core muscles. To do a dead hang, step on a bench and grab a secure overhead bar with both of your hands. Your hands should be shoulder-width apart. Step off the bench and hang onto the bar. Hold a relaxed position for ten seconds and up to a minute, if you can. Return to the bench and repeat up to three times. If your beginner shape doesn't yet tolerate this exercise, you can stay on the bench and stretch by grabbing the bar and lifting your chin up. You can then hang onto the bar with your feet resting on the bench.

- **Hanging cobra**, for which you'll need gymnastic rings. Set the height of the rings to match your chest. Grip the rings with your hands. Sink into the hand position slowly by first falling onto your knees, and then pulling the feet and legs backwards into an extended position. Then, slightly twist, first to the side that feels stiffer, and then to the other side. Hold the position for as long as you can and for as long as it feels good. You can also pull your shoulders up and hold for three to five seconds, and then relax. Give these three to five repetitions, then flip to the other position and repeat. To finish, return to the hanging position with your hands aligned with your shoulders, and head parallel with your hands. Hold for a couple of seconds and then step out of the position. This exercise is also great for those who suffer from lower back pain, as well as anyone who wants to stretch their upper back, hands, chest, and lower abdomen.

Overhead positions in calisthenics, such as with handstands, require a great deal of shoulder mobility. As you already learned, stiff shoulders not only limit your movements, but also increase the risk of injury. Overhead mobility ensures stable positioning of your shoulders when exercising, proper overhead flexion, and the ability to extend your elbows while maintaining the stability of your core and spine. As you can see, all areas and body groups are connected, and one can't function well without the strength and flexibility of the other.

Upper body exercises engage your shoulder blade as well, even when exercises don't directly target shoulders. Because of this, your ability to maintain a strong position largely relies on your shoulder stability and range of motion. You need both shoulder stability and range of motion to avoid slumped body positioning. Here are another three simple exercises you can use to boost your overhead mobility:

- **Shoulder mobilization**. For this exercise, simply circle your shoulder through its entire range of motion. Feel tension and crackling? Then circle away until your scapula rotates smoothly and effortlessly!

- **Active end range**. This time, rotate the shoulder with a fully extended arm, using your full range of motion. This exercise boosts your body alignment when doing handstands.

- **Shoulder extension with a band**. This beginner-friendly exercise is easy and fun, and will feel great if your body suffers the consequences of spending work hours behind the desk. Simply stand on a band and grab the upper part of the band with your hands. Extend the band over your head, with hands aligned with your shoulders. From there, stretch the shoulders upwards as much as you can, then bring them down, and then again up so that the shoulders are in a shrugged position. This exercise also engages your lower abdomen and lower back muscles, gently stretches the muscles of your arms, and if you do it while standing on your toes, also stretches lower body muscles and joints.

Chapter 4

Safety, Rest, and Recovery

In the previous chapter, you learned about the importance of flexibility and mobility to prevent injuries. However, doing your stretches doesn't guarantee best results and protection from injury. Rest and recovery are also necessary for the greatest health and fitness benefits. In this chapter, you'll learn why rest and recovery lead to better fitness results, and how to rest actively to allow your muscles to grow bigger and stronger.

Safety: How to Prevent Injury in Calisthenics

Injury prevention is an essential part of any training. While calisthenics carries low risk of injury due to the body's limitations in making risky movements and being in an unhealthy position, there are still things that you should do to maximize the health benefits from exercise and prevent overstrain. Training with your bodyweight itself partially prevents overuse, compared to risks with using weights.

Calisthenics training adds less stress to your joints and can lead to fewer injuries, but they can still happen if you're not careful enough. Learning how to prevent injury when exercising calisthenics is necessary if you want to progress consistently. Luckily for you, there are only a couple of simple preventive measures you can use when exercising calisthenics. Here's what you need to do if you want to prevent overstrain when working out:

- **Warm-up**. Never start an exercise session without warming up for at least 10 minutes. Bodyweight training is often thought to be light enough as to not require warm-ups by beginners, and taking extra 10 minutes to do it may seem like taking away from your exercise routine. This isn't true. A proper warm-up will boost your progress and make exercise easier and more enjoyable. I suggested a couple of interesting warm-up exercises for flexibility and mobility in the previous chapter. However, you can still choose any warm-up exercise you like. Warming up is necessary for the blood to start running through your joints and lubricating them to prevent injury.

- **Practice with a lacrosse ball**. Calisthenics doesn't require much equipment or lifting aids, but a couple of useful tools, a lacrosse ball being one of them, will maximize your exercise and performance. A lacrosse ball is useful to protect your joints from injury, particularly those in your elbows and wrists. Massaging these areas with a lacrosse ball helps remove joint pain and ease the stress from these areas. You can easily remove any joint or muscle pain by simply rolling the ball on the spots where you feel soreness, tightness, or tension. If you do this regularly, you will easily prevent post workout muscle and joint soreness.

- **Use progressions**. Start with lighter variations of more demanding exercises first to allow your muscles and joints enough time to warm up. For example, if you want to do handstands, do a couple of regular push-ups first. Only a couple of repetitions are enough to adapt your body to the movement. This way, you will prevent overstraining joints.

- **Shuffle target areas**. You should switch exercises to target different muscle groups within your workout sessions. Doing so will prevent muscles from adapting to a certain movement, which will reduce its effectiveness. Secondly, you will avoid adding too much tension on your joints, which can happen if you do too many repetitions of the same exercise. For this, it's best to come up with two weekly exercise variations. Plan for two different exercise patterns targeting desired muscle groups, and then rotate these routines. This will also keep you from being bored with your exercises, which can happen if you use the same routine session after session and week after week.

- **Focus on skills**. Calisthenics is different from weight lifting in many ways, one of them being that the progress happens due to improved physical skills, and not cranking up certain exercises and repetitions. Focusing on learning physical movements, rather than on exterior results, shifts your focus from the visual appearance of your body to a sense of inner, instinctive need to improve your body's shape and mobility. This way, when you observe your arm, for example, you won't think only about what you want the biceps and triceps to look like. When you pay attention to adding weight to your exercises and increasing repetitions, you fail to think about how it aligns with your unique physique and health. This can lead to injury.

Instead, focus on the type of movement you're trying to conquer, and ways to learn it. Muscles will grow from this approach most definitely, but focusing on the accuracy of movement, proper position, and alignment of your body will give not only better physical results, but also greater health benefits. It also prevents injuries, because your thinking revolves around the needs and limitations of your body.

Calisthenics Rest and Recovery

If your goal is to build muscle strength, become more flexible and vital, and improve overall shape and health, then resting may sound counterintuitive. It's particularly difficult not to exercise if you're high in energy, you love it, and have started seeing your first results. Still, rest and recovery are vital. They allow your muscles and connective tissues to recover and grow, and also to avoid overload. Here's a simple explanation of why.

When you exercise correctly, and even with the best exercise plan possible, your muscles and connective tissues suffer micro-tears. This minor damage done to the muscles actually produces muscle growth, because the body "fills" these tears to heal the muscle, causing it to grow in size. However, this can't happen, at least not healthily, without rest and recovery. The pattern is simple: add strain and stress to your muscles to create these minor tears, and then rest to let them heal and let your muscles grow.

The philosophy behind rest and recovery is simple, but its execution usually isn't. Beginner calisthenics exercisers are mainly confused about how often and for how long to exercise, and how long to rest and recover afterward. Other questions that puzzle exercisers also concern proper diet during workout and rest days, which we'll address in one of the following chapters.

For the time being, let's focus on the importance of rest and recovery. You may feel great after an intense workout, but your body is, in fact, exhausted and drained. The progression happens after exercising, when your brain and body start to adapt to the new circumstances. When your brain detects intense physical stress, it will trigger adaptation processes during the time you're resting. However, if you don't rest enough, you risk injury. If you overstrain consistently and for long periods of time, you risk injuring yourself so much that you're unable to train for up to a year.

Doing calisthenics will place a huge amount of stress on your body. It adds stress not only to muscles, but also connective tissues, wrists, and ligaments. As you already learned, they take nearly twice as long to recover compared to muscles. Regular calisthenics exercisers frequently suffer from elbow pain and pain in forearms. If this happens, one of the ways to ease the pain is to stop training for a while and rest.

This will release the tightness from injured tissues. If you rest regularly after training throughout weeks and months, you'll be able to exercise for years without injury. However, if you suffer a severe injury, it could stop you from exercising overall.

There are many reasons why people refuse to rest. Some feel like missing out on every opportunity to exercise will make them lose strength or put weight back on. Others simply want to take every chance they can to improve, or have become addicted to training because it's satisfying and stimulating. If you're training for a competition, it's possible for a deadline to push you into overtraining.

While all of these reasons are often hard to resist, there are also numerous valid reasons for taking a rest, despite feeling reluctant to do so. First things first, up to a week of rest won't cause you to lose strength. Instead, you could gain even more strength due to adaptation. When you rest, your muscles heal and grow.

However, it's important to adjust your diet to new circumstances to avoid weight gain.

Structured rest can even help you achieve better results. If you rest regularly and consistently between exercises, your neural and muscular systems will better adapt to the new stress. This process is called supercompensation, and it is a physiological response that happens when you get much stronger than you were.

If you become addicted to training, it can become unhealthy and dangerous, both physically and mentally. Taking some time off training will help your body and mind discover and gain a better perspective and balance.

If you're getting ready for a sporting event or a competition, your exercise program needs to include enough rest. If you fail to rest, it will only hurt your performance. Now that you know why you should rest, let's discuss how you should rest and recover from training properly.

How to Plan Calisthenics Rest Days

You should plan your rest days according to your exercise goals and intensity. The more intense and regular the exercise, the more time will be needed to rest and adapt. This means that rest days should be evenly distributed throughout your weekly plan.

What are Rest Days?

As the name suggests, rest days are the days of the week when you won't be training. You should be realistic and flexible when planning your rest days. This is a highly individual matter, and you should take enough time to decide whether you should rest every other or every third day. This will depend on your lifestyle and activity, your recovery ability, your health, and your schedule. However, this plan shouldn't be too strict. You should allow yourself more time to rest if you feel like you need it.

But how do you start making your ideal resting schedule? Typical exercise plans for regular exercisers may not be suitable for calisthenics beginners, so you'll need a lighter pace. If you're just starting, your muscles, ligaments, and tendons will take longer to recover compared to seasoned exercisers. To prevent injury, it might be good to opt-in for longer rest periods between upper body exercises.

Aside from this, you should also plan for so-called reload weeks. Your plan is best done across four weeks, with week four being lighter and lower in volume compared to the previous three. This, however, doesn't mean that the exercises should be too light, or that you should stop training completely during that week. The intensity of exercises should remain adequate to maintain progress, but with a slightly lower exercise volume and stress. During this week, you can focus more on mobility and flexibility exercises. Rest assured that these lower-stress exercises won't hurt your performance. Chances are that, after you've followed through with the correct plan, you will come back stronger and more flexible.

In this chapter, you learned more about the significance of rest and recovery in calisthenics. During rest days, your body will recover and strengthen itself. Rest is anything but the loss of precious time for exercise. In fact, as you learned, if you exercise continuously without rest, it can actually weaken you and cause long-term muscle damage. You learned that rest days are necessary for both physiological and psychological reasons. It's not only that your muscles need time to rebuild and strengthen, but you also need time to unwind from training, and to balance fitness with home and work. In fact, if you don't rest enough, you can even suffer from overtraining syndrome.

As you learned, recovery is the time when your body adapts to the stress it experienced, and that's the time when muscle strengthening and growth happen. This is also the time for you to recover the water lost from sweat and prevent dehydration, and for your muscles to replenish their glycogen supplies and energy stores, and grow by repairing the damaged tissue. In the short term, recovery, if active, will replenish your energy for long-term exercise and progress. Long-term, it will help your body adapt to physical exercise and contribute to strengthening your muscles so that you can progress.

Chapter 5

Rebalance the Scales

Calisthenics is a form of exercise that combines strength, endurance, mobility, and gymnastic exercise under one umbrella. In the introduction, we discussed why this form of exercise appeals to so many people of different ages, fitness levels, and health levels.

What makes calisthenics so amazing is that it is not just exercising that brings a wide spectrum of different benefits for every practitioner, but it is also a complete lifestyle change. As their bodies change physically, their way of eating changes, and they live a healthier and far more active lifestyle. Their mental health and emotional well-being transform, and they approach everything in their lives with mindfulness.

Life Lessons

The word calisthenics is a combination of the Greek words meaning strength and beauty. For most people, the word strength points to physical strength, and beauty means the pleasing outer appearance of a person. While this is true, these words mean much more than just physical attributes. Think of the strength of determination to go on in the face of adversity, and the beauty of caring for someone without expecting anything in return.

Physical calisthenics teaches practitioners certain fundamental life skills that do not involve physical prowess or physical strength, but have a great impact in other areas of their lives.

Discipline

We live in a world of instant gratification, where we press a button and we get what we want. Everyone multitasks, and often we do not really concentrate on any one thing at a time. Technology has spoiled us, and also robbed us of the vital life skills we all need.

When you start on your journey of calisthenics, you have a goal or goals in mind of what you want to achieve. You know you need physical fitness to achieve whatever goals you have set, but you also need mental discipline to achieve those goals.

It takes discipline to keep going when you are tired, or when you are not succeeding in a specific goal, even though you are trying very hard. Calisthenics helps you to develop discipline through the determination to reach your goals and make the targets you have set for yourself.

As your mindset develops to succeed, so does your mental discipline with each step you take forward. A chain reaction happens when you become determined to succeed. At the end of the day, the determination and discipline you have developed carry over into all other areas of your life. Your education, your career, and your personal life all benefit from strong mental discipline.

Learn to Manage the Fear of Failure

Practicing calisthenics teaches you how to manage the fear of failing at doing something. As you progress in your training, you will face failure when you don't have enough energy to complete the sets and reps you have as your goal. You will fail when you can't smoothly execute a specific hold and you end up falling. This is part of making progress in calisthenics.

Learning to accept that failure does not mean the end, but instead that it is a learning curve, is how you progress in your training and in other areas of your life. Take this lesson from calisthenics and apply it to other areas of your life. You do not have to fear failure. Embrace it, dust yourself off, and try again. You are learning, not failing. Look for and find solutions to achieve your goals.

Self-Control

Calisthenics training teaches you how to control your body physically. You'll learn how to lift it, push, and maneuver it in many different ways that you could not do before. The philosophy of self-mastery that calisthenics is based on is not a new concept. Many of the ancient religious philosophies of the world are based upon this. Self-mastery through calisthenics training extends past just the physical, to achieve mastery over our emotions and desires. Learning and achieving self-control of your emotions and desires benefits your entire life. It affects how you handle situations, and how you respond to not only good, but also bad stimuli.

Self-Reliance

People have different ways in which they strive to maintain fitness and health. They go to the gym and use the rowing machine and the treadmill, or they lift weights or use cross training equipment. They benefit greatly from this, and there is nothing wrong with their chosen methods. Yet, using these machines and equipment means they rely on external tools to maintain their levels of fitness. Remove their equipment, and suddenly everything comes to a halt.

With calisthenics, you only rely on yourself. You are not lost without a trainer or a treadmill. You only need your own body to achieve your fitness goals. You learn selfreliance without dependence on any externals.

This applies to your life in general. Think about how often you have heard someone say that they cannot feel good unless they can buy expensive things. Maybe a friend has remarked to you that they cannot feel good about themselves unless they have their partner's or their boss' approval. They have not learned to be self-reliant.

Calisthenics teaches you that you only have to rely on yourself to achieve fitness and good health, and that you already have yourself to make you feel good. All you need to do is learn how to correctly use your body and your mind.

Physical Benefits

Doing consistent calisthenics workouts has far-reaching health benefits for any practitioner. The health benefits are short-term and long-term, as many of the benefits become very important over time. Calisthenics practitioners experience a much better quality of life as they grow older.

The following benefits definitely make calisthenics worthwhile, even if it seems to be difficult at times:

Bone Density

Calisthenics promotes an increase in bone density, which is crucially important to prevent or reduce the risk of developing osteoporosis.

Chronic Conditions

Consistent calisthenics workouts help to control or prevent several chronic conditions that could be life-threatening, such as:

- Obesity
- Diabetes
- Arthritis
- Back pain
- Heart disease
- Depression
- High blood pressure
- High cholesterol
- Osteoporosis
- Certain forms of cancer
- Stroke

Cognitive Decline

Physical and mental discipline through exercise may prevent or reduce the effects of cognitive decline in senior citizens.

Energy Levels

As you progress with calisthenics, you'll grow stronger, and your energy levels will increase quite noticeably.

Flexibility, Mobility, and Balance

Calisthenics helps you to maintain balance and flexibility through increased mobility. This is important as your body ages in order to stay independent and agile.

Greater Stamina

Calisthenics creates a chain reaction of increased physical activity, strength building, better health, and wellbeing that all contribute to increased stamina.

Immune System

High levels of fitness and a nutritionally balanced diet assists the immune system to fight off illnesses.

Insomnia and Sleep

Increased fitness levels and improved mental wellbeing promotes better sleep patterns and greatly reduces the problem of insomnia.

Muscle Strength and Tone

Increased protection of your joints from injury comes with enhanced muscle strength.

Performance of Everyday Tasks

With calisthenics, you build functional strength, and not just strength for lifting heavy weights or putting muscles on display. Lean, functional muscles make doing everyday tasks much easier, with less strain on muscles and joints.

Posture

Increased muscle strength and flexibility improves posture greatly.

Risk of Injury

The risk of injury decreases with progression, muscle building, and increased strength.

Self-Esteem

When you follow a consistent workout program and you can see the improvements you are making through mastering your physical body, it increases your self-esteem.

Sense of Wellbeing

Resistance training may have a boosting effect on self-confidence and developing a positive body image. An increase in your sense of wellbeing promotes a positive mood.

Weight-Management and Muscle to Fat Ratio

Consistent workouts increase your muscle mass and burn calories even while you are at rest. This makes weight management much easier.

Mental and Emotional Wellbeing

Every human wants to be happy. In fact, happiness is part of human DNA, through a protein created by the FAAH gene that affects pain and pleasure. The best way to show you how calisthenics contributes to your mental and emotional wellbeing is to share the Action for Happiness movement's GREAT DREAM, or the

10 keys to happier living. Calisthenics ties directly in with each of the 10 keys, with great potential to improve your life and wellbeing.

Giving

Calisthenics gives you the opportunity to give to others by sharing your skills and experiences as you progress. You give your time, a precious commodity, to help others by sharing what you have learned on your own journey and to encourage others to start calisthenics training.

Relating

The calisthenics community is very close-knit in comparison with other health and fitness groups. Calisthenics is mostly non-competitive and has a culture of sharing and openness that promotes camaraderie. This is helpful especially for beginners to connect with others who share their passion, and find a lot of moral support is freely offered.

Exercising

Our bodies are not designed to live a sedentary life. Our bodies are designed for movement. The more movement we engage in, the more our bodies release endorphins, or the happiness hormone in layman's terms. So yes, when you exercise your body thanks you by releasing endorphins that make you feel good and give you an all-around sense of wellbeing.

Appreciating

Calisthenics offers practitioners two different ways in which they experience appreciation. The first way is that you literally are able to get outside to do your workouts. You are not bound to work out in a specific building or a specific environment. Depending on where you live, you may have nature at your doorstep, or you could enjoy doing your sets and reps in a beautiful park. Wherever you live, you can breathe in the fresh air while you enjoy the world around you at the same time.

The second way is through mindfulness. Calisthenics, as we said before, is not only physical exercises. It involves your mind, sharpens your focus, and hones your mental discipline. When you focus on your workout and striving toward your next goal, you do not waste brainpower worrying and stressing about things in your life that irk you, or that you can't really do anything about.

Trying Out

Doing calisthenics means that you never stop learning. There is always the next goal, or honing a specific skill. The potential for learning new things is literally endless, as you can keep on exploring new movements every time you have mastered one.

Direction

Every person needs goals to look forward to in their life, or something to strive for. This is part of human nature, and we are at our happiest when we have clearly defined goals of where we want to go. Calisthenics offers many goals you can achieve through determination, diligence, and effort.

Resilience

In the section titled Life Lessons, we discussed the management of the fear of failure. This is the mental health skill calisthenics teaches you, resilience and finding ways to bounce back again when you have failed. The physical hardships and failures you experience through training help to develop resilience to deal with failures in other aspects of your life. As your body develops, you'll learn about yourself and the ability you have to overcome whatever obstacles are in your way. This carries over to your personal relationships, your career, family, and friends.

How to Balance Healthy Eating Socially

Socializing and eating out can be harrowing for anyone still at the beginning of their calisthenics training. You work very hard for every step forward, and eating out with friends and colleagues can wipe out many hours of hard work. This sets you back and can drain your motivation, and nobody needs that. That is why it is good to have a handful of tips to help avoid the pitfalls for socializing and eating out when you are committed to building a healthy body and mind through calisthenics.

Check the Menu

Check out what is available on the menu before the meeting time. This avoids having to choose food when you might be very hungry or tired, and making unhealthy food choices on the spur of the moment.

Healthy Snack Before Arrival

When we are very hungry, we tend to overeat. If we eat out at a place where the wait for food to be served may be long, this could lead to wrong food choices and eating too much. Eat a high protein, healthy snack such as yogurt or a smoothie before you go to the restaurant.

Water

Keep a glass of water handy at all times. Drink water before the start of the meal and during, and have water instead of a sweetened drink. You will save yourself from a lot of extra calories.

Check How Food is Prepped and Cooked

The way food is prepared and cooked can have a huge impact on the number of calories and fat content of a dish. Buzz words to look for are sautéed, crispy, pan-fried, crunchy, and fried, as these dishes are usually higher in fat content and calories. Rather, look for steamed, poached, grilled, and roasted items on the menu.

Order First

We are often influenced by what other people at the table order when eating out in a group. The best way to avoid temptation and any uncomfortable moments is simply to order your food before anyone else can.

Double Up on Appetizers

Some restaurants specialize in serving huge portions, and that could mean overeating. The best way to avoid this problem is to order two appetizers instead of a huge main course. You will eat enough to be full, without an overload of calories.

Mindful Eating

Mindful eating changes eating habits, and is very helpful in social settings where overeating and bad food choices are abundant. Mindful eating means you savor each flavor and aroma of each mouthful of food, and concentrate on what feelings you experience as you taste each different piece of food. According to findings in a 2013 study, mindful eating helps gain self-control that prevents overeating, and aids in making healthier food choices when eating at social events and restaurants (Robinson et al.).

Eat Slowly and Chew Well

This tip to cope with eating out works hand-in-hand with mindful eating. By consciously slowing down how fast you eat and trying to chew each mouthful of food X number of times, your body has ample time to signal fullness before you overeat.

Coffee Instead of Dessert

Bypass the dessert trap and order a cup of coffee instead. This will greatly cut your calorie count, and you will actually enjoy the surprisingly many health benefits that coffee has.

Request a Healthy Swap

When you place your order, request to swap out high calorie items such as potatoes, fries, and pan-fried or sautéed items. Replace these items with vegetables or a salad.

Dressings and Sauces on the Side

Make it a habit to always ask that any sauces and dressings for the food you order be served on the side. Sauces and dressings are notoriously high in fats and calories, and you can control how much you have much more easily when it is served on the side.

Bread Basket

The bread basket offered before dinner is standard practice at many restaurants. If you are already hungry when you arrive, you will be very tempted to nibble and throw your eating plan out the door. Rather, send the bread basket back and avoid temptation.

Salad or Soup Starters

A 2007 study has shown that you can lower your overall calorie intake at a meal by as much as 20% when you start with soup (Flood & Rolls, 2007). The findings also showed that this works no matter what type of soup you have. This is a great way to save on calories and give you peace of mind about not interrupting your training program.

Share or Go Half-Portion

People who practice portion control often share food with another person at the table. It is a convenient way to prevent overeating, and it helps both people. If there is nobody to share with, ask the waiter for a half portion of your order. Most restaurants will allow you to order half-portions. If they don't then, tell them to pack up half your food for you to take home in a doggy bag.

Alcohol, Mixers, and Sweetened Drinks

Nobody said you have to avoid all forms of alcohol when you socialize. You simply have to think ahead and do things logically. Order a small glass of wine instead of a large glass, and ask for a diet mixer when your spirits instead of a mixer sweetened with sugar.

Soft drinks can also push up calories when eating out. It is much healthier to drink water, natural unsweetened drinks, or a cup of unsweetened tea.

Tomato-Based vs. Creamy Sauces

Try to steer clear of cheese sauces, and any sauces made with cream. Rather, go for the much healthier option of tomato-based or vegetable-based sauces for a great tasting and much lower calorie sauce.

Be Wary of Health Claims

It is not uncommon these days to see items listed on restaurant menus as "sugar-free", "keto", "gluten-free", or "paleo". Always keep in mind that sugar-free only means there is no cane sugar in the product or dish, and most of the time other forms of sweeteners have been used that are the same or higher in calories than sugar.

It is the same with items highlighted as fulfilling the needs of certain diets, as some diets are incredibly high in fats. So, have a good read through the menu and never fall for the hype.

Chapter 6

The Fuel for Lean Living

Building your body up will require a suitable diet. Well, health and wellbeing in general require a healthy diet to begin with. It's important to remember that the way you eat affects your capacity to exercise and the result of it, from before you start your exercise plan, during exercise, and while you're resting.

How much you'll have to adjust your diet depends on how proper your diet is now. If you come from a place of over or undereating and you can't maintain a regular, healthy eating schedule, your first step will be to establish a proper diet plan. Unless you eat well, you won't have enough energy to exercise, or you will, but the results will fail to show.

From the standpoint of achieving hypertrophy, or gaining muscle, your diet will have to keep up with your schedule. On the other hand, your diet mustn't be too rigorous either. You'll face life outside dieting and exercising, and daily activities and life hurdles won't care much for your need to eat properly. You'll need a simple, well-composed, sustainable, and practical diet if you want it to work for you long-term. A rigorous diet will be hard to keep up with, regardless of its perceived health and fitness benefits. Adopting a healthy diet is best done step-by-step, one day at a time, the same way as starting to exercise. We want you to be successful with your transformation, and we know that people can't tolerate too many sudden changes.

Can you slip into a strict diet and exercise schedule that's completely different than you used to have? Likely not. Health and fitness are gained one step at a time, even if it means that, on your first day, you'll exercise for only ten minutes and give up candy. Those are the kinds of little changes that snowball into a complete life transformation. One day, it's doing ten squats and switching regular pizza with the lean substitute. The next day, it will be ten lunges and two pushups, and you may eat a smoothie for breakfast instead of your usual sugary cereal. Fast forward a year from now, and you're a different person. So, be patient with yourself and snowball into your transformation.

For starters, adjusting to a healthy diet for calisthenics means introducing regular, healthy changes in your meal sizes, food choices, and eating schedule. But first, you need to think about your body, health, lifestyle, and goals to decide what kind of diet you need. Start by calculating how many calories you need on your exercise days and your resting days. Next, consider your training goal when developing a meal plan, either:

- **Muscle gain**. If you've chosen calisthenics to gain muscles, your daily calorie intake will have to be bigger than the number of calories you spend. On average, you should add 200-500 calories to your daily diet.

- **Fat loss**. If your goal is to lose fat, you should make a calorie deficit of between 200 and 500 calories in your daily diet. However, you still need to make sure that your food intake is sufficient to support daily physical activity. Remember, you'll be physically active even on your rest days, and eating too little might slow down your metabolism.

General Diet Recommendations

Eating a healthy diet for successful calisthenics shouldn't be difficult. This section will give you a couple of simple dietary recommendations to follow.

- **Focus on food quality.** Postulates of a healthy diet are often vague, and they entail eating an abundance of lean meats, healthy carbs, and vegetables. However, you also need to make sure to have enough food to keep you running. Don't fall into a trap of reducing protein, carbs, and fat to below limits just because you want to get slimmer. You still need your meats, rice, and oats, even if you're trying to lose weight. On the other hand, your diet needs to be versatile and satisfying as well. You won't feel good if you only eat lean, cooked foods, with complete disregard for your personal tastes. You can allow yourself to eat cheat meals and have some of the delicious foods you otherwise enjoy, because this will provide a break from being on a strict regimen and help you feel like all of the effort is worth it.

- **Pay attention to your appetite.** Designing your meals according to calorie charts may distract you from paying attention to your real appetite. It is possible to have a strong appetite and eat a lot but be unable to gain weight, and to have a low appetite and eat little, but still be unable to lose weight. Neither of the possibilities are excluded. If it happens that you eat a lot without weight gain, pay attention to whether or not you're eating enough protein, and also if you're overtraining. It's possible that you need more rest for hypertrophy. On the other hand, if you reduce your diet, but you're still not losing weight, it's possible that you're eating too little. In that case, you might feel sluggish and exhausted, and not even feel the appetite under the influence of overstrain. Again, revisit your diet and exercise plan to see if calorie intake and diet composition match your daily calorie expenditure. It can also happen that you don't have enough appetite for your target calorie intake. If you struggle with appetite, you can choose more calorie-dense foods to consume a greater number of nutrients with smaller food quantities. On top of that, you can also reduce fiber intake, because fibers from oats and rice are known to reduce appetite.

- **Be careful with protein supplements.** Eating a diet that's well-aligned with your exercise should supply enough protein for muscle growth and strengthening. You should only consider protein supplements if you have certain dietary restrictions, or you otherwise struggle with eating meat, eggs, and dairy.

Diet Plan Ideas

Quality nutrition is necessary for optimal fitness results, with calisthenics as well as with any other training program. Not having a good nutrient balance will get in the way of your fitness goals, regardless of your effort. If you're not used to following a specific diet program, understanding how you need to eat for healthy results with calisthenics could be a challenge. For that reason, this section will provide a diet plan that's best to follow when you're exercising calisthenics. This plan won't specify exactly what you need to eat or give precise food quantities. Instead, it will give you general guidelines for a healthy diet that supports regular exercise. With this plan, it will be easy to adjust food choices and portion sizes according to your daily needs.

To follow a diet suitable for calisthenics exercise, there's no need for you to invest in cooking equipment or fancy foods. There's also no need to spend more on food than you used to, or adjust your schedule to have enough time to cook. This diet plan will be flexible and allow you to adjust it to your individual taste and preference, as well as to your fitness goals. Weighing your food is one of the easier ways to adjust meal sizes and avoid under or overeating. Here are the basic directions to eat healthily when practicing calisthenics.

- **Eat whole foods**. You'll get the best nutrition with unprocessed foods. Processed foods don't only contain toxic chemicals. They are also heavily processed to have a longer shelf life, so they're depleted of precious nutrients that you need in order to grow your muscles and strength. Instead, get your macronutrients from organic meat, fish, dairy, seafood, and eggs. Fruits and vegetables will provide natural fibers and carbs from sugar, and grains and root vegetables will supply healthy carbs as well.

- **Cut out unhealthy food**. You need to stop eating junk food and processed fats if you want to be healthy in general, but also if you want to make progress with calisthenics. In addition to that, you should also eliminate white rice and all products made from white flour, including pastries and pasta.

- **Don't limit fruits and vegetables**. You can have as many plants as you want, and it won't get in the way of your health or exercise results.

- **Limit mealtimes**. You shouldn't scatter your meals across the entire day. Instead, eat within an eight-hour feeding window. This will help you eat when you're hungry without restrictions, but still prevent you from getting too hungry. If you don't go hungry, there's less chance that you'll feel tempted to eat junk foods. Instead, you'll eat foods that are more calorie-dense, and consume fewer calories than if you spread your meals across the entire day.

- **Supplement cautiously**. You should aim to get the majority of your nutrition from your daily meals, not supplements. In case you still feel like you'd benefit from supplementation, you should use the following supplements cautiously:

  o **Creatine**. Creatine will help you recover from injuries and supports building muscle mass.

  o **Proteins**. If you feel like you can't eat sufficient protein to build muscles, or you're a vegetarian or a vegan, then supplemental protein will be a great substitute for meat. It will also help injured muscles recover in case you over train.

- o **Branched-chain amino acids**, or BCAA, can help you gain muscle and maintain the muscle growth you achieved so far.

- o **Vitamins**. Although you will easily eat sufficient vitamins when consuming fruits and vegetables, multivitamin supplementation can help obtain those nutrients that are otherwise hard to gain through diet, like Zinc, B complex, and vitamins E, D, and C.

To understand how to eat healthily when doing calisthenics, you should first learn how to balance out macronutrients in your diet. Your carbs, fats, and protein require a good proportion in your meals for optimal performance effects. Here's how to eat to get sufficient healthy macronutrients:

- • **Carbohydrates.** You should focus on eating complex carbohydrates, which won't spike your blood sugar and cause excess blood glucose to be stored in fat cells. You'll find complex carbs in fruits and vegetables, whole grains, and nuts and seeds. Fiber from fruits and vegetables also breaks down into carbohydrates when consumed.

- **Fats.** Aside from fats naturally found in meat, dairy, nuts, and seeds, you should also use healthy fats while cooking. Ideal choices include extra virgin olive oil and coconut oil. Saturated fats are found in meats and tropical plants like coconuts, while unsaturated fats are present in fish, nuts, and vegetables. You should reduce your intake of saturated fats by choosing lean meats, because human bodies can produce them on their own. However, essential fatty acids, like omega 3 and omega 6, must be obtained through diet. This is why it's advised to have at least two servings of fish each week, and to use scarce amounts of extra virgin olive oil when cooking. Still, even these fats can cause obesity when consumed in excess amounts.

- **Proteins.** Proteins form your muscles, nails, hair, and ligaments, and serve to keep your body moving. They are amino acids that serve as building blocks for muscles. When looking for sources of healthy protein, look for lean meats and fish, but also lean dairy, eggs, mushrooms, legumes, and beans. These foods can be eaten in large amounts without contributing to weight gain.

- **Micronutrients.** Last but not least are vitamins and minerals found in fruits and vegetables. Vitamins are necessary to support biological processes in your body, and in terms of calisthenics, they secure strong and safe movements. Vitamin deficiency often affects metabolism, your energy levels, and your appearance.

Eating Tips and Meal Ideas

So far, we've given you general recommendations for how to eat properly when practicing calisthenics. In this section, you'll find a couple of meal ideas for breakfast to dinner, to help you get a sense of what your daily meals should look like.

Breakfast

Oatmeal with Fruit

Ingredients:

- 1-2 cups whole oats

- 1-2 cups regular, almond, or coconut milk

- 1 cup berries

- Up to 1 cup crushed nuts

Instructions:

You need a strong breakfast to get you going, and oatmeal with berries of your choice (strawberries, blueberries, or mixed berries,) with the addition of fruits like bananas, mangoes, and oranges, is a great option. One bowl is usually a good measure regardless of gender and lifestyle, but you can adjust your breakfast to add or reduce calories as needed.

For example, if you want a leaner breakfast, go for coconut or almond milk instead of regular, or cut back on the fruit serving. On the other hand, if you want to increase the caloric value of the dish, you can add up to a cup of nuts. Keep in mind that nuts are calorie-dense and could add up to 200 calories to a meal. Berries and fruits are important to supply enough sugar, but in a healthy way, and of course to add fiber that supports the health of your digestive system.

Fruit Salad

Ingredients:

- Chopped fruits (bananas, avocado, apples, oranges, pineapple, strawberries, or raspberries)
- 1 tbsp. raw honey
- 1 tbsp. lemon juice

Instructions:

If you prefer a lighter breakfast, you can have as many bananas, avocados, oranges, berries, apples, and citruses as you please. The secret to eating the right amount of fruit is simple: chew and eat slowly, and only eat to the point where you feel full.

Breakfast Tortilla

Ingredients:

- 1 whole wheat tortilla

For fruit topping:

- 1 cup chopped fruit
- 1 tbsp. peanut or almond butter
- Up to 1 cup crushed nuts

For vegetable topping:

- Chopped vegetables (tomatoes, spinach, kale, or onions)
- A drizzle of olive oil
- 1 tbsp. lemon juice
- A pinch of salt
- A pinch of pepper
- A pinch of each of the spices of your choosing
- (parsley, basil, dill, etc.)
- 1 slice cheddar cheese
- Greek yogurt

Instructions:

A whole wheat tortilla is a great breakfast option, regardless of your gender and fitness goals. Your breakfast will be light if you top your tortilla with fruits (berries, bananas, and avocados) or vegetables (sliced tomatoes, leafy greens, olives, cucumber, etc.).

If you want to increase the caloric value of your breakfast, you can add a layer of almond or peanut butter if you choose fruits, or add a cup of Greek yogurt to your vegetable wrap. This will add fat to the meal in case you're doing higher volume training. Optionally, you can substitute some of the ingredients with cheddar cheese and kale, or add them if you want to boost your breakfast with extra healthy calories.

Green smoothie

Ingredients:

- 1 handful spinach
- One apple
- 1 handful kale leaves
- One banana
- 1 tbsp. lemon juice
- 1 cup almond or coconut milk
- Water, as needed

Instructions:

Opinions are divided regarding whether or not a smoothie is the best breakfast option. It can be if you add enough carbs to the mix. You can pop any leafy veggies you like into a blender, but an apple with a handful of spinach leaves, some lemon, kale, and a banana is a safe bet. If your smoothie is still too lean, you can add fruit, like a half or a whole banana, or berries to add flavor, vitamins, and calories. Lack of carbs? Add up to a cup of whole oats, and if you're doing high volume training, you can also add a cup of almond or coconut milk. As you can see, there are many healthy ways to add or deduce the caloric volume of your smoothie, and the choice is all yours!

Lunch and Dinner

The beauty of healthy cooking is in its versatility. Lunch and dinner combine meats, vegetables, herbs, and spices that can be eaten both during the day and in the evening. For the sake of simplicity, we recommend cooking a double measure of a meal and simply having one serving for lunch, and another for dinner. On the other hand, if you don't want to eat the same meal twice a day, you can always pre-make a couple of meals in advance. Mid-day meals do require a careful balance of carbs and protein. This is because the foods that carry most macronutrients also have quite a bit of fat, and all of that combined can easily spike your blood sugar and make the meal too heavy.

As always, make sure to use whole, organic, non-processed foods. Here are a couple of ideas for healthy, balanced, and satiating meals:

Fish with Vegetables

Ingredients:

- 1 -2 salmon, or any other fish of your choosing (a palm-sized serving)
- 2 cups or more chopped kale, cauliflower, broccoli, onions, zucchini, and eggplant
- 1 tbsp. extra virgin olive oil
- 1 tbsp. lemon juice
- ½ tbsp. chopped parsley
- 1 tsp dill
- 1 tsp basil
- A pinch of salt
- A pinch of pepper

Instructions:

Cooking fish is never too much trouble. If you don't enjoy cooking too much, you can simply grill a palm-sized piece of fish, or boil it. If you want to add flavor, on the other hand, simply top the fish with extra virgin olive oil and sprinkle with spices, like powdered onion, parsley, or dill. For this recipe, you'll make a piece of salmon with a vegetable side-dish made from chopped and sautéed broccoli, spinach, zucchini, cauliflower, and eggplant. Don't forget your avocado! You can have it with your vegetables if you enjoy such a blend, or have it as a dessert.

Meat with Vegetables

Ingredients:

- 1-2 chicken breasts
- 2 or more cups chopped kale, broccoli, spinach, cauliflower, paprika, and zucchini
- Extra virgin olive oil
- A pinch of salt
- A pinch of pepper
- 1 cup vegetable stock
- ½ tbsp. chopped parsley
- ½ tsp basil
- ½ tsp dill
- ½ tsp ginger

Instructions:

The same process for making a healthy, protein-dense meal can be used to cook meat. All you need is a palm-sized piece of meat, which you can grill or chop and sauté however you please! Remember to only use up to one tablespoon of extra virgin olive oil.

To make a side-dish, you can either stir-fry chopped sweet potatoes (up to two cups), or chop veggies of your choosing all together (e.g. kale, broccoli, cauliflower, and spinach), and stir-fry with a little bit of water or a cup of vegetable stock.

Want to spice it up? Add chopped parsley, onions, basil, or dill, or drizzle with a tablespoon of lemon or lime juice.

Beans/Legumes with Stir Fry Vegetables

Ingredients:

- 2 cups quinoa, brown rice, or beans
- 2 cups or more chopped vegetables of your choosing
- One sliced onion
- 1 tbsp. extra virgin olive oil
- A pinch of salt
- A pinch of pepper
- 1 cup vegetable or chicken stock

Instructions:

Now, hold on. Who says you have to eat meat each day to become ripped? Really no one, not even nutritionists. For this meal option, you'll substitute a palm-sized piece of meat with up to two cups of beans or quinoa. Lean meals usually feature a cup-sized measure, while those who want to gain weight and muscle often go for two cups or two small cans.

First, boil your legumes for 30 minutes. They'll be ready to eat, but not very tasty. Grab a pot and add a tablespoon of extra virgin olive oil. Add chopped onions and let simmer briefly, adding a half-a-cup of water or vegetable stock. To increase lean calories, you can use chicken stock. Then, add your rice or quinoa, mix it in, and let simmer for about five minutes. Your meal is nearly finished, and all you need to do is to add up to two cups of finely chopped vegetables, top with more water or stock (up to a glass), and let simmer up to ten more minutes. Enjoy!

In this chapter, you learned how to cook your basic meals to support fitness and muscle growth. But what about your pre-and post-workout snacks? In the next chapter, you'll learn more about the health benefits of smoothies, and how to make them quickly and easily.

Chapter 7

Getting Started with Smoothies

Smoothies are not only for bodybuilders, weight lifters, and dedicated gym junkies. Smoothies are great tasting and pack a protein punch when you need it, whether they are for breakfast, post-workout, or as a delicious snack. The variety you can make is truly endless, and you can adapt the level of sweetness or add savory ingredients as per your personal preference.

A word on protein powders is to take note that protein powder supplements are not FDA regulated. Therefore, the very large number of options and brands available on the market can vary radically from each other. Do your research to find which of the protein powders suits your needs the best.

There are many ways to gear up for making smoothies that will save you time and needless effort. For the majority of people, life is busy, and any possible way to spend less time preparing food is a huge bonus.

Frozen Fruit vs. Fresh

Unless you have a constant supply of fresh fruits and products available at all times, your first shortcut is to start building your supplies of frozen fruits. You can buy containers of frozen fruit in most supermarkets, or you can start your own supply. It is a good idea to freeze your favorite fruits in single-servings in jars, plastic containers, or zip-lock bags in the freezer. This way, you can just grab a container and make a smoothie without first having to think about portion sizes.

Make-Ahead Smoothie Packs

You can take your containers of frozen fruit a step further and actually prep your smoothies ahead of time. This is hugely helpful in any household with more than one person using smoothies, as well as an economical step when buying fruit and vegetables in bulk.

Wash and clean all the fruits and vegetables. Then, measure out all the ingredients for each specific smoothie you want to make, and place the ingredients in single smoothie packs in the freezer. The smoothie packs can also be placed in the refrigerator for use within the next few days.

This is the fastest way possible to make a smoothie, as you simply have to add the liquid because all the fruits and veggies have been prepped.

Quick Fix Remedies

Often, we have a smoothie that is either too sweet, too thick, or lacks the amount of tartness you prefer. Here are a couple of quick fixes to help when things go wrong. Add the ingredients to adjust taste or thickness, and blend for an extra 10-20 seconds to incorporate everything.

Too thick: Add a small amount of juice, milk, or water, and blend. Repeat if the mixture is still too thick.

Too thin: Add any of these ingredients to help thicken the mixture:

- Banana
- Strawberries
- Frozen yogurt
- Extra ice
- Chia seeds
- Raw oats
- Protein powder
- Xanthan gum
- Avocado
- Silken tofu

- Nut butter

Bitter taste: Mature greens often have a bitter taste, and the best way to lessen the bitterness is to use baby greens, as they have a much milder taste. You can add any of the following ingredients to lessen the bitterness:

- Bananas, because they have a neutralizing effect on the bitter taste

- Strawberries sweeten green smoothies very well

- Vanilla extract or vanilla bean

- Agave

- Cocoa, or unsweetened cocoa powder

Too sweet: Add frozen lemonade concentrate or fresh lemon juice

Not sweet enough: Add sweeteners or ingredients to sweeten the smoothie little bits at a time, so as to not make it overly sweet. Ingredients include:

- Watermelon, instead of water

- Agave, honey, sugar, or maple syrup

- Stevia, or artificial sweetener of your own choice

- Grapes

- Dates

Not creamy enough: Try any of the ingredients on this list to help create a creamier taste:

- Avocado
- Ice cream
- Vanilla yogurt
- Frozen yogurt

Substitutions

Most smoothie recipes available tell you to use only specific organic ingredients. You can, however, substitute just about any ingredient listed in a smoothie recipe with an ingredient better suitable for your personal needs and tastes. Also, using plant-based ingredients instead makes the recipes vegan and vegetarian friendly.

The following ingredients and their substitutions can be used to mix up really good-tasting protein smoothies that will please everyone.

- Dairy milk
- Soy milk
- Hemp milk
- Almond milk
- Oat milk
- Cashew milk
- Rice milk
- Sorghum milk

- Coconut milk
- Flax milk
- Nuts
- Sunflower seeds, or the butter made from sunflower seeds (sun butter)
- Pumpkin seeds (pepitas)
- Tahini
- Flax seeds
- Chia seeds
- Hemp seeds
- Sugar honey
- Maple syrup
- Brown rice syrup
- Agave nectar
- Barley malt syrup
- Sorghum syrup
- Stevia, or artificial sweetener of your own choice
- Dates
- Grapes
- Whole eggs
- Store-bought Ener-G egg replacement
- 1 tbsp. agar flakes

- 1 tbsp. applesauce
- 1 mashed banana
- ¼ cup silken tofu
- ¼ cup of coconut yogurt
- 1 tbsp. ground flax or chia seeds, simmered for 2 minutes in 3 tbsp. of water (or left to chill in the fridge for 15 minutes)
- Egg whites/aquafaba
- Any of the substitutes listed for whole eggs
- Spinach, bok choy
- Kale
- Radish greens
- Parsley
- Dandelion greens
- Arugula
- Turnip greens
- Celery
- Celery greens
- Collard greens
- Swiss chard
- Mustard greens
- Romaine lettuce
- Broccoli

- Beet greens
- Broccoli rabe (rapini)
- Carrot greens
- Dairy yogurt
- Protein powder
- Coconut cream
- Almond milk yogurt
- Chia seeds
- Ripe avocado

Blending Tips and Tricks

We always want the best-tasting smoothies in the shortest time possible, so a few tips can come in handy to make things easier and speed the process along.

You can use a high-speed electric stand blender, or a jug and an immersion blender to make smoothies. The biggest difference between the two is that a stand blender has a more powerful motor. This allows the stand blender to more easily blend firmer ingredients like cruciferous vegetables, frozen ingredients, and ice cubes.

Load the blender jug with your ingredients in the following order:

1. First, pour in the liquid.
2. Then add soft and small ingredients.

3. Place any greens on top of that.

4. Place vegetables and frozen fruit on top of the greens.

5. Lastly, add any ice cubes you would like to use.

A great tool to purchase, if your stand blender does not have it as an accessory, is a blender tamper. You use the tamper to remove any air pockets that might be in the blender jug and to push the ingredients down onto the blender blades.

Be patient, and do not over blend the ingredients. Remember, the motor and blades will heat up fast, and will start melting the frozen ingredients. Blend in bursts of 30-45 seconds and repeat if necessary.

Depending on the ingredients used for a specific smoothie, you may have to stop the blender, scrape the sides clean, and give it another short burst of blending.

If you use coconut, different types of seeds, oats, or whole nuts, add them to the blender with the liquid. Blend these ingredients and the liquid until you have a creamy paste, for approximately 30 seconds. Then add the rest of the ingredients.

If you are not using a high-speed blender, it works much better if you grate vegetables such as zucchini, beets, and carrots before adding to the blender jug.

Smoothie Recipes

Orange and Mango Recovery Smoothie

This smoothie is sweet, with turmeric that adds anti-inflammatory properties that aid recovery. This recipe is vegan and has no added sugar, and is high in vitamin C and antioxidants. The primary source of protein is protein powder.

Prep Time: 5 minutes

Total Time: 5 minutes

Serving Size: 1

Ingredients

- 1 cup almond milk, unsweetened, or other plant milk of your choice
- 1 cup mango blocks, frozen
- 1 scoop (2 heaping tbsp.) vegan protein powder, vanilla
- ½ banana, frozen
- ½ tsp turmeric (optional, to add anti-inflammatory properties)
- 1 naval orange, frozen, peeled and cut up
- ½ tsp vanilla extract or essence
- 1 tbsp. hemp seeds (optional)

Directions

- Layer all the ingredients into a high-speed blender.

- Blend until completely smooth.

- Pour into a glass and enjoy it.

Green Breakfast Protein Smoothie

This is a good smoothie to start the day with vitamins and minerals, plus healthy fats from hemp hearts and pumpkin seeds. You can add protein powder as an optional extra for an increased protein boost.

To make this smoothie nut-free, substitute the almond milk with oat, coconut, hemp, rice, or soy milk.

Prep Time: 5 minutes

Total Time: 5 minutes

Serving Size: 2 cups (1 large serving)

Ingredients

- 1 ripe frozen banana (can be substituted with 2/3 cup peach chunks)

- 1 cup almond milk, unsweetened, or substitute with milk of personal choice

- ½ cup frozen mango chunks

- 1-2 big handfuls of baby spinach, or destemmed kale

- 2 tbsp. hemp hearts (hemp seeds that have been hulled)
- ¼ cup pepitas (pumpkin seeds)
- ½-1 scoop (1-2 heaped tbsp.) protein powder, vanilla flavor
- ¼ cup water (optional)

Directions

Place all the ingredients into the blender jug and blend until the pepitas are completely blended in and smooth.

This is a large serving, so you can either have it for breakfast, or split it into 2 smaller servings and have the second half as a morning snack.

Cinnamon, Oats, and Apple

If you are an oatmeal lover, this is definitely the smoothie for you. It is suitable for breakfast, a morning snack, or lunch. Oats give a slow release of energy that will last several hours, and the oats and almond butter are your main sources of protein. You can also add hemp hearts for higher protein intake, and the hemp does not affect the taste of the smoothie. For a hefty protein boost, you can add vanilla protein powder as well.

Prep Time: 5 minutes

Total Time: 5 minutes

Serving Size: 1 large serving

Ingredients

- ½ cup oats, rolled
- 1 small-to-medium sliced apple
- ½ tsp ground nutmeg
- ½ tsp cinnamon powder
- ½ cup coconut milk, unsweetened
- 1 tbsp. almond butter
- 2 tbsp. hemp hearts (optional)
- 1 scoop (2 heaping tbsp.) vanilla protein powder (optional)
- ½ cup water, cold
- 3-4 ice cubes

Directions

- Place the water and oats into the blender jug and pulse a few times. Set the jug aside for 2-3 minutes to give the oats time to soften.

- Add the rest of the ingredients to the blender and process for roughly 30 seconds, until the mixture is smooth.

- Pour into a large glass and sprinkle with extra nutmeg and cinnamon as garnish.

- Enjoy immediately.

Acai Berry and Mint

This is a smoothie for literally any time of the day, for breakfast, post-workout, or as a morning snack. Using unflavored protein powder allows the mint and fruit taste to stay in the foreground. Adding ground seeds makes this a thick smoothie with a very good protein supply. The mango and tart cherry puree and acai berry puree can be store-bought in single-serving packets, or you can use your own frozen fruit from your freezer.

Prep Time: 5 minutes

Total Time: 5 minutes

Serving Size: 1 large

Ingredients

- 1 frozen banana, sliced

- 1 orange, fresh (Cara Care, Valencia, and Navel oranges work well)

- ½ cup mango, frozen, or 1 packet tart cherry and mango puree, frozen (3.5 oz.)

- 3.5 oz. of frozen Acai berries, or 1 packet of frozen Acai puree (3.5 oz.)

- 1 tbsp. flax seeds, ground

- 1 tbsp. chia seeds, ground

- 1 scoop (2 heaping tbsp.) protein powder, unflavored

- 2 tbsp. hemp seeds, ground
- ½ cup coconut milk, unsweetened
- 4-5 mint leaves, fresh

Directions

- Place all the ingredients into the blender jug and blend until the mixture is smooth.
- Pour into a large glass and serve immediately, while still cold.

Avocado and Matcha with Vanilla

This smoothie is energizing, and the matcha, which is a form of powdered green tea, has great health properties. This recipe is gluten and soy-free. You can keep this smoothie with just the basic ingredients, or add any of the optional ingredients as preferred.

Prep Time: 5 minutes

Total Time: 5 minutes

Serving Size: 1

Ingredients

- 1 cup almond milk, or milk of personal preference
- ½ avocado
- ½-1 tsp matcha powder (start off with ½ tsp, as it is potent)

- 1 scoop (2 heaping tbsp.) protein powder, vanilla (rice or pea protein works well)
- 2-4 ice cubes
- ½ cup frozen fruit of personal choice (optional)
- 2 tbsp. chia seeds, flax seeds, or pepitas (optional)
- A few dates for sweetness (optional)
- 1-2 tsp maple syrup for extra sweetness (optional)

Directions

- Place all the ingredients into the blender and blend until smooth.
- Serve immediately.

Cranberry, Banana, and Peanut Butter

Cranberries are a winner in any smoothie because they are high in vitamins and antioxidants, and have anti-inflammatory properties as well. The banana and cranberries are sweet, so it is suggested that you use unsweetened ingredients with them. Should you prefer to make it sweeter, use peanut butter with added sugar, and add optional sweetener to the smoothie, such as honey or maple syrup. The source of protein for this smoothie comes from the peanut butter and the protein powder, and gives you roughly 1.2 oz. of protein.

Prep Time: 5 minutes

Total Time: 5 minutes

Serving Size: 1 large portion

Ingredients

- 1 large frozen banana, sliced
- 1 cup coconut milk, unsweetened, or milk of own choice
- 2 tbsp. of peanut butter, unsweetened
- ¼ cup dried cranberries, unsweetened, or sweetened with fruit juice only
- 2 heaping tbsp. unflavored protein powder
- 1 ½ tbsp. ground chia seeds
- 1 tbsp. ground hemp seeds
- 3-4 ice cubes
- Shredded coconut as an optional topping
- Cacao nibs as an optional topping

Directions

- Grind the hemp and chia seeds in a coffee grinder before adding them to the smoothie mixture.
- Place the milk and ground seeds into the blender and pulse until combined.

- Add all the remaining ingredients and blend until the mixture is smooth.

- Pour smoothie into a large glass, add the optional topping if using, and enjoy.

Quinoa with Strawberry and Banana

Quinoa is very high in protein and contains all of the nine essential amino acids that your body needs, and is also high in magnesium and fiber. Chia seeds are the richest plant-based source of Omega 3, and provide more Omega 3 than salmon. Wheat germ adds fiber and vitamin B to the smoothie to make this an all-round protein and vitamin-packed smoothie for any time of the day. You can cook the quinoa beforehand and then measure it out into single portions and freeze it to save time and effort.

Prep Time: 6 minutes

Total Time: 6 minutes

Serving Size: 2 (4 cups)

Ingredients

- ½ cup cooked quinoa, cooled down

- 1 ripe banana, large

- 2 tbsp. honey

- 6 oz Greek yogurt, vanilla

- 1 tbsp. wheat germ

- 1 tbsp. chia seeds

- 2 cups frozen strawberries (if using fresh strawberries, freeze them first)

- 1 ½ cups almond milk, vanilla flavor (or milk of own choice)

- 1 tsp xanthan gum (optional if you prefer a thicker smoothie)

- 1 cup ice cubes

Directions

- Place all the ingredients into a blender jug and blend for roughly 45 seconds, until the mixture is smooth.

- Pour into two large glasses and serve immediately.

Banana, Peach, and Honey

This smoothie is popular with adults and children for breakfast or a snack. The main source of protein is cottage cheese. Unflavored protein powder can be added for an extra super protein boost. The recipe makes 2 large smoothies, or 3 medium-sized ones.

Prep Time: 5 minutes

Total Time: 5 minutes

Serving Size: 2 large smoothies

Ingredients

- 2 ½ cups of peach slices, frozen
- 1 banana, ripe and fresh or frozen

- 1 cup milk (full cream, non-fat, or fat-free,) can be substituted with any plant-based milk

- 1 cup of cottage cheese, preferably cultured

- 2 tbsp. honey (more or less, can be used as per personal preference)

Directions

- Place all the ingredients into the blender and blend until you have a smooth consistency.

- Pour into two large glasses and serve.

Pineapple and Raspberries

This recipe yields 3 cups as a single serving. If you find this too much, you can optionally add in plain cottage cheese and more milk, and then split the smoothie into 2 servings. The source of protein comes from the protein powder, and the cottage cheese if you add that.

Prep Time: 5 minutes

Total Time: 5 minutes

Serving Size: 1 very large serving (3 cups)

Ingredients

- ½ cup frozen or fresh raspberries

- 1 cup frozen pineapple chunks

- 1 cup of unsweetened coconut milk

- ½ tsp Stevia or honey (optional)

- 2 tbsp. vanilla protein powder of your own choice

- ½ cup ice

- ½ cup cultured plain cottage cheese (optional extra)

- ¼ cup extra coconut milk (optional extra if you are adding cottage cheese)

- Shredded coconut, unsweetened, as a topping

Directions

- Place all the ingredients into the jug of a highspeed blender and blend until the mixture has a thick, creamy texture.

- Pour into one very large glass, or into two medium-sized glasses.

- Top with shredded coconut or any other topping of your own choice and serve.

Cantaloupe and Ginger Smoothie

This smoothie recipe focuses mainly on cantaloupe instead of the usual assortment of fruit, nuts, seeds, and vegetables that go into most smoothies. The main source of protein here is from Greek yogurt and cottage cheese. Unflavored protein powder can be added if you need to add extra protein to your diet.

You can turn this smoothie into a smoothie bowl by adding an extra ½ cup of Greek yogurt and topping with toasted coconut, chopped kiwi fruit, and chia seeds.

Prep Time: 7 minutes

Total Time: 7 minutes

Serving Size: 2 cups (2 servings of 1 cup or 1 large serving)

Ingredients

- 2 ½ cups of peeled cantaloupe, cut into blocks
- 1 cup Greek yogurt, plain
- ½ cup cultured cottage cheese
- 1 tsp fresh ginger, peeled and grated
- ½ tsp lime zest, finely grated
- ½ scoop (1 heaping tbsp.) unflavored protein powder (optional)
- 2 tsp honey or maple syrup

Directions

- Pack all the ingredients into the blender and process for about 30-60 seconds, until the mixture is smooth and thick.
- Serve immediately as one large smoothie, or two servings of 1 cup each.

Chapter 8

7-Day Training Guide Plan

The following is a 7-day training guide to walk you through the first week of calisthenics.

Monday

These exercises are calisthenics building blocks that will help you build strength and endurance. They'll set a basis for performing the more demanding movement in the future. Perform four cycles of the following exercises:

- A plank:

    o Put your hands underneath your shoulders.
    o Ground toes into the floor so that your body is in a neutral position.
    o Hold for 30 seconds.

- Eight squats:

    o Stand straight, feet slightly wider than the hips, and point toes outwards.
    o Look straight in front of you, with a straightened, but not stiff, neck.
    o Raise your arms parallel to the ground with a neutral spine.

o Squat with spine, with the core slightly flexed.

o Push hips back.

o Squat.

o Stand back up in the right position.

- Eight lunges on each leg:

  o Stand tall, with feet aligned with hips.

  o Step forward with one leg.

  o Lower the body until the thigh parallels the floor.

  o Stand back up.

- Eight pushups:

  o On the ground, place hands slightly wider than shoulders.

  o Make feet well-balanced.

  o Keep spine and core in a neutral position.

  o Lift yourself up until your arms are straight.

  o Go back down.

- Eight lay-down leg raises:

  o Lie down with your legs extended and arms flat against your body.

  o Join legs together and lift them up.

  o Keep core flat against the floor.

  o Lower back down and repeat.

- 20 mountain climbers on each leg:

- o Position into a plank.
- o Pull one knee into the chest.
- o Straighten the leg out.
- o Repeat.

- Eight pike push-ups:

  - o Get in a push-up position.
  - o Lift your hips and form an upside-down V.
  - o Bend arms at the elbow until you nearly touch the floor.
  - o Push yourself up and repeat.

Tuesday: Basic Exercises

Today, you will introduce yourself to more basic calisthenics exercises. These exercises will require a bar for you to hang from. A quality bar will be an investment, but you can find many that are reasonably priced so that you don't have to overspend.

You'll do four cycles of the following exercises:

- Seven close-hand chin-ups:

  - o Stand in front of a pull up bar.
  - o Grab it with an overhand grip.
  - o Lift your body, with hands around a foot apart.
  - o Pull yourself up until your chin is above the bar.

- o Return to the starting position and repeat.

- Five pull-ups

- Six dips

  - o Stand between parallel bars and jump up while holding onto the bars.
  - o Lower your body with arm-bending and dip until your elbows are slightly below the bars.
  - o Lift yourself back up.
  - o Repeat.

- Fifteen push-ups

- Five leg raises

- Nine jump squats:

  - o Stand straight, feet shoulder-width apart.
  - o Jump up.
  - o Lower the body into the squat position when landing.
  - o Repeat.

- 15 Australian pull-ups:

  - o Wrap a towel around a door knob on each side of your door.
  - o Stand aligned with the door edge, one foot on each side of the door.

- o Squat down while holding onto the towel, with your elbows parallel to the ground.
- o Pull yourself as far back as you can without extending the arms.
- o Pull yourself back towards the door.
- o repeat.

Wednesday: Rest

Remember how we talked about the importance of active resting? Today, you shouldn't actively exercise, but instead opt-in for up to an hour of light walking in the fresh air, or up to fifteen minutes of light jogging. Remember to adjust your meals to your activity levels! On rest days, you should eat slightly less than when you're working out, but still enough to support muscle recovery.

Thursday

Today, you'll do four cycles of:

- Wide push-ups, 20 repetitions:

  - o Position for regular pushups, hands wider than shoulders.
  - o Bend elbows outwards.
  - o Lift yourself up, pause, then pull yourself down.

- Mountain climbers, 20 of each

- A one-minute wall sit:

  - Stand against the wall with a flat back.
  - Hold feet shoulder-width apart.
  - Bend down with back flat against the wall, until your thighs parallel the ground.
  - Hold the position for 60 seconds.
  - Repeat.

- A one-minute plank

- Clap push-ups, 15 repetitions:

  - Start off by lifting yourself up in a regular push-up position.
  - Propel yourself to lift hands off the ground.
  - Clap once your hands lift off the ground.
  - Return to the starting position.
  - Repeat.

- A half-minute superman hold.

- Lie down on your stomach.
  - Extend arms and legs.
  - Lift arms and legs up so that your body is in an arched position.
  - Hold for 30 seconds.
  - Return to the starting position.

- Squats, 30 repetitions

Remember to hydrate while exercising!

Friday: Fat Loss

It's time to do a little bit more cardio to get rid of excess fat. Today, you'll do four cycles of:

- A 100-meter run

- Five dips

- Eight push-ups

- Jumping jacks for 45 seconds:

    o Stand straight.
    o Keep your legs together and arms at sides.
    o Jump and spread your legs while lifting arms over the head.
    o Return to the starting position.
    o Repeat for 45 seconds.

- A 15-second plank

- Mountain climbers with alternating knees, 30 repetitions

Saturday: Cardio

Not going to work today? In that case, it's a great time to do some more cardio. It may not be what you hoped for, but remember that cardio exercises benefit your cardiovascular health and endurance of physical stress. Today, you will do:

- Four cycles of 15-second sprints, followed by a 45-second walk

- One cycle of a 30-minute sprint and a 90second walk

- Four cycles of a 15-second sprint followed by a 45-second walk

- One cycle of a 30-second sprint and a 90second walk

Now, you will break a sweat—don't doubt it.

Sunday: Rest

Chapter 9

Calisthenics Workout:

Muscle Groups and Body

Splits

The beauty of calisthenics lies in the fact that it never engages just one single muscle. It always engages one or multiple muscle groups, giving you a gracious, natural form that grows straight out of the natural shapes and forms of your body. In the previous chapter, you learned how to plan and track your progress with calisthenics. Now, the fun begins! In this chapter, you will learn which exercises train specific muscle groups, so that you can choose depending on your personal goals.

While the calisthenics exercises are too numerous to explain in this beginner manual, you can roughly divide them by the muscle groups they activate:

- **Upper body push**. These exercises stimulate the chest, anterior and medial shoulders, and triceps. They are beneficial for stabilizing shoulder positioning when you're performing pushing-away movements. These exercises can be further divided into horizontal and vertical.

- **Upper body pull**. These exercises train your posterior shoulders, biceps, lats, trapezius, and rhomboids muscles. They help you balance shoulder muscles and pull yourself up when exercising.

- **Knee flexion**. These exercises include different variations of squats, and they train muscles involved in squatting, like adductors, quadriceps, glutes, and hip muscles. Training these muscles enables you to squat in the right position.

- **Single leg**. These exercises help you balance your body when standing on one leg. They strengthen your core, adductors, and quadriceps, and improve your coordination and balance.

- **Hip extensions**. Stretching and flexing hip muscles engages the lower back, glutes, and hamstrings. They help you maintain a straight posture and prevent injuries when exercising.

- **Core stabilizers**. These exercises include the famous plank and its many variations. They engage your upper and lower core muscles.

The so-called upper-lower body split is quite popular among calisthenics exercisers. While there are many principles and methods you can use and apply as you advance your training, this method might be the most beginner-friendly, because it's most concise. The upper-Lower body split splits your training sessions to target each muscle group at least once during the week. Research shows that exercises using traditional split methods lead to better progress and fewer injuries. However, research also shows that targeting one body part for each day of the week is a less successful method, because the individual body parts get too much resting time.

How Much Should You Exercise?

Optimally, you allow for up to three days for each of the muscle groups to recover. This means that you should target a specific muscle group at least twice a week. The best way to progress is to exercise multiple times each week. Research shows that those who exercise twice a week show better muscle growth than those who exercise only once. If you train twice per week and do it accurately, you should see a 6.8%

muscle growth after a couple of weeks (Peterson et al., 2004).

But how many, and which muscle groups should you target each week?

You can successfully add a training session for each muscle group without increasing the number of sessions. Instead, you can do this by focusing on a single muscle group per each training session. If you split to the upper and lower body, this means that one session will be dedicated to the upper body, and another one to the lower body. Still, you should make sure that all of the muscle groups have enough time to recover.

How to Train Different Muscle Groups?

So, how do you do upper-lower body split workouts? The answer is simple. One day of the training is dedicated to upper-body exercises, and the other to the lower body.

- **Upper body exercises** engage chest muscles, upper and middle back, forearm, arm muscles, and shoulders. Exercisers usually have to find a way to incorporate forearm exercises into their body routine, which can be done by adding pull-ups and deadlift exercises.

- **Lower body exercises** engage the muscles in your stomach, lower back, quads, hamstrings, glutes, and calves.

One of the greatest advantages of this exercise model is that it maximizes the gains from engaging individual muscle groups once per week. As you progress with the exercises, you can add more repetitions and sets.

When you engage the muscles of a certain group, they grow in the size of the muscle cells. This is called hypertrophy. Muscle hypertrophy in the upper body is achieved mechanically, by adding physical stress to the muscles, or muscle damage, that stimulates muscles to grow stronger and bigger, and metabolic stress, which happens when chemical products of anaerobic metabolism build-up.

This is important to keep in mind, because targeting muscle size doesn't always improve muscle strength. You'll use different strategies to become bigger and to be physically stronger. You should aim to do exercises that cause hypertrophy if you want to increase the size of your muscles.

The following beginner fundamental exercises engage main muscle groups and enable you to move onto other, more demanding exercises:

- **Push-ups** engage your hands and consist of using your hands to push yourself up and then let down slowly. They engage upper chest muscles, triceps, and shoulders, and stabilize your abs, back, legs, and traps. Aside from the famous handstand, push-up exercises give you stability when lifting heavy objects. They are compound horizontal exercises. A correct pushup is done by letting your chest get as close to the ground as possible. Aside from the mentioned muscles, proper exercise will also engage your upper and lower back.

- **Pull-ups** include compound vertical pulling exercises that are done on a bar, pulling your body upwards. These exercises engage abs, biceps, and shoulders mainly, and other muscle groups, like those in your legs, when you're pulling your body up. Doing these exercises strengthens muscles needed to climb and pull down objects. Aside from being able to maneuver shelf objects with much grace, pullups will also help you perform other activities and exercises that demand you to grab, pull, and climb. Beginner pull-ups include leg assisted, half pull-ups, and full pull-ups.

- **Squats** are compound exercises that engage your lower body. A proper squat is done by bending your knees until you touch your hamstrings with your calves. After that, you press back up. These exercises engage your abs, side abs, and lower back, aside from leg muscles. They stabilize your whole body, strengthen your core, and help you stay balanced. Modified versions include assisted half and full squats, half squats, and full squats.

- **Leg raises** strengthen both the front and back core. Exercising them requires lifting the legs until they are parallel with the floor. They mainly target abdominal muscles and improve hip flexion and extension. They also stabilize your legs, making your core strong and creating visible abs.

- **Planks** strengthen your core and train abs while stabilizing muscles. To do a plank properly, you should get into a push-up position with your feet joined together. Your forearms should rest on the ground, and the position should be held for as long as possible. Planking is one of the most demanding exercises, but best known for its results.

- **Dips** are among the most effective and most important calisthenics exercises. They are done using parallel bars. The easy-looking exercise requires you to push your body in while holding onto the bars. To do them correctly, your brachialis should point forward and your elbows should be right next to your body. Your scapula should remain tense and be slightly pressed down, with your neck straight. Your pelvis should be tipped back, and your legs straight to keep your spine straight and stable. This exercise will engage your triceps and strengthen mainly core muscles, but also your thighs.

What is Hypertrophy, and How to Achieve It?

To achieve muscle hypertrophy, you'll need more repetitions than you'd need for muscle strength.

Metabolic stress is mainly triggered by an increase in exercise volume, and it is the main factor that causes hypertrophy. Up to 25% of muscle growth happens because of metabolic stress.

However, simply increasing exercise volume won't be enough for the desired result. Research shows that you should work on each muscle group three times per week. This is a measure best suited for both athletes and nonathletes. More precisely, four sets per muscle group at 60%, one-repetition maximum, will provide the best result, combined with proper intensity and adequate split.

Athletic physique, on the other hand, if you want to maintain or progress, will need a higher volume training, done twice per week. Athletes usually exercise eight sets per each muscle group at 85%. This training regime gives greater volume, and best-optimized hypertrophy.

How to Schedule Your Workout Sessions

But how to schedule your sessions for the best results? Your schedule should be simple and attainable. It should be easy to follow by keeping up a three-to-four-day exercise schedule. Here's a suggestion for your exercise days:

- Monday and Thursday - upper body exercises

- Tuesday and Friday - lower body exercises

- Wednesday, Saturday, and Sunday - rest days

During the rest days, you should be recovering actively by doing light cardio and other low-intensity activities. For example, you should take light walks or jogs. You can vary this schedule if you want to, to introduce more variety into your routine, or adjust your workout schedule to your weekly schedule. Here are some suggestions for how to vary your three-day routine throughout two weeks:

First week

- Monday and Friday - lower body

- Wednesday -upper body

- Tuesday, Saturday, and Sunday - rest days

Second week

- Monday and Friday - upper body

- Wednesday - lower body

- Tuesday, Saturday, and Sunday - rest days

This schedule will give you similar efficiency to the four-day split, at a lower frequency for different muscle groups. It will work well for those who have a busy schedule and can't find the time to work out four times a week.

How to Include Cardio Exercises

Cardio exercises are usually more popular with people who are after weight loss than muscle and strength building. You should still include cardio training into your routine even if you're not looking to lose weight, because they are good for your cardiovascular health. If you are trying to lose weight, you should keep in mind that strength exercises are often equally or even more effective than cardio.

When you're working with limited time capacity, you should do around twenty minutes of cardio training after each session of strength training. High-intensity intervals will help maximize workout time. You can also add cardio training to everyday activities, like jogging from and back to your home, and whenever the occasion is suitable.

When you start doing your exercises, it's very likely that you'll experience some stress and loss of motivation. However, there are things you can do to prevent and improve this. You should make sure to keep up with your schedule, because results that will show will most certainly help improve your motivation.

How to Exercise Your Core

Core strength will give you not only stability with other exercises, but also joint flexibility and motor control. And, let's face it, everyone wants a tight stomach with prominent chest muscles. While the majority of popular core exercises belong to the intermediate level, there's still plenty for beginners to enjoy. Core exercises strengthen the three important elements of successful calisthenics, which include joint flexibility, motor control, and core strength. Here are some of the beginner-friendly exercises that address all three important aspects:

Core Flexibility

- **Hip rotations**. Start the exercise by lying with bent knees and feet together, with a flat back. Drop both of your legs to one side and hold for up to 30 seconds. Bring legs to the center and move to the other side. Repeat the exercise three times.

- **Lumbar extension**. Lie on your stomach and place your hands underneath your shoulders. Your glutes and pelvis should touch the ground as you push your chest up from the floor. Hold the position up to ten seconds, and repeat up to five times.

- **Hip stretches**. Kneel and step forward with your left leg, so that it's in a lunge position. Tilt your pelvis forward and hold the position for 20 seconds, after which you'll repeat with the other leg. You should do this exercise three times.

Core Strength

- **Leg lowers**. Lie on your back with your legs up at a 90-degree angle. Your back should be flat, not arched, as you lower one of your legs until it touches the ground. Pull the leg back up and repeat with the other leg. You should practice 10 times with each leg, while making sure that your back doesn't arch. Take a minute break after each set.

- **Arabesque**. Stand on one leg and bring the other back. Lower your trunk to parallel the floor, then return to the standing position. Complete two sets of 10 repetitions on each side.

- **Single leg squats**. Stand on a pillow with one leg and lower your body by bending at your knee and hip. Complete two sets of 20 repetitions.

Core Control

- **Arm and leg alterations**. Position yourself into a four-point kneel. Make sure that your lower back is parallel to the floor, and not arched. Lift the opposite arm and leg at the same time and extend them, while making sure that your back and pelvis are aligned. Practice two sets of 20 repetitions.

- **Bridge**. Lie flat with your knees bent. Lift your bottom from the floor by engaging core muscles. Practice two sets of up to 20 repetitions.

10 Tips for Making Motivation Last

Now you know what calisthenics is all about, what you need to do to exercise properly, how to eat, when to rest, and all the other essentials. Still, if regular exercise was so easy, the world would be much fitter and leaner, and obesity would've been eradicated. But it's not like that, is it? One of the bigger challenges with calisthenics lies in the fact that it's done independently. There's no one to supervise you and give direction in case you're not exercising correctly.

Why Have You Lost the Motivation to Exercise?

There are several reasons why people lose motivation to learn calisthenics. The first reason is that they repeat the same exercises and routines over and over again, and become bored with it after a while. To a certain degree, this can be due to the lack of knowledge about how to alter exercises to achieve a good result. A repetitive exercise regimen no longer stimulates your body, and so you don't feel like doing it anymore. You stop seeing results and lose your motivation. Another important reason is that exercisers become too focused on targeting the core and forget that, in calisthenics, each exercise serves a purpose, and all of them affect different muscle groups indirectly.

The third reason for the loss of motivation could be that you're over-exercising and not getting enough rest. If training consumes your daily schedule and you get too caught into planning and measuring progress, it becomes an obsession. A sport that once served to deepen your physical awareness and sharpen your skills falls victim to self-policing, so you feel like a prisoner of it in a way. The lack of time to rest and unwind, listen and observe your body, and more importantly, forgetting that calisthenics is more than exercise, kills your motivation.

So, what do you do when you get stuck in a rut? The best way out of it is to reflect on the meaning of calisthenics and its significance for your life and health. This way, you will again find beauty and fun in it. Should the aforementioned happen to you, there are numerous ways to regain your motivation. The following sections will give you some suggestions to regain your motivation and start exercising devotedly once again.

When You Feel Like Giving Up, Remember to...

Start Small

When you're just starting out with calisthenics, it may look as if achieving progress and seeing results is too far away. The beginnings are arguably most difficult. You're just getting used to regular exercise, it's possible that your weight is a point of contempt in your daily life, and you've yet to figure out how to fit exercise into your lifestyle. Although the idea of exercising at home and achieving great results sounds appealing, the lack of knowledge and experience can make you doubt your abilities. With this, you can begin to lose motivation to exercise.

First thing's first, focus on getting into a habit of exercising. You don't have to start with a pitch-perfect routine the very first time. You can start with as little as a 10-minute workout, as long as you start getting used to doing physical activity at that time of the week. You shouldn't think in "all or nothing" mode, but instead do whatever you can of your exercises, even if you feel like you can't push through an entire workout. Because you're starting from scratch, you'll feel all the aches and pains beginners go through before they build the fundamental skills.

Stick to the Basics

There are numerous strategies you can use to keep your motivation high while exercising. However, it's important for you to first know some of the mental principles and training misconceptions. The first is that calisthenics isn't a program for you to build muscle and strength quickly and effortlessly. It will take devotion and time, just like any other program. The only way for you to see quick changes is to follow an expensive program that covers specialized equipment, diet, and supplements. Even with this, chances of failure would be quite high, since it would be up to you to make major changes in your diet and activities.

Focus on Consistency Over Intensity

One of the things to consider is that calisthenics is more than simply an exercise program. It is a lifestyle that demands the following essential principles. The first thing you need to understand is that calisthenics doesn't promise overnight success. It requires devoted exercise, tracking your progress, and using your body weight to the maximum if you want to see results. If you are willing to invest time and put effort into training, you'll eventually witness how much your strength, health, and performance can improve. However, this doesn't happen quickly. Safe to say, it will take a couple of months for you to see the first results. Calisthenics has a long history, and has been used by many historic strongmen to make exceptional achievements.

Remember Why You Started

Calisthenics isn't only about exercise and physical strength. It is also about creating a healthy connection with your body and being willing to invest in yourself so that you grow your potential. It will help you become the best version of yourself, so that you can contribute to the world and to those around you. However, most people who become successful because of calisthenics spend over ten years not only exercising, but studying physical strength and learning about this form of exercise. This way, they were able to build themselves up to the greatest levels of success, and are now able to perform push-ups with one arm, or squats with one leg. However, the road there isn't easy for anyone, and it won't be easy for you.

Don't Take an All-Or-Nothing Approach

The second thing you need to understand is that you have more strength than you think. Most people tend to underestimate their capacities and overestimate limitations. Nowadays, people want to see instant success, and feel like they're not capable enough if what they do doesn't show results right away. As with many other things in life, this approach won't help with calisthenics. You simply need to give it time. You'll need to develop devotion and mental toughness going forward, because learning and patience, aside from regular training, are all you need to get where you want to be.

Stick to the Basics

Even reaching the fundamental goals might test your patience and motivation, and there's nothing wrong with that. Keep in mind that you're neither the first nor the last person to doubt their abilities at the very beginning. If you want to succeed, you need to decide that you will push through obstacles and limitations and stay focused on following through with your plan, more than you'll be paying attention to the results you're trying to see. Calisthenics will require a lot of hard work, and it should, because you'll learn devotion and discipline that will transfer onto other areas of your life.

Remind Yourself What's at Stake

You will often find yourself wanting to quit. Whenever you start thinking about giving up, you should think about the health benefits of doing exercise, even if the desired results fail to show. Even if you're exercising and not getting the results you want, you will still be doing better compared to not exercising at all. If you get stuck and start to feel like you want to switch onto another program, focus on the fact that you will most likely have to commit to going to the gym or buying equipment before you can even start, let alone before you see results.

Every workout you do, regardless of how you feel, just for the sheer discipline, strengthens your body and your mind. People who have anxiety or stress-related health issues often find it difficult to perform daily tasks without getting upset at every little unpleasantness, and it is that growing sensitivity that only worsens your health issues. The more you face this overwhelming feeling of not wanting to exercise and just leap into your workout instead, the more you will develop the skills to cope with and overcome other challenges and unpleasantness in life.

Make it Fun!

Another important thing to think about is making your workouts fun. You will most definitely lose your motivation if you only focus on the number of repetitions. There are ways for you to have fun while exercising. If you find yourself bored by doing exercises or they feel too difficult, you can play some music or listen to an e-book. Regardless of your goals, you should have an action plan when you start exercising. Your exercise plan will prevent you from being bored or confused because you don't know how to exercise, or which exercises to use. Having a clear, progressive plan will tell you exactly what to do to see progress. Making your exercise plan is a great first step, but actually following through with it is a different story.

You'll need to develop strategies to fight off sluggishness, stress, tiredness, or boredom before and while working out. Aside from creating an interesting setting for exercise, you should also make sure that you're well-rested and have properly eaten.

Aside from this, tracking your progress will boost your motivation as well. In the next chapter, we'll talk about the importance of keeping track of how many exercises you've done, the repetitions, difficulty, weight loss, and the visible changes in your physique. All of these activities will have a beneficial impact on your motivation as well. You will be able to see how far you've come. Most importantly, you'll be able to tell how exercises that once posed a great challenge have now become easy, and you've moved on to greater challenges. Aside from this, measuring your progress will help you remember just how many new things you learned to do, despite having started with zero knowledge and skill.

This way, whenever you get stuck again and start to feel like you've encountered a challenge you won't be able to overcome, you will look in your workout log and remember which approaches and strategies you used to overcome previous challenges. You will understand which areas you need to improve before moving forward.

Aside from this, you should also be aware of the fact that success is a momentary experience. You are becoming more successful, stronger, fitter, and leaner with each new workout. Knowing what you want to achieve with calisthenics and keeping that image in your mind will keep you going when you get stuck. This way, you will gradually progress day after day.

Last but not least, make sure to have some versatility in your exercising so that it's fun. You should shuffle and change up exercises to add variety and boost muscle strength and endurance. You can do this by changing the order of your exercises, changing the range of repetitions, switching volume, doing variations of different exercises, setting medium goals or milestones, changing the frequency of your training, adding cardio, flexibility, and mobility exercises, training other sports you like, or boosting repetitions.

How to Avoid Future Mistakes

Ultimately, you will regain your motivation if you manage to figure out what went wrong with your training and commit to doing things differently in the future. Tracing your footsteps and realizing where you made a mistake could be useful to prevent future failures. Ask yourself if you made some of the following mistakes:

Hating on Fat

If one of your goals was to lose weight, you could've made the mistake of thinking that all fat is your enemy. Fat loss is essential to gain visible muscle, but you will still need enough body fat to keep your body building strong muscles. Fat is an energy reserve, and although you shouldn't have too much of it, you mustn't become fat-depleted either.

Poor Diet and Cardio Optimization

If the beginning of your journey was marked by the difficulty to control eating and engage in cardio, the initial results and improvement could have driven you to over-exercise while eating too little. This loss of balance in diet and exercise may not only slow down your metabolism, but also cause psychological stress and mental tiredness, aside from physical. So, ask yourself, is it possible that you haven't been eating enough for the amount of exercise you want to do? If needed, increase your meal sizes, and the energy replenishment should, and most likely will, result in a better mood to exercise.

Focused on Result, Not the Process

The first thing one learns about calisthenics, and the thing that is easiest to forget, is that its primary goal is to improve your health and physical skills, not necessarily your looks. If you forget this, chances are that you may over train the exercises that produced the most visible results, and forget about the rest of them. To avoid this, always focus on the process of exercise, and on how you want to exceed your body's limitations with physical movement. This way, your choice of exercise will be different, and better adjusted to the needs and possibilities of your body. They will stimulate both body and mind, so you'll never get tired of them.

Chapter 11

How to Track Your Progress

All beginnings are difficult, and doubting whether or not the exercise gives results can make you doubt whether it's worth doing at all. On the other hand, those who are passionate about exercise and physical activity might enjoy it too much, and eventually burn out. How to prevent this? The answer is by keeping track of your progress.

Intuitive vs Planned Training

Should you exercise based on your intuition, or should you develop an exercise program? Some people prefer to follow the wills of their body and do exercises that feel most comfortable, relying on their intuition to tell them what type of movement their body needs. There's logic to that, of course, and the school of intuitive fitness is gaining traction as much as other exercise programs do. Oftentimes, and for certain people, measuring progress is a challenge. Whether because of health limitations or personal circumstances, some just can't commit to a schedule or prioritize their training. Nothing wrong with that, unless your intention is to pursue a skill and make visible progress.

The so-called "autoregulatory training" relies on your body to provide direction for how you shoulder exercises, which exercises to do, and for how long. It relies on "biofeedback evaluation" for the choice of number of sets, repetitions, and types of exercises. Of course, this type of training doesn't guarantee a certain result.

Intuitive training might be wise from time to time, or used with other activities that are more a hobby than they are expected to produce results. If you have a particular goal with calisthenics, and you have an intention to achieve a certain result, then keeping track of your progress is a must. Training without tracking progress keeps you from tracking your goals and noting whether or not you're advancing in the desired direction, and at the desired pace. If you keep track of your exercise, you'll know how many of which exercise you did in your workout sessions, which is especially important when you're aiming to increase training intensity.

Planned training begins with evaluating your starting point and informing yourself of the amount of progress you can achieve given your training background, lifestyle, and health situation. Aside from this, planning helps you build a habit to exercise. If you haven't exercised regularly, making a commitment to work out might be challenging. Planning helps you make physical activity a part of your daily life, and it helps you develop a realistic perspective and expectations for your progress. Planning also helps you keep track of how far you've come, compare current progress with your long term goal, and pay attention to whether or not your time is spent doing exercises that bring progress.

Writing down your workouts helps track how much you should increase the difficulty of an exercise to progress. After you've spent some time tracking progress, for example after six months, you'll be able to see how close you are to your goal, which mistakes you made, how much you've effectively exercised, and how attainable your goal is. This will help you make better decisions regarding training and bring you closer to your goal.

Tracking your progress will also help you feel more accomplished and boost your motivation to move further. This will assure you that you're investing time and effort wisely, and be satisfied that you're taking enough time to train.

How to Plan Your Calisthenics Training

As a beginner, it's best for you to make a 6-month plan for learning calisthenics. A good plan will contain the workout routines that will serve to produce weight loss or build the amount of muscles you want. Aside from that, it will also include life lessons that you want to learn, and the way in which you will start as a beginner. You'll start making your workout plan by determining how many of each exercise you want to be able to do in six months. However, you will plan for setbacks and failures as well. What if it turns out that your evaluation was wrong, and you don't master the skills you thought you would? In that case, you should plan for so-called regressions, which means using easier modifications of chosen exercises that are a better fit for your body.

Your plan will also determine the types of exercises you should do to increase pulling strength, pushing strength, lower body, and core. After that, you should make a workout plan for one month, and then a weekly plan (which will be given in this book) to follow. Finally, you'll plan progressions, and decide which advanced exercises you'll focus on when increasing the difficulty and volume of training. When you're planning ahead, there's a good chance that you won't make accurate evaluations. That will most likely happen if you plan on your own. But, if you consult a calisthenics expert, they will give experienced advice for what kind of expectations you can set for yourself.

Here's a short example of a six-month plan you can use when planning your training:

- **Basics**. Which warm-up exercises do you want to use, and for how many repetitions? Account for making up to a minute-long break between exercises. Start by mapping out your ability to do five of each: squats, dips, shoulder-width chin-ups, knee raises, and push-ups. If you can't meet these beginner demands just yet, give yourself more time to practice said exercises, and then move to progressions intended for the first month.

- **First month (weeks 1-4)**. At the end of your first month of exercise, you should be able to do ten squats, five push-ups and shoulder chin ups, eight knee raises and chair dips, and at least a minute-long rope jump. A monthly plan should include three workout days, and four (active) rest days.

- **Second month (weeks 5-8)**. By the time you've completed eight weeks of exercise, you should be able to do at least five L-sit chin-ups and decline push-ups, eight dips and hanging leg raises, twelve lunges, and at least three minutes of running. As you can see, these exercises are different compared to the first month, as diversity is important to avoid boredom.

- **Third month (weeks 9-12)**. If you achieved your previous goal, you're now entering the intermediate level. By the end of your twelfth week, you should be able to do five high chest pull ups and straight-on-bar dips, eight leg raises and decline push-ups, twelve calf raises on each leg, and duck-walk for thirty seconds.

- **Fourth month (weeks 13-16)**. You should set your mind to doing ten horizontal jumps, eight pike push-ups and Australian pull-ups, six straight bar dips, five jump muscle ups, and a minute of mountain climbers.

- **Fifth month (weeks 14-17)**. You are approaching your six-month goal! By the end of week 17 of your program, you should set your mind to doing a half-minute frog stand, a minute-long rope jump, three muscle-ups, skin the cats, and chin-above-bars, and 10 vertical jumps.

- **Sixth month (weeks 18-21)**. After six months of training, you should manage four muscle ups, fifteen dips and pushups, and ten jumping squats on a three-minute limit.

The 7-day training guide given in this book will be adjusted for beginners, but feel free to adjust it to your abilities. Keep in mind that practicing below your ability won't show results, and trying to do exercises that are too difficult could result in overstrain and injury.

How to Track Your Progress

Here's what you should track regarding your progress in calisthenics:

- Entire workout sessions and exercises with date, and start and finish time

- Number of sets and repetitions

- Rest and recovery periods and practices

- Warm-ups

- Cool-downs

You can also rate your degree of discomfort, forms you achieved, and levels of exhaustion on a scale from one to 10. When it comes to doing exercises, your pain should be below grade three. If it exceeds it, you should switch to a different variation or better observe your form.

When it comes to your form, you should be tracking how accurately you performed an exercise. Your form score should be at least a nine.

These scores will help you decide how to repeat each consecutive workout or set. When it comes to more difficult exercises, you should pay better attention to the form. The proper form protects against injury, and doing more difficult exercises with an improper form increases your risk from injury. If you can't perform at a score of at least nine, you should consider doing an easier variation of the exercise.

With proper tracking, you should be able to reflect on the quality of your training accurately and note what you can do differently with the next workout to improve. Your exhaustion levels can vary with your exercise program and each individual exercise. However, your exhaustion level should still be between six and eight. Aside from this, you can also keep track of how you feel and what you think about while exercising, and your ideas and suggestions for future workouts.

At the very least, you should keep a workout journal. You can take notes during the workout to trace your performance. Don't lose count of repetitions, and you can also write down your exercise scores. It's also wise to lay out your workout structure before you start. This way, you can just add multiple sessions without putting too much thought into the process.

After the workout, you can write down the notes and observations that you weren't able to write during exercise. You can also write down your notes after the exercise, but the sooner the better. If you wait too long after you've exercised, you can forget some of the important details.

If you don't feel like keeping a journal, there are many other ways for you to track your progress. You can write in a regular notebook that you can take with you anytime you're working out, or you can write down your notes on your phone or tablet. You can also use tracking on your computer to log your exercises. However, make sure that logging doesn't take up too much time, or distract you from exercising. Experienced exercisers find simple notebooks to be the best option because they are the least distracting.

Optionally, you can get a workout log. This log is essentially a notebook, with a template designed to log exercises and other relevant items.

Aside from logging, there are a couple of other ways to keep track of your performance and progress. You can take your measurements if you're pursuing muscle gain or weight loss. You should do this weekly or monthly by measuring the circumference of your arms, waist, forearms, neck, and other parts of the body. You can also take pictures and observe your transformation over the years. You should take three monthly pictures, front, rear, and back. Your muscles shouldn't be flexed or pumped on these images, but natural and taken in natural light.

You can also keep track of your weight by measuring it on a scale. Depending on your goals, you can also do this as often as daily, or once a month. Your body-fat composition is another important item to measure. If you want your body fat to reduce, you should get a body-fat caliper and document your percentages on a monthly or weekly basis.

How to Evaluate Your Progress
with Calisthenics

Ultimately, you should work out a method for measuring your progress. So, which metrics should you use with bodyweight training? There are three types of measurements to evaluate your improvement:

- **Exercise progress**. You should track your total training volume, or number of repetitions done per training session, how much time it takes to perform the same number of repetitions, and the quality and accuracy of your exercises (how well you're aligned, how you maintain form, how difficult it is to make repetitions, and how slowly you can do a movement).

- **Physique progress**. Here, you will track and evaluate how much your progress is notable in your shape and size. In calisthenics, physique improves with other improvements of skill, so it is a side-effect in a way. You can measure your weight and follow with body circumference measurements to see how much regular exercise affects your physique.

- **Performance progress**. Lastly, you can track how much your speed, strength, and other physical abilities have improved since you started training. If you're training calisthenics to improve not only looks, but also health and productivity, you can note your energy levels, stress resilience, and how exercise affects your emotional and psychological stability. These can be valuable in case visible changes fail to show significantly, because they remind you of how the quality of your life improved with regular exercise.

Chapter 12

11 Biggest Myths About Calisthenics

There are so many myths and misconceptions out there, and especially on the internet, that it will make your head spin. The biggest problem with these myths is that they can cause harm and frustration, especially for people starting out on the journey of getting their bodies into shape.

It is important to go through all these myths and misconceptions, as many of them are so ingrained in the fitness scene that they are accepted as truth. The last thing any person starting out with calisthenics needs is to have their progress sabotaged and their fitness goals delayed. The other reason to debunk myths is to not fall into the trap when well-meaning friends and family give advice based on misconceptions and myths. This can easily lead to strained relationships, whereas when you are armed with facts, you can politely and graciously defuse any situation.

Where there is more than one myth concerning a topic or action, they are listed under one heading for easy reference and clarity.

Myth #1: The Best Workout Time is Early Morning

Early mornings are great for doing your daily workout, and if you are a morning person, it is the perfect way to start your day. You also do not have to then make time during your day for your workout, because it is all done with. There is, however, not really a difference whether you prefer to do your workout first thing in the morning or later during the day, at a time more suitable to your personal schedule.

According to a 2019 study, there is no difference in the quality of a workout done first thing in the morning or, for instance, between 1 p.m. and 4 p.m. in the afternoon (Youngstedt, Elliott, & Kripke, 2019). The best time depends on each individual and their daily schedule.

Always Do Cardio First

Many people prefer to do the cardio portion of their exercise at the beginning of their workout so that they can concentrate on other aspects of their session. Cardio exercises draw heavily on your body's glycogen stores within your muscles, whereas other forms of exercise do not. Doing cardio first, in reality, leaves your body with a shortage of glycogen for the rest of your training session. Your weight and strength training will be of poor quality, so switching to doing cardio at the end of your workout gives you a better and more effective workout overall.

Minimum of 20 Minutes Cardio

Often, people fixate on cardio and swear by the 20minute minimum cardio rule. It is not the time factor in cardio, but instead the intensity of training. You can pack a serious cardio workout into doing high-intensity interval training for a much shorter period. High intensity interval training is a double plus, as it keeps burning calories once you have completed the workout session.

Another great option to look into for your calisthenics cardio workout is Tabatha training. Tabatha is a form of HIIT, but it takes it to the next level and packs a punch into 4-minute routines that are simply incredible. So, there is no rule that says you must do 20 minutes of cardio for it to be beneficial for you.

More Cardio, More Weight Loss

The idea behind this misconception is that the more cardio you do, the better chance you have of shedding those extra pounds. We are all aware that to lose weight, you must create a calorie deficit, and cardio does contribute to that on a day-to-day basis. However, that is not the smart way to go about losing weight. The smart way is to combine the following things:

Lean muscle mass burns calories while your body is at rest. To create this effect, you need to combine strength training with high-intensity cardio routines.

All your efforts need a solid foundation of a good nutrition plan based on your personal needs.

Cardio Machines Record Calories Burnt Accurately

If you use an elliptical trainer or a treadmill, you should not take the calories burnt display at face value. According to a 2018 study, these machines have a tendency to overestimate the calories burnt per 30minute workout by at least 100 calories (Glave et al., 2018). This lulls you into a false sense of security, and over time the discrepancy can be quite significant.

Myth # 2: Crunches and Sit-Ups Equal 6-Pack Abs

All ab exercises are great for building and strengthening the muscles of your core. That said, sit-ups and crunches do not automatically give you those sought after 6-pack abs. You have to have a decent eating plan to back up your exercises. You cannot follow a diet high in calories and unhealthy fats if you wish to achieve that ripped look. A thick abdominal subcutaneous layer of fat will hide the tendinous inscriptions completely. Crunches and doing sit-ups alone are not going to work, and even if you can deadlift a significant amount, you need to eat a balanced diet as well.

Myth # 3: Crunches for Core Strength

Crunches are not the beginning and end of core strengthening exercises. Instead of focusing solely on crunches, concentrate on multi-muscle exercises that target all the areas of your core, and not only one.

Fat Is Able to Become Muscle, and Vice Versa

Nobody really knows where this myth started, but muscle tissue and fat are definitely two very different things. Yes, you can lose muscle and gain fat tissue, just as you can build muscle and lose fat. However, there is no magical process that turns the one into the other.

Muscle Loss Starts After 7 Days of Being Inactive

When you have recently started a workout routine and you take a week off, the progress you have gained will be eradicated in a short time. This is logical. It is very different, however, if you have an established workout routine and have been doing it for several months. A study done in 2007 with athletes showed that their performance showed very little deterioration for a period of up to 3 weeks of being inactive (McMaster et. al., 2013).

Myth #4: No Pain, No Gain

Pain warns the body that something is wrong, so the myth that your workout was not effective unless you are sore afterward is a total misconception. Yes, muscle stiffness can be felt after an intense workout, but sharp or intense pain means to stop whatever you are doing and consult your healthcare provider.

Should you feel discomfort and muscle aches after a workout, you should refuel your body, stay hydrated, and rest to allow your body to recover.

Myth #5: Running Is Better Than Walking

This is a misconception that often causes confusion. Running and walking target the exact same groups of muscles, and the only difference is the intensity. The health results of walking and running are the same when you look at the energy expended and calories burnt. The difference is that it takes twice the amount of time for walking to achieve what running does.

So it really is up to the individual whether you want to run, for instance, for 15 minutes, or have a brisk walk for 30 minutes. The only real difference is the time allocated to this activity. Often, a brisk walk with a loved one or a friend has many social and interactive benefits as well.

Myth #6: Sports Drinks Are Healthy

Hydrating after a workout is a great idea, but downing a sports drink is not the greatest idea. Sports drinks are loaded with lots of sugar, and the sugarless ones are loaded with artificial sweeteners. You are basically loading up on unnecessary sugar, sodium, and carbs.

Myth #7: Treadmills and Running Outdoors Are Equal

Running outdoors is different as you encounter uneven terrain, run up and down hills, and encounter wind. This means your body uses more energy than when you run on a treadmill inside a gym or at home. You will burn approximately 10% more calories running outdoors than over the same distance running on a treadmill.

Myth #8: Exercise Makes You Hungry

People often confuse their body signals, especially when they have worked out. They need liquid, and confuse it for hunger. Another reason why people think they are ravenous after a workout is that their sugar levels drop. Your body signals your brain about the drop in blood sugar, and we associate this with hunger.

There are also countless conflicting myths about working out and when you should or should not eat.

Never Do Workouts on an Empty Stomach

There are absolutely no scientific or medical facts to support the misconception that you must eat before you start your workout.

Myth #9: Toning My Muscles Is All I Need to Do

Your muscles are actually well toned, as you use them all the time in everything that you do. You don't see the muscles because they are covered by a layer of fat. The problem lies with your diet. Once you start on a balanced diet, you can use workouts to boost your calorie consumption. Soon, those muscles you want to tone will no longer be hidden under a layer of fat.

Myth #10: Men and Women Cannot Do the Same Workouts

It is a total myth that men and women need different exercise routines. Men and women are the same species and have the same physical design. The difference lies in the fact that men carry much higher levels of testosterone than women. This gives men a strength advantage, but there is no reason why men and women cannot do the same workouts.

Women Should Lift Lighter and Do More Reps

This myth is kept alive because in general, women worry about how lifting weights will affect them, and that it will make them bulk up. Logically, though, women don't lift the same weight as men because of their lower testosterone levels. This also means they do not bulk up in the same way that men do, and women have no need to compensate for this by doing more repetitions.

Men and women should do weight lifting workouts that challenge them, but not overtax or injure them without taking myths to mind.

Yoga Is Not Proper Exercise

The misconception that yoga is not a proper workout and is all about gentle routines with stretching is perpetuated by people who have never taken any yoga classes. The media also portrays yoga as this spiritual and gentle activity. Yes, there are gentle yoga routines, but there are many intense and rigorous routines, for example, power Vinyasa and Bikram yoga. Yoga takes dedication and working out regularly.

Myth #11: Stretching Is a Must to Prevent Injuries

Everyone has heard this at some time during their lives, that you must do stretching exercises before you start your workout, and the dire warnings that you will injure yourself if you don't. Numerous studies over the past decades have found absolutely no proof that doing static stretches before a workout in any way reduces any form of injuries related to exercise.

Yes, it is true that you should not just jump into your calisthenics workout routine without preparation, but you do not have to do stretches. What you need to do is warm-up exercises for about 5-15 minutes, to increase the blood flow to your muscles and loosen the tendons. This is the way to lower the risk of injury during any workout.

Conclusion

Congratulations! You know the basics of calisthenics, and have a good idea of how you can create your exercising plan and start transforming your life, health, and body right now.

The goal of this book was to introduce you to the basics of calisthenics. First, you learned that calisthenics is different from your usual gym workout program. You learned that it is a form of exercise that improves health and beauty most naturally, simply by using the weight of your body and the force of its movement. As you learned, the nature of exercises in calisthenics is such that they don't require lifting weights, only light tools such as bars, rings, bands, and others. You also learned that calisthenics carries a low risk of injury, and that is because your body won't allow you to make movements that are beyond its capabilities. As such, calisthenics is much safer for you and far more effective compared to other forms of exercise.

After that, you learned about the numerous benefits of calisthenics. You first learned that the main benefit of calisthenics comes from the body's own need to move. Our movements are complex and affect both our bodies and minds. You learned that calisthenics utilizes these movements strategically to activate muscles of the entire body in a natural way that grows your muscles and physical strength. As you learned, the lack of movement may cause physical weakness and chronic pains, and calisthenics is a great way to prevent this. You learned that you benefit from calisthenics in numerous physical and mental ways, from losing weight and growing muscles, to regaining emotional and mental balance, regaining healthy sleep, and building discipline, self-responsibility, and accountability. All of these traits, as you learned, will quickly and easily transfer to other areas of your life, affecting not only your fitness and physical ability. They will affect your work and relationships as well, because you'll have strengthened your self-esteem, become a sharper thinker, faster both with work and on your feet, and in better control of your feelings and impulses.

You also learned that to start with calisthenics properly, you need to do it slowly and methodically. You learned that you must start from the simplest exercises and move your way up. You learned that there is no use in comparing yourself to others because your body is one and only. It has its unique abilities, features, and needs. More importantly, you learned that you will do better with calisthenics if you focus more on the process of exercise and enjoy movement, rather than waiting to see the result. As you learned, this type of natural movement deepens your bond with your body and awakens your bodily awareness. The more you exercise, the better you'll recognize the true needs of your body.

As you learned, there's always a risk from injury in sports, even if you practice calisthenics. You learned that there is a risk from overtraining, and that skipping your rest days can not only slow down your progress, but also lead to overtraining syndrome. As you learned, pushing yourself too hard may easily result in temporarily losing the ability to exercise and diminishing the progress made so far.

After that, you learned how exactly calisthenics trains your body. You learned that the three most important principles include the SAID principle, overloading, and progressive overloading. These principles explain that growth of your muscles happens when you add stress or strain that's greater than the level you're used to. When you increase activity levels and load, your entire body, from your brain to the nerves and muscles, adjusts to respond to that stress. That's how the body becomes stronger. You learned that progressive overloading, or increasing the intensity and volume of your exercises once you conquer one level, secures long-term growth and progress.

If you read those sections carefully, you probably came to understand why accurate, well-measured exercises are so important to target muscles by groups and strengthen those you wish. You learned that too little resistance doesn't produce results, and too much leads to burning out. So, what does one do to secure longterm healthy exercise?

The answer is: rest and recover. Upon learning how calisthenics exercises look and which movements to do to target desired upper and lower body muscles, you learned about the enormous importance of rest and recovery. You learned that your muscles don't grow while you exercise, but afterward. You learned that, while you exercise, you cause tiny tears in muscle and ligament tissue. After exercise, rest is vital to allow the body to grow that tissue and fill the micro-tears, hence creating more muscle tissue. You also learned that rest and recovery are vital for the health of your joints and ligaments. You learned that the organs that connect your muscles and tie them to the bones are less supplied with blood, so they need more time to heal compared to muscles.

As you learned, diet and lifestyle play an enormous role in succeeding with calisthenics. You learned that the diet provides fuel for your muscles to grow, and that you need a healthy eating regimen regardless of whether or not you're trying to lose weight. You learned that there's more to your diet than calories. How much protein, carbs, and fat you eat greatly affects how effectively you will learn new skills, and how well your muscles will grow. You learned that both too little and too much of macronutrients gets in the way of healthy exercise. Insufficiency will prevent muscle growth, and too much will deplete fat loss. You learned that you need to balance your macronutrients well if you want to support and stimulate the progressive growth of your muscles and the development of skills.

You learned that eating healthy for the sake of your calisthenics training isn't at all difficult, or expensive. You learned that you only need clean and lean meats, vegetables, fruits, dairy, eggs, nuts and wheat, and legumes, and that you can have them in the amounts that match your exercise goal. You learned that only 200 calories can make a difference between fat gain and fat loss, meaning that adjusting your diet to your goals is much easier than you think.

In this book, you also learned about the importance of defining your goals and planning your exercises and progress. You learned that you need to establish whether your main goal is to lose weight, build muscle, or gain skills. While the chances are that you'll eventually do all three, your primary focus determines your exercise schedule. Those who target weight loss will do more cardio than those going after strength, for example.

Aside from having a clear goal, you also learned how important it is to have an exercise plan based on your goals. You learned that your exercise plan should consist of the types, number, and volume of advanced exercises and abilities you want to achieve for six months. But, as you learned, tracking your progress is vital to know whether you've completed your goals. You learned that you can simply track your progress by writing down how many repetitions you're able to do, how difficult they feel, whether you feel any pain, and how your body has changed during the process.

In this book, you also got a week's-worth of calisthenics exercises to get you going. We focused on the exercises that have proven to be most effective for beginners, and to introduce enough versatility for different types of people to enjoy. You also learned what other exercises you can use to target the muscles of the upper and lower body, and how to exercise and target your goal. With the given exercises, you can now begin the exercises and set your own goals based on what you perceive to need improving.

In terms of improvement, you learned that the lack of flexibility and mobility can get in the way of progress as well. You learned that your tendons, joints, and ligaments can get depleted of blood due to lack of mobility or too much strain. To prevent this, you learned that you need to do flexibility and mobility exercises regularly. You also learned that you need to constantly work on the so-called overhead mobility. You learned that your shoulders can become stiff for numerous reasons, and exercising overhead mobility guarantees that you'll be well-coordinated and strong enough to perform more demanding, advanced exercises.

Finally, you learned about the importance of motivation for exercise. You learned that you may hit a plateau for numerous reasons. It can happen because you followed a too repetitive exercise schedule, because you over trained, because you haven't paid attention to your diet, or because you didn't have enough rest. Either way, you can find yourself stuck, bored, and without the motivation to move forward. As you learned, the solution for this lies in reminding yourself of why you began training calisthenics in the first place, and looking into your unique strengths and needs to find out what's the best way forward. You also learned that there's no need to compare yourself to others. You learned that everyone progresses at their own pace and that your journey is yours alone. You learned that you can bounce back by re-evaluating why you fell in love with calisthenics in the first place, what you wanted to achieve, and also how you might have done things wrong.

You learned that long-term motivation requires finding out where you made a mistake so that you can prevent that mistake from happening in the future. Finally, you learned that there are many misconceptions about calisthenics. You learned that both men and women can do the same exercises, that yoga can be as effective an exercise as all others, that cardio exercises don't always guarantee weight loss, and that you're best off exercising in the fresh air whenever you can.

We want to leave you with a final message to never forget what calisthenics is all about: the harmony between your body and its need for movement. Remember that the best results will come when you focus on your body's natural need to push itself harder, to stretch, pull, and stimulate its tissues. By doing so, you won't worry about your weight or the looks of your abs. You will progress to an amazing level of physical ability, have superb mental and emotional health, and prominent muscles to serve as a cherry on top of the cake.

References

Basso-Vanelli, R. P., Di Lorenzo, V. A. P., Labadessa, I. G., Regueiro, E. M., Jamami, M., Gomes, E. L., & Costa, D. (2016). Effects of inspiratory muscle training and calisthenics-and-breathing exercises in COPD with and without respiratory muscle weakness. *Respiratory care*, 61(1), 50-60.

Beecher, C. E. (1867). Physiology and Calisthenics: For Schools and Families. *Harper.*

Flood, J. E., & Rolls, B. J. (2007). Soup preloads in a variety of forms reduce meal energy intake. *Appetite*, 49(3), 626-634.

https://doi.org/10.1016/j.appet.2007.04.00 2

Gist, N. H., Freese, E. C., Ryan, T. E., & Cureton, K. J. (2015). Effects of low-volume, high-intensity whole-body calisthenics on army ROTC cadets. *Military medicine*, 180(5), 492-498.

https://doi.org/10.7205/MILMED-D-14-00277

Glave, A. P., Didier, J. J., & Wagner, M. C. (2018). Calorie expenditure estimation differences between an elliptical machine and indirect calorimetry. *Exercise Medicine.*

https://doi.org/10.26644/em.2018.008

McMaster, D. T., Gill, N., Cronin, J., & McGuigan, M. (2013). The development, retention and decay rates of strength and power in elite rugby union, rugby league and American football. *Sports*

Medicine, 43(5), 367-384.

https://doi.org/10.1007/s40279-013-0031-3

Peterson, M. D., Rhea, M. R., & Alvar, B. A. (2004). Maximizing strength development in athletes: a meta-analysis to determine the dose-response relationship. *The Journal of Strength & Conditioning*

Research, 18(2), 377-382.

https://doi.org/10.1519/R-12842.1

Thomas, E., Bianco, A., Mancuso, E. P., Patti, A., Tabacchi, G., Paoli, A., ... & Palma, A. (2017). The effects of a calisthenics training intervention on posture, strength and body composition. *Isokinetics and exercise science*, 25(3), 215-222.

Youngstedt, S. D., Elliott, J. A., & Kripke, D. F. (2019). Human circadian phase-response curves for exercise. *The Journal of Physiology*.
https://doi.org/10.1113/JP276943

Book 2

Beefy Calisthenics

Step-by-Step Guide to Building
Muscle with Bodyweight Training

Introduction

How do you imagine building strong, well-defined muscles? Do dumbbells, barbells, kettle weights, and pushing and pulling weights with cables in a crowded, noisy, unclean gym come to mind? It doesn't have to be that way. Instead, consider the impressive physiques of male Olympic gymnasts: well-shaped bodies from head to toe and sharply defined muscles but not excessive like some muscle-bound weightlifters' builds.

The ideal body is not created by pumping iron; there is an easier, safer, better way without the gadgets, gimmicks, and risks of injury. You are in the right place to learn how to achieve the body of your dreams.

Long before fitness centers came into being, men who wanted to get strong have relied on a regimen of bodyweight exercises—called calisthenics—to build muscle, become powerful, and create a natural-looking overall shape. The key for you to achieve the same results is to become functionally strong with bodyweight calisthenics training.

This book will give you the confidence to get started and keep going with enthusiasm as you see impressive improvements and feel stronger, fitter, and more toned every day.

There's a chapter dedicated to nutrition that will give you guidance on carbs, proteins, and fats and will show how the right diet can help build muscles, while the wrong diet can actually lead to muscle loss. You will become knowledgeable about calories and the various diets that do—and do not—help you manage your weight and build lean muscle mass.

You will also learn how to develop the optimal workout routine to build your ideal body faster and easier than traditional, often painful, weightlifting. You will master the nine fundamental calisthenic movements that use your own bodyweight to strengthen your upper body, core, and lower body to ensure a full-body workout. Our 21-day workout plan will get you started and keep you on track every day for optimal results.

Cardiovascular exercise is an essential component of physical fitness and is credited with helping prevent heart disease, obesity, diabetes, and many other diseases. You will learn to select the right cardio routine and learn how long and how intense your cardio workout should be.

You will learn methods for measuring your progress as you try to maximize the results of practicing bodyweight calisthenic exercises. You will be taught the correct way to perform each exercise and how you can progress quickly, transitioning from beginner to intermediate sooner than you think.

There's a comprehensive troubleshooting section with a Q&A to guide you through issues, problems, and challenges, concluding with a review of the myths and misconceptions that people make when trying to build muscles.

Yet, first, the book will begin with the science of muscle building so that you can understand why proven techniques, good nutrition, and healthy rest and sleep habits form the basis of building muscle and achieving your overall fitness goals.

Fig. 1

Chapter 1

The Science of Muscle Building

There is science behind building stronger, impressive muscles, and by following basic principles, you can start down a path that will lead to tangible, visible results. Knowledge is the key to your success in building a great physique as you grow measurably stronger and look and feel better.

Knowledge begins with understanding what muscle is, what it's made of, how it builds, and how it deteriorates. As you will discover in this chapter, our bodies are designed to build muscle by creating tiny injuries to muscle fibers as you exercise, and these tears, at the cellular level, build new muscle tissue as they heal. But it is important to train correctly so that the correct amount of stress is placed on the muscle fibers.

The right kind and amount of rest and proper recovery time are also critical following each workout so that the muscles can heal and grow. The muscle-building process is also dependent on supplying your muscles, as well as the rest of your body, with the best kind of nutrition.

Is the Gym Really Necessary?

The short answer is, no, gyms aren't necessary, especially not when you can use your own bodyweight to build muscle and get toned with calisthenic exercises. It's more than possible to skip the gym, weights, and machines and still get in great shape.

Further, gyms cost money, and unless you have a fitness center in your home or apartment building, getting to and from the gym takes time. Then, there's the crowding, all those people and too few weights and machines.

Take a good look at many of the guys pumping the big weights in your gym. You can hear them moaning, sighing, and often dropping the weights. That's for your benefit, you know. These are narcissistic people who like to show-off. Is all that noise and drama necessary? Isn't it better to be able to concentrate on your own exercises, not theirs? As you will discover, a good calisthenics workout puts you into the zone of concentration without disturbing distractions.

The Natural Calisthenics Body

Now that you know you don't really need the gym, the next issue is what kind of muscles you want to build. You could purchase a home gym and do weightlifting at home. But why pay for weights when your own bodyweight will provide all the resistance you need for a natural calisthenics body? Look again at the heavy lifters and decide if that kind of bulked-up muscle mass is really what you want.

When our ancestors built muscle through the hard work of their daily lives (chopping, carrying, heaving, fighting, and hunting), they were doing many of the calisthenic bodyweight exercises you'll be learning about here. Their bodies responded naturally and developed the kinds of muscles they needed to live and survive. They became immensely strong, and today, we'd describe their physiques as cut, defined, and powerful.

Respected calisthenics trainer Danny Kavadlo (2017) described how pressing, pulling, and lifting in their daily lives was a hardwired part of their DNA and that the naturally-achieved "calisthenic body is a uniquely impressive physique," which is rippled and muscular with good balance, erect posture, and no superfluous body fat. Contrast this with the weightlifters who are stooped, curved, over-bulked, and muscle-bound. Sure, they're strong, but they've become dysfunctional, unlike the naturally built body that has strength, flexibility, resilience, and good tone.

The Importance of Muscles

We're all aware of our muscles, whether it's when we step out of the shower and see ourselves in the mirror or when we feel the warm glow in our arms, shoulders, chest, abs, and legs after resistance exercises. We're also aware of our muscles when we've overdone exercise or any form of lifting, and our overworked muscles are screaming out with pain. However, muscles are not just for lifting, walking, running, and jumping: our muscles affect our overall health, our metabolic rates, and even our longevity. Having good lean muscle mass is a key component of your well-being, apart from your goals of building muscles and increasing strength.

While there are various types of muscles in our bodies, including the myocardium (heart muscle) and the diaphragm that supports breathing, we're focusing on the 650 skeletal muscles. These are the muscles we see and feel and that contract each time they receive a signal from motor neurons, which are the nerves that connect the muscles to the spinal cord and brain. The better the communication between motor neurons and muscles, the greater the strength of the muscles.

Hypertrophy: How Muscles Grow

Every skeletal muscle is made up of thousands, or millions, of tiny muscle fibers; each fiber is actually a muscle cell built of links known as sarcomeres, which are the foundation of muscle fibers that contract to actually make you move. Each muscle is constructed of these sarcomeres, which contain thread-shaped contractive components called myofibrils, myosin, and actin. When your brain sends a signal for a muscle to contract, it activates the contractile fibers, notably actin and myosin, within the sarcomeres.

The growth of skeletal muscles is called hypertrophy. It's a complex process that begins with the myosin and actin fibers building up the sarcomeres, which, in turn, build up muscle fibers, and ultimately, grow the muscle itself.

According to physiology professor Len Kravitz, PhD, and grad student Young Kwon at the University of New Mexico's Exercise Science Program (2004), when muscle tissue is subjected to intense exercise, there is trauma inflicted on the muscle fibers, defined scientifically as injury or damage to muscle organelles. As a result, satellite cells on the outside of the muscle fibers reconstruct the damaged tissue by fusing with the muscle cells. This action builds the muscle cells, enlarging the muscle fibers; this is the muscle growth process of hypertrophy.

This repair process begins after intense workouts, and with each repair, the muscle fibers become slightly thicker so that, over time, the muscles become visibly larger as well as stronger. Muscle gain occurs if the muscle protein fusion is greater than muscle protein loss or breakdown. Muscle growth is enhanced by additional cell nuclei being added to the muscle fiber cells. Importantly, the repair and growth process of muscle cells and fibers only takes place during rest after working out; growth never occurs during exercise.

There are three elements that contribute to muscle growth, which include:

1. **Muscle Tension**, which is created by stress that is more intensive than muscles are accustomed to.

2. **Muscle Damage**, which results from the stress of extreme muscle tension.

3. **Metabolic Stress**, which is a process where muscle cells become swollen by the addition of the energy-supplying glycogen, creating the pumped-up sensation. (To be clear, this muscular swelling or pumping-up is temporary, as the actual muscle growth occurs after the exercise when the muscles are in their rest-and recover phase.)

The Role of Hormones in Muscle Growth

Hormones play an important role in muscle regeneration and growth. You have probably heard about the male hormone testosterone, which is pivotal, as is another hormone called insulin growth factor. Most of the body's testosterone is dedicated to various bodily functions, but during resistance strength training, some testosterone is released and is able to activate muscle cell receptors. The role of testosterone, in this situation, is to increase muscle protein growth, slow the breakdown of protein, and direct neurotransmitter chemicals to damaged muscle cells to activate growth of new muscle tissues.

Insulin growth factor hormone further encourages muscle growth and glycogen release for energy and sends amino acids, which are the building blocks of protein, to the skeletal muscles.

Do these findings suggest that you should ingest hormone supplements to increase the effects of calisthenics? Most likely, not. Medical professionals generally advise not taking hormones without close medical supervision and only when blood tests confirm a deficiency. Your increase in muscle size and strength should come from natural workouts and not from taking potentially risky hormone supplements.

Okay, the scientific part is over and behind us. Now that you are armed with the knowledge of how your muscles grow, you are better able to appreciate the vital role nutrition plays in rebuilding and strengthening muscle fibers and cells. It's time to get you on the right track to eat more nourishing, healthier meals without having to give up your enjoyment of eating so that you can bulk up muscle mass while losing body fat. Ready?

Let's start eating right.

Chapter 2

Nutrition

Nutrition is the process of eating, and the *quality* of nutrition is a function of what we eat, how well we digest and assimilate it, and how it affects us. The expression, "You are what you eat," pretty well sums up the concept of nutrition. Of course, it's not that simple. Our gastrointestinal system digests and breaks down foods into basic components so that assimilation does not take place at the granola or Twinkie level but at a more fundamental chemical level. Still, each food we eat has its own nutritional values, calories, and other components that our bodies process and react to. Some foods we eat may also contain chemicals or ingredients that can be potentially harmful.

Good nutrition is everyone's business, since our health, well-being, and longevity depends on it, but it plays a specifically pivotal role for those wanting to build lean muscle mass and get into good physical shape. As you learned in the previous chapter, muscles grow by repairing the cellular damage resulting from calisthenics and other resistance activities, and this growth requires an adequate supply of the amino acids, proteins, and other essential nutrients the repairers utilize. Learning the essentials of nutrition and constructing an ideal diet for optimal overall health and disease prevention is vital in your quest to build a strong, well-defined muscular body.

Carbohydrates, Protein, and Fats

The energy values of the foods we eat are expressed as calories; a calorie is the amount of energy needed to heat one gram of water by one degree Celsius. Every gram of carbohydrates contains four calories, and every gram of protein also contains four calories. Fats (including oils) are different; nature designed fats for storage, so each gram of fat contains nine calories. Carbohydrates and fats have the primary roles of providing energy, while protein rebuilds cells. Indeed, proteins rebuild every one of the trillions of cells in our bodies from muscles to red corpuscles in our blood.

Now, let's look at the three fundamental food groups. We'll begin with a normal basic diet. The daily number of calories needed to gain, maintain, or lose weight is based on current bodyweight, so take an average adult male who needs 2,000 calories per day to maintain a current, normal weight (that is, not overweight or obese). Our source for the following diet is Kathy Lee Wilson (2018), a certified trainer and athlete, and she recommends that:

Quality carbohydrates should account for between 45% to 65% of total caloric intake. To build lean muscle, you will be at the lower end of the scale so that you can leave room for more protein. Most people are surprised that carbohydrates are so important, but we're basing this need on quality carbohydrates, including the vegetables, fruits, berries, whole grains, and cereals that are in the Mediterranean diet, which you'll read about below.

Lean proteins can range from as low as 10% up to 30% of total daily calories. In seeking lean muscle mass, you will be closer to the 30% protein level. The protein that everyone needs to repair cells throughout the body, including restoring blood cells, body organs, skin, hair, and nails, is only part of the equation. Your body will need additional protein to repair and build the skeletal muscle fibers and cells that are broken down during your bodyweight calisthenic exercises. Sources of protein are lean chicken, turkey, fish, low-fat milk and yogurt, and good plant-based proteins, such as nuts, beans, seeds, grains, and cereals.

Healthy fats may account for 25% to 35% of your daily caloric intake, and with the great need for protein to build muscle, your fats may be on the lower end, closer to 25%. The good news is that you will be getting the healthy fats you need for good health from other parts of your diet, including fish, olive oil, nuts (like walnuts and almonds), avocados, and flax seeds. Because fats contain more than twice the calories of proteins and carbohydrates (nine calories per gram vs. four per gram), it doesn't take much to reach that 25% goal for healthy fats.

So, given the above considerations, to optimize building lean muscle, your caloric ratio target should be close to:

➤ 45% quality carbohydrates

➤ 30% lean protein

➤ 25% healthy fats

How many calories does this equal? That depends on your daily caloric input. As we stated above, an average adult male needs 2,000 calories to maintain weight. Remember, there are four calories in each gram of carbohydrates and protein, and nine calories in each gram of fat. On the basis of 2,000 calories per day, that means:

➤ **Quality carbohydrates** are 45% of daily intake = 900 calories per day (425 grams)

➤ **Lean proteins** are 30% of daily intake = 600 calories per day (150 grams)

➤ **Healthy fats** are 25% of daily intake = 500 calories per day (56 grams)

(Look for the *Fitness Calculator* at the beginning of this book, which you can download and use to determine your daily protein and calorie requirements to build strong, lean muscles.)

Ideal Sources of Protein

These foods are good sources of protein:

Food	Serving Size	Calories	Protein (grams)	% Daily 150 grams
Eggs (large)	1 (50 gm)	70	6	4%
Barley, Peas, Lentils, Rice	2 oz(dry)	180	7	5%
Beans, Chickpeas	4 oz	120	7	5%
Nuts (peanuts, walnuts, cashews)	1 oz	170	8	6%
Skim Milk	8 0z	80	10	8%

Greek Yogurt (0 % fat)	6 oz	100	19	14%
Sardines	3 oz	200	22	15%
Chicken, Turkey, Beef (lean)	4 oz	106	24	16%
Tuna (one can)	4 oz	260	26	17%

Calories In, Calories Out, and Building Muscle

As mentioned, a calorie is the amount of energy needed to heat one gram of water by one degree Celsius. What science has proved unequivocally is that weight is gained, lost, or maintained based on *calories in* (ingested) and *calories out* (burned). While no two people digest, metabolize, and assimilate foods at an identical rate, the physics tells us that if your caloric *intake* exceeds your caloric *output*, you will retain the difference, either as muscle (if you work hard at building muscles, that is) or, as is more typically the case, as fat.

If you follow this book's guidance and perform the bodyweight calisthenic exercises, you will not gain weight or fat when you increase your protein intake or even consume more calories than normal. But protein alone won't do the work of muscle building for you. Those four calories per gram will be stored as fat if they aren't assigned to rebuilding muscle fibers and cells that have been stressed and damaged by your good resistance workouts. A diet composed of a 30% daily intake of protein is ambitious and will require increasing normal servings of high-protein foods. These calorie counts you are seeing are approximate, and since no two people have an identical metabolic rate, only through trial and error can you ensure you are managing your weight effectively.

Your Basal Metabolic Rate

When you are at rest without movement or stress, your metabolism is at its lowest level; this is called your basal metabolic rate (BMR). It refers to the minimal number of calories your body needs to survive and sustain itself under the least challenging conditions. Imagine your metabolic rate while you've been lying down for hours, doing nothing. As you are aware, your body is still using calories while you are at rest to perform involuntary functions to support your heartbeat, breathing, digestive organs, brain function, and central nervous system, and, of course, to repair damaged muscle fibers.

While you cannot raise or influence your BMR through activity, it can be raised when lean muscle mass is increased. As a consequence, you can actually burn more calories when at rest, even when you are asleep. Muscle mass has an appetite for calories that supply energy to the continuing rebuilding process, which happens when muscles are resting.

According to Bodybuilding.com ("Calculate Your Basal Metabolic Rate," 2020) the total calories you use every day is known as the "total daily energy expenditure," and it factors in your BMR plus all the activities you perform over the course of a 24-hour day. The total expenditure depends on your activity level, age, and gender. Activity includes everything you do physically and mentally (you may be surprised to learn that your brain accounts for about 3% of your bodyweight but uses around 15% of your caloric energy).

Ideal Sources of Nutrition: The Mediterranean Diet

Nutritionists may have different dietary preferences, but they tend to agree on this basic principle: The best, healthiest diet is based on groups of real foods. What are real foods? They're unprocessed, close to their natural form, rich in nutrients, and free of preservatives, sugar, and other highly refined carbohydrates. Another major agreement is that diets should limit foods containing saturated and trans fats.

Among many ways to eat naturally, the **Mediterranean diet** has emerged in recent years as the ideal diet for keeping healthy, maintaining weight, and generally feeling better. And while this diet is not specifically targeted to building lean muscle, you are free to shift the emphasis to muscle-building protein while keeping within the Mediterranean diet guidelines.

This diet is based on the eating practices of those who live in southern France, Italy, Greece, and other regions close to the Mediterranean basin. It has been shown that the residents of these regions live longer and are healthier compared to those in the rest of the world. They tend to avoid obesity and sedentary lifestyles, being active throughout their lives.

They eat a healthy, balanced, natural diet in moderate portions. You will appreciate the pleasures these practitioners experience from eating real, delicious, minimally processed, and wholesome foods. There's no need to become a vegetarian or vegan; with the Mediterranean diet, you can benefit from a combination of plant-based and animal-based foods.

> ➤ **Plant-based foods** provide essential vitamins, minerals, nutrients, moderate amounts of healthy unrefined carbohydrates, some protein, and healthy fats. Plant-based foods include a wide range of vegetables, fruits, nuts, seeds, beans, whole grains, cereals, and vegetable oils.

> **Animal-based foods** are essential sources of protein and are higher than vegetables in the muscle-building proteins you need. Yet, they should be consumed in moderation and only when lean. Animal-based foods can include fish, low-fat dairy products, and eggs, which are all high-quality proteins that offer a good source of nutrients.

Let's take a closer look at the groups of **plant-sourced** foods within the Mediterranean diet.

1. **Vegetables** are low in calories and carbohydrates, yet are a storehouse of vitamins, minerals, nutrients, beneficial fiber, and even a moderate supply of protein.

   Vegetables the Mediterranean diet encourages you to eat include broccoli, bell peppers, and asparagus, which are low in carbohydrates and calories and supply vitamins K and C as well as fiber and antioxidants. These same nutrients are provided by carrots, Brussels sprouts, cucumbers, beets, and kale. Tomatoes, technically a fruit, contain vitamin C and other nutrients.

   In fact, almost all vegetables you'll find at the grocery store are low carbohydrate sources of vitamins, minerals, and antioxidants. Also look for artichokes, celery, cabbage, leeks and onions, Swiss chard, green zucchini, and yellow squash.

Experts say that a mix of colors is ideal for supplying different minerals.

2. **Fruits and berries** are nutritious as well as naturally sweet and delicious.

    Apples are filling and high in fiber, antioxidants, and vitamin C. They're an ideal healthy dessert or a nutritious snack between meals. Bananas are a great source of the electrolyte potassium, vitamin B6, and fiber. Blueberries have these same nutrients and are also a good source of antioxidants.

    Avocados are also in the fruit category but are low in carbohydrates and high in nutritious polyunsaturated avocado oil, potassium, and vitamin C. Other good sources of vitamin C and fiber are oranges, strawberries, grapes, and most other fruits, melons, and berries.

3. **Grains and cereals** have been with us since early hunter-gatherers harvested wild wheat and later when the first farmers began to cultivate wheat, rye, barley, rice, and other grains. In a nutritious diet, grains are whole, rather than refined, retaining the bran, fiber, minerals, and vitamins.

    Brown rice, whole-grain breads and cereals (unsweetened), and quinoa are the most popular healthier grains and contain good levels of magnesium, vitamin B, and fiber. Be aware that "multi-grain" does not mean whole grain; read the labels and stick with unpolished, unrefined grains, cereals, and whole-grain breads.

Oatmeal is credited with lowering LDL (bad) cholesterol, thanks to its beta-glucans and soluble fiber content. Opt for regular, not precooked oatmeal, since it's higher in nutrients and only takes three minutes to cook.

Grains and cereals provide moderate levels of protein, but given their high carbohydrate levels, those on medically-recommended low carbohydrate diets may need to limit their grain consumption.

4. **Beans and legumes** are within a family of plant foods called pulses. We're most familiar with the dried variety, but peas and string beans are pulses, too. For their small size, beans are very high in protein and other key nutrients.

    Beans include pinto beans, kidney beans, chickpeas, black beans, lima beans, navy beans, cannellini beans, and soybeans. There are also split peas and lentils. All provide about 7 to 8 grams of protein in a ¼ cup serving (measured dry). You may use the pre-cooked canned versions or begin with dry. (If using dried beans, be sure to presoak before cooking.)

    In addition to protein, beans provide complex carbohydrates, fiber, folate, iron, phosphorus, and linoleic and oleic unsaturated acids. Clinical studies cited by Harvard's T.H. Chan School of Public Health (2020) show the phytochemicals in beans help reduce the risks of Cardiovascular disease, digestive diseases, diabetes, obesity, and cancer.

5. **Nuts and seeds** are used mostly in snacks, as additives to cereals, and when baking bread, and they are a surprisingly good source of nutrients.

   Nuts, including almonds, walnuts, peanuts (actually a legume), pecans, and cashews, are high in beneficial antioxidant oils and fiber. Nuts are an above-average source of protein, copper, magnesium, folate, potassium, vitamins B6 and E, and niacin. Nuts have been shown to help prevent heart disease, diabetes, and cancer.

   Seeds include familiar pumpkin seeds, sunflower seeds, chia, and flax seeds, which have become popular recently and may be sprinkled on cereals and fruits to add fiber, magnesium, calcium, and antioxidants.

6. **Olive oil** and most other plant-derived oils are an ideal, beneficial source of necessary fats.

   The molecular structure of olive oil is primarily monounsaturated oleic acid, an unsaturated fat that studies cited by Joe Leech (2018) in Healthline.com show is good for heart health, especially preventing the build-up of LDL (bad) cholesterol, which can clog arteries. Findings also credit olive oil with good levels of antioxidants and anti-inflammatories. It can reduce your risk of developing diabetes, strokes, and Alzheimer's disease.

Be sure to use extra virgin olive oil, which is the least processed and most nutritious form. Many other plant-based oils, including soybean, sunflower, corn, and safflower, are polyunsaturated and are also beneficial. Be careful of a few plant-based oils that are high in saturated fats, such as coconut oil.

Now, let's look at **animal-sourced** foods that are part of the Mediterranean Diet.

1. **Meats**, in limited quantities, are an excellent source of muscle-building protein.

   The meats you choose should be on the lean side, including white meat chicken, white meat turkey, lean pork, and lean beef, which is a good source of iron. Be careful to avoid meats marbled with saturated fats, which are to be avoided for cardiovascular health as well as to manage caloric intake.

   Portions of meats should be smaller than you may think. Nutritionists and the American Heart Association (2020) propose the serving of lean meat should be about the size of a deck of cards or three to four ounces. But with a goal of building bigger, stronger, and leaner muscle mass, you may need to increase the portion size of lean meat but not too much. There are plenty of healthy proteins in plant-based foods and in fish.

2. **Fish** is a highly recommended source of quality protein and of valuable nutrients.

Ideally, your diet will include at least two servings of fish per week. Salmon, cod, sole, seabass, tuna, sardines, swordfish, and mackerel are excellent protein sources. The fats and oils in these cold-water fish are unsaturated. Fish also contain valuable omega-3 fatty acids and iodine.

There have been studies that link diets rich in seafood with living longer and healthier with less chance of developing heart disease, depression, and anxiety.

3. **Dairy** products, including milk, cheese, and yogurt supply good amounts of protein plus vitamins.

   You should limit your selection to fat-free or low-fat milk and yogurt and limit your overall consumption of cheese. Try to avoid or limit full-fat cheeses and cream, which are high in saturated fats.

   Greek and Icelandic yogurts are increasing in popularity due to higher protein levels compared to traditional yogurts, thanks to the straining process that removes excess water.

4. **Red wine** is generally included in the Mediterranean diet, and studies point to healthier hearts and health when the consumption is moderate.

   Some findings suggest that moderate drinkers of red wine and other forms of alcohol are better off than non-drinkers and heavy drinkers. But caution is advised. Moderate for adult men means no more than two 5-ounce glasses of wine, two servings of 1.5 ounces of alcohol, or two 12-ounce servings of beer per day. Doctors advise that if you do not currently drink alcoholic beverages, you should not start.

You may be wondering about eggs. Despite warnings issued decades ago about the cholesterol levels in eggs, nutritionists now rate eggs high on the nutritional chart and recommend up to two eggs per day as a rich source of protein and nutrients.

Now that we've covered the ideal diet for overall health and for building lean muscle mass, we can conclude this chapter with a brief look at the negatives of bad diets.

Risks of Bad Diets

We humans evolved over the millennia, eating a variety of the foods you have just read about in the Mediterranean diet: all-natural, unprocessed or minimally processed, diverse, providing the full range of essential amino acids, full of proteins, and containing healthy carbohydrates and oils. They did not eat greasy, fried foods, overly processed foods containing artificial preservatives, foods with added sugar or other refined carbohydrates, or food full of saturated and hydrogenated fats and trans fats.

They did not eat junk food, and neither should we.

Take the hamburger as an example of how foods can be good and bad, depending on the ingredients. Imagine a hamburger with two simple ingredients: 95% lean unprocessed chopped meat and a whole-grain bun. The lean meat is supplying about 22 to 24 grams of protein, or 16% of your daily need, plus a small amount of fat. The whole-grain bun adds fiber, vitamins, and minerals that come from the bran layer, plus needed healthy carbohydrates and (surprise!) 2 or 3 grams of protein.

In contrast, take the typical hamburger from a fast-food joint: fatty meat loaded with calories and unhealthy saturated fats, and with fewer grams of protein, since the amount of protein-rich lean meat is less. The bun contributes to the empty calories, too, with overprocessed white bread, which is made from refined white flour that has had its natural nutrients removed. Like most white breads, its ingredient list is filled with flavor enhancers, stabilizers, and preservatives.

You can see the huge difference between these two hamburgers, and how one (the healthy version) gives your body what it needs to produce lean muscle.

Beyond that, an unhealthy diet is full of sugar, which is a source of excessive empty calories and is present in many foods and beverages, such as soft drinks and sports beverages. Read the labels and learn to give up sugar-laden foods and drinks.

Fried foods are bad news. The breaded coating absorbs cooking oils, which can become toxic through reheating with trans fats. Like our hamburger example, frying good lean foods deprive them of all their benefits. Frying potatoes, chicken, and fish add hundreds of fat calories. A donut exemplifies a bad diet of unnecessary, overused oils and trans fats, plus loads of sugar.

Become aware of which foods are more natural and which are overly processed. Get in the habit of reading labels and asking yourself, "Do I want to eat all that sugar and those chemicals?"

You have a good start on developing the right diet, and it's time now to move on and learn much more about the value of rest, recovery, and consistency.

Chapter 3

Rest, Recovery, and Consistency

Doing calisthenic exercises and nothing else won't allow you to build the lean body you want. Rest and recovery (along with diet) are just as important. The optimization of recovery and rebuilding, through the discipline of consistency, within your daily, weekly, and long-term routines is key to your success in fine-tuning your muscle mass and body.

As you prepare to begin a serious bodyweight calisthenics program and are committed to achieving your bodybuilding goals, the first step (perhaps the biggest step) is mental: Your commitment to perform the exercises, as instructed, on a regular, consistent basis and, just as importantly, to observe the discipline of rest and recovery.

If you just completed a marathon, would you consider hitting the road again tomorrow and running another 26.2 miles? Of course, you wouldn't. Beyond the sheer fatigue, there would be something important— essential—going on in your body. Thousands of muscle fibers are beginning to repair the damage you just imposed on your muscles, and you are recovering from the stress many of your body's organs and functions experienced. Even if you woke up feeling great, your body isn't prepared or ready for more exercise. The same principles apply to serious resistance exercise.

Further, protein also plays a role in helping to build muscles bigger and faster through recovery. And rest and recovery mean nothing if you're not getting a good night's sleep every night.

The Importance of Rest and Recovery

Recovery shouldn't be an afterthought, something you underestimate, or a part of your calisthenics plan you ignore. That's why we want you to understand the great importance of rest and recovery *before* you even get into the actual body weight calisthenics techniques. It's natural to believe that the calisthenics movements you'll be performing are all that matter. But the truth is that all the hard work you do on workout days can be wasted if it's not followed by adequate rest and recovery time. Some athletes actually feel a sense of guilt on days when they don't exercise hard or at all but this is contrary to the fact that adequate recovery time is needed if your damaged cells, fibers, and muscles are to repair and grow in size and strength.

Workouts break down muscle fiber and cells, cause loss of fluids, and deplete stored muscle glycogen energy. During recovery, the body is able to repair and rebuild the muscles and other damaged tissues, replace missing fluids, and recharge the energy supply. But without rest, recovery can't take place, and the body will continue to break down. Closely scheduled hard workouts coupled with no rest and recovery can become detrimental to health and well-being.

Overtraining syndrome is a potentially serious downside to not providing yourself adequate recovery time. In the online fitness journal, *Very Well Fit,* exercise physiologist and sports medicine consultant Elizabeth Quinn (2020) explains that overtraining syndrome occurs from training beyond the body's ability to recover. The result is a reduction in strength and conditioning, rather than growth. Symptoms of overtraining syndrome can include compulsive exercise, reduced immunity (leaving the person susceptible to infections, colds, and flu), continuing sore muscles, aching joints, and a reduction in exercise performance, such as fewer push-ups and pull-ups than normal. Other symptoms may include a loss of energy, irritability, insomnia, and a loss of enthusiasm for workouts.

You can self-diagnose for overtraining by checking your resting heart rate each morning, just after waking. Under normal conditions, your heart rate should be fairly consistent from day to day, but if you record a distinct increase in the resting heart rate, it may indicate that full recovery from the previous workout has not been achieved, and it will be important to make that day one of rest and recovery. Depending on the degree of overwork, several rest days may be necessary. Don't rush it; stay well-hydrated and do not exert yourself. In extreme cases, when overtraining has occurred over a sustained period, it may take several weeks of taking it easy and reducing stress.

Now, let's look at how much rest and recovery is needed.

Maximize Muscle Growth With Rest Days

Recovery takes place in stages, each of which plays a role in resting and rebuilding your muscles. In the hours after completing an intense resistance session, the recovery process enters its first phase, referred to as short-term or active recovery, where you can be performing low-intensity walking or light lifting activities (including housework, gardening, or hiking at a comfortable speed). These light activities should continue into the next day, keeping you active but without exerting yourself. You will also be recharging protein, fluids, and energy stores.

During this active recovery phase, many things are happening inside of you. The strained and damaged muscle cells that you challenged during your workout are going through the recovery process and muscles, ligaments, and tendons are being repaired. Chemicals, including lactic acid, that have built up in the muscle cells are removed. You should allow a minimum of one rest day after a moderate calisthenics workout and at least two consecutive rest days after a hard workout. Rushing the rest and repair process can reduce or negate the positive effects of the hard exercise.

Not only do recovery and recuperation give you the ability to regain strength and energy after each workout, but the faster you are able to recover, the faster muscle mass and greater strength will occur.

Here are the fundamentals of creating faster, more complete recoveries to build more muscle mass in a shorter time:

> **How fast and how fully** you are able to recover is unique to you and is based on your genetic profile and overall physical condition. The intensity and duration of the calisthenics exercise you performed also determines the recovery time needed. Also, you must consider how much rest time you had *between* each workout.

> **How often you exercise** each week is very important. Fewer resistance workouts and more rest time can lead to fuller recovery periods.

> **Your diet** plays an influential role, and not just in terms of protein intake. A balanced, healthy diet of diverse, natural, and minimally processed foods (the Mediterranean diet, for example) will supply the vitamins, minerals, antioxidants, and anti-inflammatories needed to optimize the repairs of muscle fibers and cells.

➤ **Stress** can disrupt the rest cycle by activating the sympathetic nervous system's fight-or-flight response and kicking adrenaline and cortisol production into high gear, which elevates heart rate, breathing rate, and blood pressure. It's best to avoid stress always but especially as you recover.

➤ **Rest days** can be any days where you take it easy and are not engaged in high-intensity workouts. Do other things, like hobbies or family time, as opposed to physically challenging activities.

Ideally, you want three workout days per week. At the popular bodybuilding site, Barbell.com, physical trainer Randy Herring (2019), who has over 40 years of conditioning, building solid muscle, and training experience, recommends three good resistance workouts per week. More than three can result in too few rest and recovery periods, and fewer than three may not be enough to achieve the muscular physique you are seeking.

Recuperation time may be divided into three segments:

1. During the workout, take a 30 to 90 second pause between sets (a set is a continuous series of repetitions, or reps, like 15 nonstop pushups). As you go from exercise to exercise, the 30-90 second pause should be observed, especially if you are repeating sets of the same exercise.

2. Immediately after the exercise is over, take a 2 to 4 hour pause in any other heavy exercise, lifting, climbing stairs, or carrying heavy objects. It's okay to walk and be normally active, however.

3. During the two to three days following exercise, do not perform any resistance exercises, heavy lifting, pulling, or pushing activity. This is the period when the serious rebuilding and recovery takes place, and if you respect this recovery period and limit workouts to three per week, you will be doing the best you can to build lean, large, and well-defined muscles.

The Role of Protein in Recovery

We already know how important nutrition is for building a lean, muscular body, but diet is also an important factor in recovery. The right diet can help replenish energy stores and fluids and optimize the synthesis of protein (a process where amino acids form chains of peptides, which then form complex chains of proteins). Each unit of protein is programmed by our DNA to repair muscles, tendons, ligaments, or any of the trillions of other cells in our bodies. Amino acids and proteins are also essential to building hormones and enzymes. So, if protein is the building block of our muscle cells, fibers, tissues, and organs, having adequate protein in our daily diets is of considerable importance to the recovery process.

Since the damage to muscle cells is actually caused by a depletion of protein, it takes more protein to make the repairs and contribute to the slight overbuilding of the muscle fibers that lead to bigger muscles. And that protein, which contains amino acids, needs to come from our diets. As you learned earlier, you should aim for a 30% caloric intake of lean protein, which can come from plant and animal sources. Having adequate protein available for the recovery also helps prevent the body drawing on healthy protein for repairs (a destructive process called catabolism).

Research published by the International Society of Sports Nutrition (ISSN) shows that athletes following an intense training program can benefit from consuming twice the daily recommended amount of protein or up to 2.0 grams per kg (2.2 lbs). For example, someone who weighs 165 lbs would consume 150 grams of protein per day with or without using a supplement (Kerksick et al., 2018).

Since you will be taking in more than the average amount of daily protein (that 30% of total calories is about 150 grams), it helps to have a protein-rich meal soon after your workout ends. For example, if you workout before breakfast, follow your work out with a breakfast that includes Greek yogurt, two eggs, wholegrain bread, and oatmeal with nuts, flax seeds, and skim milk. You may add meat for added protein but be careful of bacon, which is high in saturated fats, preservatives, and more salt (sodium) than you need. Similarly, if your intense workout is before lunch or dinner, follow with a protein-rich meal afterward.

Should you consider a protein supplement? There are many plant and dairy-based powders and liquids that can provide an average of 15 to 20 grams of protein per serving. According to *Medical News Today*, protein powder may be used to help repair damaged tissues and muscles, and many athletes rely on protein power to accelerate recovery from muscle soreness (Leonard, 2018). Protein supplements taken after intense exercise can speed recovery and improve performance by contributing to muscle protein synthesis (Leonard, 2018).

If amino acid and protein supplements are of interest to you, check the labels for ingredients and try to avoid the brands with a long list of chemical-sounding words. If you're not comfortable with taking supplements, consider getting 18 or 20 grams of natural-sourced protein with a serving of Greek or Icelandic yogurt, which also provides probiotic bacteria that are beneficial to the microbiome in your gut.

Another benefit of a higher-protein diet is weight loss. This is not due to protein being less fattening than carbohydrates, but rather because protein is slower to digest, so it stays in the stomach and gives a feeling of fullness for a longer time. In contrast, carbohydrates and fats are more readily digested, so they pass more quickly through the stomach, leading to hunger pangs.

The Underestimated Importance of Sleep

If we spend eight hours asleep in bed each night, we might think we are wasting valuable time. This attitude encourages many people to sleep fewer hours by staying up late and getting up early. Today's digital age even tempts people to bring their cell phones, tablets, or laptops into the bedroom to keep their days going a little longer.

But it turns out that the traditional advice of "getting a good night's sleep" is medically and scientifically validated. We need eight hours or so, and this is especially true for those, like you, who work out and are trying to build bigger, stronger muscles. Your body needs this full night of restful sleep to rebuild and recover, and so does your brain.

Sleep, it turns out, is as important as intense calisthenics exercise because during sleep, your body initiates the recovery and rebuilding process and gets to work healing the microscopic rips and tears your muscles experienced as you pushed, pulled, and challenged them with hard exercise. The reason for this is that as you sleep, your body is in a high anabolic state, meaning it is better able to fabricate the larger protein molecules that are needed to repair your muscle fibers, your body tissues, your nervous system, and your immune system.

Also, compared to your waking hours when you are active and your muscles are in use, when you are sleeping, your body metabolizes protein more effectively and faster. A full, uninterrupted night of sleep is especially important following an intense workout when cell damage is maximal and protein synthesis is most needed.

When you are asleep, your body is producing testosterone and melatonin, which are human growth hormones crucial for cellular regeneration. The protein production stimulated by these hormones then exceeds protein destruction (because your muscles are inactive), so there is a net gain in muscle fiber size. But upon awakening and throughout the day and evening, protein is being broken down faster than it can be repaired; this is true even on days you do not work out. You probably recognize melatonin for its ability to induce sleep; now, you can appreciate the relationship between melatonin, sleep, and regeneration of muscles.

Physiologist Barry Lumsden (2019), a Level 2 Gym Instructor with 20 years of scientific research supporting his perspectives, recommends a protein-rich beverage before bed on nights following a hard workout. This will ensure that the body's protein stores are not depleted during the night and maximum rebuilding of muscles can occur. Lumsden (2019) suggests that either whey protein or casein protein supplements are excellent for inhibiting protein breakdown during sleeping. Both elevate amino acid levels; however, casein-derived protein tends to last longer.

A further benefit of sleep is stress reduction. Our bodies react to stress by elevating our cortisol hormone levels, which then prompts surges of energy-producing glycogen to the muscles that counter the growth hormone testosterone. It's the familiar fight-or-flight reaction. Stress can be responsible for breaking down muscle tissue and preventing regrowth. A full night's sleep diminishes stress and keeps cortisol levels low and testosterone levels high.

With the need for a full nights' sleep to build muscle and maintain good physical and mental health, how do we establish good sleep habits and stay with them?

Here's how:

1. **Be Consistent** - Go to sleep and wake up at the same time every day. Don't make exceptions on weekends, because the goal is to condition your body to make sleep habitual and regular.

2. **Don't Oversleep** - Oversleeping can reset your internal clock, making it harder to wake up on time the next day. Oversleeping will also make it harder to fall asleep at the prescribed time.

3. **Don't Nap** - Yes, Winston Churchill napped and some people advocate a little siesta after lunch, but naps will leave you less tired at

bedtime. A cup of coffee after lunch is a better option.

4. **No Caffeine in the Evening** - It takes four to six hours for the caffeine in your body to diminish sufficiently to not keep you awake. So, that means no caffeine in the evening or before bed.

5. **No Alcohol Before Bedtime** - If you drink (and do so in moderation), do it early enough so that it's out of your system before bedtime. During sleep, alcohol suppresses stage 2 REM (rapid eye movement) sleep, which is when dreaming occurs and the brain resets itself.

6. **Avoid Sleeping Pills** - Sleeping pills can become a hard-to-break habit, and you don't want to become dependent on them. Like alcohol, some sleeping pills can interfere with dreaming and the resetting of the brain.

7. **No Digital Visitors** - Do not bring your mobile phone, tablet, or laptop into the bedroom. First, whatever you are watching or reading may cause you stress, making it hard for your central nervous system to calm down. Also, the bluish light from these digital screens tend to counter our melatonin production, which normally activates when it is dark. For all these reasons, do not watch television in bed as well.

8. **Keep Your Evenings Calm and Relaxed** - It's best to avoid any stressors before bed. Avoid arguments, confrontations, or emotional talks with family and friends. If you watch TV or stream movies in the evening, steer clear of violent programs, which can raise your pulse rate and breathing rate, simulating the release of cortisol and adrenaline.

9. **Reduce Tension** - If you are feeling tense before bed, take a warm bath or shower. Have a warm beverage, but instead of coffee or tea, consider warm milk (better than you may think) or hot chocolate.

10. **Make Your Bedroom Conducive To Sleep** - Your sleeping area should be dark and quiet with a good airflow of cool air. If the airflow isn't good, consider a small fan that will also provide a light white noise effect. Keep your bedroom uncluttered so that you don't end up tripping in the dark.

With all the knowledge you have about how to rest and recover correctly, we can now get to the heart of beefy calisthenics and dive into the bodyweight calisthenics exercises and routines you will follow to reach your physical goals, starting with the proper exercise selection.

Chapter 4

Proper Exercise Selection

Your calisthenics exercise program will be based on the experiences of many different athletes who have experimented and tested, under a wide range of conditions, every type of movement imaginable. Consider the almost infinite number of exercises that are open to you: pushing, pulling, lifting, bending stretching, arching, extending, and compressing among others. Consider how much resistance should be used for each exercise: a lot, a little, or none at all. Consider the element of timing: the speed of performing each movement, the number of repetitions, the number of sets, the time between each set, and the sequence of the exercises. These are all things you will learn to master through the art of proper exercise selection.

Compound vs. Static Exercises

Calisthenics exercises can either involve movement with more than one muscle group working at the same time (compound exercises) or involve no movement with only a single muscle or muscle group working (static exercises). On the whole, compound movements are far better in helping you achieve your fitness goals than static ones.

Compound Exercises

Compound exercises work and challenge multiple muscle groups simultaneously. When you perform a squat, for example, it is a compound exercise that involves working the glutes, the quadriceps, and the calves. A push-up is a compound exercise that engages abdominal muscles, shoulders, triceps quadriceps, and glutes all at the same time. Another type of compound exercise is performing two separate or unrelated exercises at the same time, such as a leg raise while doing lunges. If done by itself, the leg raise would be categorized as an isolation exercise, since it's working only one muscle group (the abdominals). The advantage of compound exercises is working more muscles or muscle groups at the same time, while isolation exercises may be appropriate when a specific muscle needs strengthening, such as during post-injury rehabilitation.

The benefits of compound exercises are based on getting more done in a shorter time, resulting in more muscles worked, more calories burned, better intramuscular coordination, greater strength building, more muscle mass, and increased flexibility. There are cardiovascular benefits, too, since compound exercise raises the heart and breathing rates. Experts consider compound exercises to be the ultimate form of strength training and recommend these multiple exercises to be the central focus of a workout.

Static Exercises

Static exercises, commonly known as isometrics, are distinctly different from compound exercises, as they do not involve movement (that is: there is no shortening or lengthening of the muscles). The muscles are tensed and flexed but are not compressed or expanded. As a result, only moderate amounts of work are being performed, leading to limited improvement in strength and muscle size. While static exercises can work different muscle groups at the same time, they do not challenge the full range of muscular motions and need to be supplemented with the movement of compound exercises.

However, certain static exercises can fit within a bodyweight calisthenics workout; the side plank is a good example of a bodyweight exercise that works multiple muscle groups—abdominals, anterior part of the deltoid, and quadriceps—at the same time. Static exercises can also be used to target the entire body, including challenging several different muscle groups at the same time.

Static exercises are also good for those recovering from injuries or suffering from health conditions who need low-impact exercise. The Mayo Clinic reports that isometric or static exercises may be prescribed to help rehabilitate rotator cuff injuries and arthritis (Salyer, 2016). The online medical journal Healthline.com reports that static (isometric) exercises may be the safer alternative to more strenuous exercise under certain conditions, such as when someone is recovering from knee surgery, a shoulder injury, or a general surgical operation (Salyer, 2016).

Summing up, given your goal of using bodyweight calisthenics to get into great shape and build a physique you are proud of, your workouts should be based primarily (if not exclusively) on compound exercises, rather than relying entirely on single isolation or static isometric exercises.

Whole Body Workout

The best way to achieve a full body workout is to perform a prescribed series of compound exercises, which is known as circuit training, that target the upper body, the core, and the lower body. This way, different muscle groups can be worked sequentially. For example, after doing exercises that challenge your upper body, it is better to move on to the core and then lower body before returning to the upper body again.

You may wonder why a full body workout is necessary. Perhaps, a great set of biceps and shoulders is all you want. Well, first of all, you want to look great from head to toe, but the rationale for a full body workout is about more than aesthetics. You want to have a strong, well-developed body for your health and so that you can tackle all aspects of your life. Further, you want a well-conditioned body that has adequate strength for all types of activities.

The major advantage of bodyweight calisthenics over weightlifting is that you avoid overdeveloping certain muscle groups, which means you will have more movement and flexibility.

The following sections describe the nine fundamental bodyweight calisthenics, including the body sections and muscle groups that are worked and how to perform the exercises. In the following chapter, there are further descriptions of the exercises and how to perform them, plus images and links to online videos that demonstrate the movements.

Pull Exercises for Upper Body

Pull exercises develop and train your arms, upper body, back, biceps, and forearms. These pull exercises are very demanding and should be performed two times per week to permit sufficient recovery and rebuilding time.

Pull-Ups

Yes, the pull-ups you may have done in high school are a highly effective exercise for building your upper body. A pull-up is performed by hanging from a bar with your arms shoulder width apart and palms facing forward as you grip the bar. You then pull-up until your head reaches over the bar.

If you have ever found pull-ups tough to do, it's for good reason: A pull-up forces you to lift your entire body weight without assistance. As you think about doing pull-ups, consider the importance of good form. Be more concerned about your technique rather than how many you can perform. You may recall a trainer or coach advising you to go "all the way up and all the way down," and that advice remains solid today. Speed should be moderate, and a slight pause when you reach bottom will prevent a "bounce" back up.

Chin-Ups

These movements appear identical to pull-ups, but the hands are a bit closer together and the palms are facing backward; otherwise, it's the same movement. One key difference in the effect of this movement is the additional work being done by the biceps as well as the shoulders and forearms. As with pull-ups, form is important here. You want a full range of motion: All the way up, head over the bar, all the way down, and not racing through the movements.

Unless you have been doing pull-ups and chin-ups regularly, you will find them tough when first getting started. There is no trick or shortcut; the only way to master these two versions of the pull-up is to do them consistently. You may not be able to do many reps, and that's okay, as long as you do as many as you can and do them correctly. Rest between sets and do the required number of sets. Within a week or two, you will be increasing your reps and after a month, you will be impressed with your progress.

Push Exercises for Upper Body and Core

Push exercises develop and train your arms, chest, triceps, and shoulders, as well as the complexity of central muscles that comprise your core. Push exercises should be performed two or three times per week, depending on intensity, to permit sufficient recovery and rebuilding time.

Push-Ups

Most of us have done push-ups as part of our workouts at some time, but this simple reliable exercise is often overlooked. It deserves our attention and adoption as part of a serious calisthenics workout. Using your bodyweight for resistance, push-ups work, all at the same time, the arms, shoulders, upper body, core, and even lightly the quadriceps. As such, they are an excellent compound exercise. Push-ups super target the chest muscles (pectoral), shoulder muscles (deltoids), upper arms (the triceps), the so-called wing muscles below the armpits (serratus anterior), and the stomach (abdominals).

While there are variations you can try, the basic pushup is a good way to start. Hands are placed shoulder width apart while the back remains straight (no sagging!). You lower your chest to the floor, pause for an instant, and raise up fully on extended arms.

Be less concerned about how many push-ups you can perform during one set; keep the pace slow and the form correct. Push-ups will become easier to perform in greater numbers within a short time.

A challenging variation is to go very slowly, taking 15 or 20 seconds to reach bottom, pause, and then take the same slow time to raise all the way up. Someone who can do 20 or 25 push-ups at normal speed may be challenged to do more than three of these slow versions.

As a starting movement, you can do planks, which are performed by simply assuming the starting push-up position with arms fully extended and back straight. Hold this position for at least 20 seconds, and over time, up to one minute. It gives the core a good workout and prepares the shoulders and arms for later efforts to perform push-ups.

Dips

A dip is a simple movement that helps tighten the core, strengthen the shoulders, and especially works the triceps at the back of your upper arms. Since push-ups also work the same muscle groups, do not perform push-ups and dips in close proximity. Allow some time in-between by doing exercise for the upper body or lower body.

If you have access to parallel bars or any furniture that will allow you to lean forward and lower your upper body, you should be able to perform dips without a problem. But as an alternative, you can do bench dips these two ways:

1. **Option 1**

   Place two benches or chairs parallel to each other and a bit more than your shoulder width apart. Stand between the benches, place your hands on them, and walk your feet forward so that you are in a nearly seated position. Your arms should be fully extended.

   Lower your body directly downward, as if you are trying to sit on the floor. You won't reach the floor, but drop down as far as you can, and then rise back up. Perform the planned number of reps, if you can.

2. **Option 2**

   Sit on a bench or heavy chair (that will not tip forward) and place your hands on the front edge of the bench or chair wide enough apart to allow room for your body to pass between them.

   Slide your bottom forward so you are now suspending your upper body in front of the bench. Lower your body directly downward as far as you can and then rise back up. Perform the planned number of reps or as many as you are able.

However you are able to perform dips, you will be impressed at how well they work the triceps behind your upper arms. If you find your elbows are getting sore, don't descend quite as far during your next set of dips.

Exercises for the Core

The core is the network of interlocking muscles that control and stabilize the body's central torso. It includes the abdominal muscles, the transverse abdominis (technically speaking, the broad and paired muscles on the lateral sides of the abdominal wall), the internal and external abdominal obliques, the erector spinae (a group of muscles and ligaments that straighten and rotate the back), and the right and left lower lats.

Weakness or injury to the core muscles can lead to imbalance, strains, and lower back pain. Further, a weak core will allow abdominal muscles to sag and will result in a protruding waistline and a stooped posture, which is the opposite of what you are hoping to achieve with solid, rippled abs.

Core training exercises can strengthen and develop the core's stabilizing muscles. In addition to the core strengthening push exercises, like push-ups and dips, there are other exercises that isolate the core muscles, including leg raises, side planks, and Supermans.

Leg Raises

This simple movement is recommended to strengthen the abdominal muscles and the lower back. Leg raises are considered to be more effective and safer than crunches and sit-ups, which may strain lower back muscles. The key to effectively and safely building the abdominal muscles, especially the lower abs, is to perform leg raises slowly and deliberately, being more concerned with form than with how many you can perform in a short time.

To perform leg raises, lie down on your back, either on a mat or carpeted floor (if you have neither a yoga-style foam mat nor carpet, you may spread out a folded blanket so that it's thick and cushioning). Your legs should be extended fully forward. Slide a folded towel under your bottom to raise it slightly. Begin the exercise by raising your head and shoulders a few inches off of the ground. If this feels like it's straining your neck, use your hands to hold your head up.

Now, inhale and raise your legs about 30 degrees or about a foot and a half above the ground. Hold that position for a few seconds and then exhale as you slowly lower your legs. But be sure that they do not touch the ground. Hold them just above the floor. Repeat this cycle for the desired number of reps. If you need to lower your legs all the way to the floor, that's okay; you'll get stronger with time and repetition.

A leg raise variation that can create a compound exercise entails doing leg raises while performing pullups or chin-ups. For this, you lift your legs from the vertical position to the horizontal position as you pull yourself up and lower them as you descend. Athletes in top condition can hold their legs in the vertical position throughout the full cycle of reps. An easier version is to lift your knees to your chest as you pull yourself up and then lower the knees as you descend.

Side Planks

This exercise is good for strengthening the core, especially the oblique abdominals, which are not well challenged by crunches or even by leg raises. Side planks also stabilize your hips by strengthening the gluteus maximus and gluteus Medius, which are the muscles we sit on! Unlike some other core exercises, side planks do not pressure your neck or lower back, which could lead to strains and injuries. This exercise also helps build balance, leading to ease of movement.

Begin the exercise by lying on your right side with your legs fully extended and the left leg lying directly on top of the right leg (or "stacked") from your thighs to your ankles. Your right elbow should be below your right shoulder. Let your left arm extend along your left side. Pull in your abdominal muscles. Rest your weight on your right elbow and forearm to hold your upper body up. Try to keep your legs and torso aligned and hold the position for as long as you can.

When first starting out, try to hold the side plank for at least 30 seconds. If you feel up to it, raise your left arm and point it to the ceiling. Try not to sag while holding the side plank position. Also, don't roll or fall forward or hold the position for too long. Keep your balance and maintain the correct position. When you feel fatigue or the inability to hold the position, let yourself down carefully. Repeat the exercise lying on your left side.

Depending on your condition, this may be difficult when first starting your bodyweight calisthenics program. If it's too hard to raise up on your right elbow, use your left hand to add to the upward pushing effort. Repeat this two-handed effort on the other side. Other variations to ease into side planks include raising the upper leg (while not trying to push your body up) or lying on an exercise ball. Be patient; this will become easier over time as your balance improves and your strength increases.

Superman

Does "Up, up, and away" come to mind? Can you picture Superman flying through the air with his arms and legs fully extended? That is the position of the Superman pose that you will use to develop your core. This exercise helps build the muscles in the shoulders, the frontal and oblique abdominal groups, and the muscles of your back and legs. The

Superman exercise looks easy, but you may find it takes time and practice to master this important movement, which is often adopted by yoga and Pilates practitioners because of its benefits. This exercise both strengthens and increases mobility to help prevent both lower back and upper back injury while giving the entire core, shoulders, and legs a good workout. Sean Alexander, an ACE-certified trainer, says that the Superman is a very effective movement that uses body weight to strengthen the posterior upper and lower back muscles, the abdominals, the glutes, and the hamstrings (which means lower body benefits, too) (Weiner, 2020).

Begin by lying on your stomach on a mat or carpeted surface, not on a hard floor, and extend your legs straight back and your arms fully forward along the sides of your head. Look down, not forward or up. Imagine Superman surveying the ground below and tuck your chin down towards your chest (you'll avoid straining your neck this way). Raise your arms a few inches upwards and, at the same time, raise your legs upwards a few inches as well. Manage the tempo and don't go too fast. Hold the position at the top of each rep for several seconds and then lower your limbs. Pause and repeat.

Here are some suggestions to help performance and create good results:

1. If you find it too hard at first to raise both arms and both legs simultaneously, raise only one arm and one opposite leg at a time (for

example, right arm and left leg) and then reverse. You may only be able to lift your limbs slightly, but this will improve.

2. Work on extending the range of motion. Keep breathing slowly and deeply. Do not be tempted to hold your breath. Inhale deeply when you raise your limbs and exhale fully as you lower them.

3. Avoid overextending your arms and limbs, which puts too much strain on them. Instead, maintain a slight bend in your limbs as you perform the exercise.

Lower Body Exercises

The importance of strong legs cannot be overstated. Almost everything we do involves our legs, from walking to running and from climbing to lifting. So, it's good to know that our thigh and calf muscles respond well to bodyweight calisthenics. In fact, as our bodyweight calisthenics program proceeds, they will become bigger, stronger, and more defined.

Squats

This is the definitive bodyweight exercise for the set of quadriceps thigh muscles that extend down the front of our upper legs from hip to knee and for the gluteus maximus, minimus, and medius, better known as the buttock muscles. Squats also work the hamstrings (at the back of the thighs), the adductor groin muscles, the hip flexors, and the calves. Squats are also credited with working the range of core muscles. As these are the largest muscles in our bodies, we burn more calories when we work this group compared to any other.

As important as squats are, they are comparatively easy to perform. You can get through most of the required reps easily with some harder work needed for the last few. But then, you'll feel a rewarding burn or glow when you've stopped.

Begin by standing upright with good posture. Place your hands on opposite shoulders, crossing your arms in front of your chest (this is to help with balance). Your feet should be shoulder width apart, and your weight shifted slightly to your heels.

Now, keeping your back straight, slowly lower downward into a squat position, which is about halfway down. Your thighs should be parallel to the ground, but you have some latitude here. Go down far enough to work the muscles but not so far that your knees begin to hurt (a little crackling of the knees is normal, especially when we mature).

In case you have balance issues and find yourself having to step forward or to the side, simply hold lightly to a chair, table, or counter without using it to relieve any of the weight you are lowering and raising. With practice, you will find it easy to keep from falling over.

Don't lean forward; maintain good posture throughout the movement to ensure keeping your balance.

Maintain a slow, consistent pace and don't try to go too fast. Pause when you reach the full squat position, instead of bouncing right back up. Don't hold your breath. Inhale deeply as you squat down. Exhale fully each time you rise back up to the standing position.

Calf Raises

If you have ever seen runners warming up or cooling down by pushing against a tree or a wall, chances are they are stretching their calves. Our calf muscles work hard to propel us forward and help us stand, so they are important to keep strong. The calf raise is one of the easiest exercises to perform, yet it is effective in strengthening and shaping the calf muscles and helping to prevent injury.

Stand with feet close together or slightly apart with weight distributed evenly. Rise up on the balls of your feet and your toes by raising your heels. Stand upright, and you should be able to perform calf raises without holding on for balance. But if you need a little assistance, lightly hold on to a table or chair. Rise fully, pause, and lower for the prescribed number of reps.

For increased extension and compression of the calf muscles, stand with the front part of your feet on a stair, a book, or anything that keeps the heels lower than the toes. When you rise, a greater effort is required to achieve the longer range of motion.

Another calf raise variation is to bend your knees slightly as you perform the raising and lowering. This shifts the workload to the soleus muscle, which is smaller but equal in importance to the larger gastrocnemius muscle (the one we see as the major calf muscle).

With this orientation to proper exercise selection now completed, we are ready to move to the specific details that will more completely familiarize you with these nine fundamental exercises and enable you to perform them with confidence.

Chapter 5

Nine Fundamental Movements to Master

Now that you have become familiar with compound exercises and the fundamental bodyweight calisthenic movements, you are ready to master these nine exercises and build a solid foundation that will fulfill your expectations of achieving a strong, muscular body that you can be proud of.

Each of these nine calisthenics exercises was reviewed in detail in the previous chapter; however, here, they are presented in a streamlined format with images and videos so that you can start practicing them quickly and correctly.

> ➤ Take advantage of the links provided that lead to online demonstrations of the exercises, positions, and movements. You may click on the link in the *How* section to start each brief *YouTube.com* video presentation. (You will see a brief commercial when most of the videos begin; look for the small "Skip Ads" button on the lower right to begin the demo.)

Pull-Ups

Fig. 2

Where: You will need a horizontal bar that is at the height of your extended arms, and if there is nothing available at home, you can usually find a bar to use in a park or recreation area. There are pull-ups/chin-up bars that can be purchased, too (this is the only equipment you might need to buy for this complete workout).

How: Reach up to grasp the bar with both hands, palms forward. Your arms should be shoulder width apart. Pull slowly up until your head is above the bar. Pause for a split second and then lower back down. Extend fully. Repeat the pull-up cycle up to the plan limit or as many as you can without jerking, kicking your legs, or failing to reach the bar.

Link to the video demo:

https://www.youtube.com/watch?v=eGo4IYlbE5g

Result: This is primarily an upper-body exercise. You will feel the effort in your upper arms, lower arms, and especially the shoulders. There is usually some additional work performed by the core muscles, such as the back and the abdominals, if the legs are engaged by pulling or raising them up during the pull-up cycle.

Chin-Ups

Fig. 3

Where: The chin-up is the fraternal twin of the pull-up and is performed under the same "where/what" conditions with a horizontal bar that is at least armreach height.

How: The movement is the same as pull-ups with the exception of the grip: The backs of the hands are placed face forward and the palms and fingertips are facing toward you. The hands may be placed closer to each other than shoulder width. As with pull-ups, the movements should be slow and steady without jerking. Try to fully reach the bar with your head (ideally, your chin) and fully extend at the bottom.

Link to the video demo:

https://www.youtube.com/watch?v=brhRXlOhsAM

Result: Compared to pull-ups, there will be more work done by the biceps with chin-ups, and you may feel a warm glow and heat (due to blood and hormones accumulating) as the bicep is being pumped up. Shoulders, lower arms, and core muscles will also be worked.

Push-Ups

Fig. 4

Where: Perform push-ups on any flat surface.

How: Begin with your legs fully extended behind you and your body supported by your fully extended arms.

Your hands should be under your shoulders so that hands, elbows, and shoulders are in a straight vertical line. Slowly, lower your chest to the floor, keeping your back straight (no sagging!). Push back up to the beginning position, remembering to keep your back straight. Repeat for the planned number of reps and sets. Don't bounce right back up when you've fully lowered, but there's no need to pause, either. If you're finding it tough when starting out and want to make your push-ups easier, drop down on both knees. To make push-ups more challenging, slow the pace down, taking longer to lower and raise.

Link to the video demo:

https://www.youtube.com/watch?v=IODxDxX7o i4& feature=youtu.be

Result: This classic compound exercise is great for building up your core strength as well as challenging and building strong shoulders.

Dips

Fig. 5

Where: Dips can be performed at home using chairs, boxes, benches, or countertops, as shown above. Just be sure that whatever you will be dipping with is steady and won't easily tip as you lower yourself.

How: Place your hands on the two separate surfaces so that you can lower yourself between them. Lift your feet and cross your ankles. Slowly, lower yourself as far as possible without straining and then push yourself back up to complete one rep. An alternative form of a dip is to lower yourself on a single chair, bench, or countertop. To do this, grasp the edge of the surface and extend your legs forward. While holding your weight with the palms of both hands, slide your body forward far enough so that your bottom can pass in front of the surface. Lower your body by bending your elbows, going as low as you can without straining and push back up. Repeat as specified in the plan. To make it easier, slide your feet back so that your knees are bent.

Link to the video demo:

https://www.youtube.com/watch?v=isikOOF0W3k

Result: You will feel the workout mostly in your triceps (the back of your arms), plus your shoulders.

Leg Raises

Fig. 6

Where: On the floor with a yoga mat (or any foam mat) or carpet (a folded blanket should work well, too).

How: Lie on your back with your legs fully extended. Place a folded towel under your hips so they are slightly elevated (or you may slide your hands under you to lift your hips, as seen above).

The movement begins by raising your heels about 18 inches off of the floor. You should feel a slight tensing of the abdominal muscles. Now, raise your legs all the way up so that they point at the ceiling and pause. Slowly, lower to the starting position. Keep your heels from touching the ground and raise the legs for each of the reps in the set. Try to keep your legs straight throughout the movement, but if you're finding it hard, bend your knees. As mentioned previously, you can make this a compound exercise by performing leg raises while doing pull-ups or chin-ups.

Link to the video demo:

https://www.youtube.com/watch?v=l4kQd9eWcl
E

Result: Leg raises are great for the core, including the frontal abdominal muscles, the lower abs, and the lower back muscles. If you find your neck has become sore, place a small folded towel under your head to avoid the strain.

Side Planks

Fig. 7

Where: On the floor with a foam mat, carpet, or a folded blanket for support.

How: Roll over onto your right side, extend your legs fully, and place your left leg on top of the right leg. Rest your upper body weight on your right forearm and right elbow, which should be directly under the right shoulder. Place your left hand on your left hip. Now, push your hips upwards, supporting your body with the right elbow and forearm. Align your legs and body in a straight line. One option is to raise your left arm and point it toward the ceiling. You may find this movement difficult when first starting out, so you can use your left hand to press down on the floor, which will assist considerably in getting your hips up in the air. You may also find it easier if your left leg remains on the floor in front of your right leg. Do your best to raise your hips even a little, knowing you will get stronger with practice. Hold the side plank position for up to 30 seconds starting out (you'll do it longer as you develop). Once you complete the side plank on the right side, roll over and repeat on the left side.

Link to the video demo:

https://www.youtube.com/watch?v=NXr4Fw8q60o

Results: Once you are able to perform this movement even partially, you will be improving your core, the oblique abdominals, and the glutes, which stabilize the hips and improve balance. Your shoulders will get some work, too.

Superman

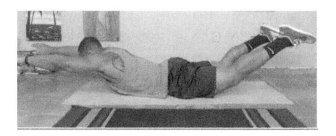

Fig. 8

Where: On the floor, supported by a foam mat, carpet, or folded blanket. Allow enough room so that you can fully extend your arms and legs.

How: Reach as far forward as you can with arms against your head and legs stretched behind you with toes extended back. Raise your hands and arms a few inches. Do the same with your legs. Ideally (and this may take some time and practice), the arms will be raised from your shoulders and your legs will be raised from your hips. An interim version to build strength is to raise one arm and the opposing leg and then reversing the sequence (right arm and left leg and then left arm and right leg). Keep the emphasis on raising the arms and legs and not arching the lower back.

Link to the video demo:

https://www.youtube.com/watch?v=VUT1RHyM Euc **Results:** This is one of the finest exercises to develop the core, including the front abdominals and upper and lower back. It also benefits your upper arms, shoulders, and the lower body, such as the hamstrings, hip flexors, and glutes. Just be careful not to over flex or strain the lower back.

Squats

Fig. 9

Where: Any flat, hard surface. A chair or table is optional for assisting with balance. Also, you can perform the movement with a wall close behind as to prevent accidentally falling backward.

How: Stand upright with your feet shoulder width apart and with your weight shifted slightly back toward your heels. Angle your toes outward. Keeping your back straight, bend your knees and squat as if sitting down in a chair. Keep your knees pointing forward. If done correctly, your knees will remain over your toes and should not extend past them. To keep your balance, you may extend your arms forward, or if balance is still challenging, place the fingers of one hand on a nearby chair, table, or counter. Don't place any weight on it; it's just to steady yourself. Try to lower until your thighs are parallel to the floor. Keep alert to maintain upright posture throughout the movement. Rise from the squat with the same good form and repeat the required reps.

Link to the video demo:

https://www.youtube.com/watch?v=aclHkVaku9U

Result: A well-performed set of squats will be felt warmly in the quadriceps at the front of your thighs. They will also tone your hamstrings, calves, and hip flexors.

Calf Raises

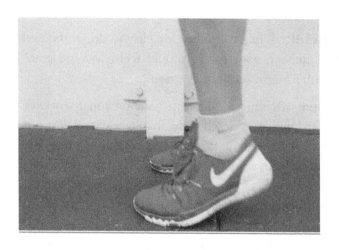

Fig. 10

Where: Any flat, hard surface or on a step, if a longer movement is desired. A chair or table is optional for assisting with balance. This exercise may also be performed by standing on a flat surface that is 1-2 feet from a wall, tree, or pole.

How: It's as simple as raising up on the balls of the feet and toes, pausing, and lowering to the floor. At the top of the raise, you will feel the muscles of your calf compressing. If you are standing on a step with your heels extended, lower all the way down so your heels are well below the level of the step and your toes. An easier version of calf raises is to perform them while seated in a chair.

Link to the video demo:

https://www.youtube.com/watch?v=TZrBb5M1C
dM

Result: While calf raises are easy to do, at the end of the set, your calves should feel good (no pain) with a warm sense of exertion.

Now, it's time to develop your personal workout plan, which is a schedule that takes into account your level of conditioning and establishes how the next three weeks will unfold. Each of the nine bodyweight calisthenic exercises will be scheduled with sequences per day, repetitions, and sets. You will do exercises most days of the week, because you will be rotating different muscle groups. So, while one group rests, another gets to work. The important rest periods are included but don't expect time off. Calisthenics are a daily commitment, but as indicated, hard workouts will be separated by two or three recovery days.

Chapter 6

Your 21-Day Workout Plans

We have so far provided you with the foundation of how to build muscles and get fit and stronger with bodyweight calisthenics. The next step is learning how to schedule your workouts so that each day you know *what* to do and *how* to do it. Here, you will explore two 21-day plans that will get you going right away and keep you going over the long haul. In addition, your planning will integrate two other key elements of your conditioning: cardiovascular exercise and a healthy, protein-rich diet.

The Importance of Planning

Extensive experience has convinced generations of trainers and physical therapists that planning plays a decisive role in determining how effectively an individual will train and achieve their fitness and strength goals. If you have been to a gym or fitness center, you have probably seen trainers working with their clients by following a prescribed schedule of exercise movements, day by day, week by week, and month by month. When it's done right, planning ensures steady progress without imposing excessive strain or causing injuries. In fact, many coaches believe that overdoing workouts and pushing and pulling too much, too fast leads to burnout, strains, or pulls that can set back bodyweight training programs by weeks or months.

To achieve the muscular body you desire, while avoiding injury and overwork, trust the plans that you will be following here. They have been designed with your success and well-being in mind. Even though you will not be using weights and resistance machines, do not underestimate the benefits of using your own bodyweight to perform each exercise. Yes, bodyweight calisthenics are safer than dumbbells, barbells, cables, and machines. When done correctly in the right form with the prescribed reps, sets, rotations, and resting phases, you will build bigger, well-defined muscles with distinctive "cut" musculature. You will also become stronger and faster than you could imagine.

Cardio Exercise and Diet Plan

Your bodybuilding plan would not be complete without the two additional elements of cardiovascular conditioning and a responsible, nutritious diet. There is a strong medically proven basis for performing cardiovascular exercises that systematically raise your pulse rate and breathing rate for a sustained period. These exercises can be performed at least several times a week and in a variety of ways, such as walking, hiking fast, jogging, running, swimming, biking, and using an elliptical machine among the more popular options. Cardiovascular training is important for your overall conditioning and health and will be included in your planning,

If you did not spend too much time digesting (pardon the pun) chapter 2's discussion of nutrition, make sure you give it a second look and also review the role of protein in your diet to optimize muscle building that's covered in chapter 3. Eating a great healthy diet will support and enhance the results of your training. Or, you can ignore good dietary practices, which can slow your bodybuilding results and risk your health.

By including the life-enhancing benefits of bodyweight calisthenics resistance exercises, regular cardiovascular conditioning, and a healthy diet, you will not only be achieving your primary goals of looking good, feeling good, and getting much stronger but you will also be making yourself more resistant to obesity, diabetes, heart disease, and even cancer. Regular intensive resistance and cardiovascular exercise along with a Mediterranean (or similar) diet can reduce or eliminate stress, anxiety, inflammation, and depression. There are encouraging findings that these combined disciplines can slow or stop the onset of dementia, Alzheimer's disease, and Parkinson's, among other degenerative disorders as well.

Taken in the holistic sense, your adoption of and commitment to a comprehensive exercise and diet plan is the most important investment you can make.

A Note of Caution

The UK's respected School of Calisthenics has built their training programs around the concept of hypertrophy, which you may recall refers to building the skeletal muscle fibers by working them hard so they are damaged and need to be rebuilt by the protein in our bodies ("Bodyweight training and workouts," 2020). This healthy damage is caused by forceful tension, which, of course, we supply through resistance exercises. The levels of resistance must be sufficient to truly work the mussels hard, yet not so forceful or long-lasting as to cause serious damage, such as tears, strains, and pulls. That brings us to some practical words of caution to help prevent injuries that can sideline you and your bodybuilding schedule.

It's important to listen to your body, not too closely, or you may overreact. But generally, pain is a warning that should not be ignored. With experience, you will learn to recognize the difference between the normal feeling of exhaustion, like a burn, when you are nearing the end of a set and you're pushing out a few more reps and the real pain that signals that serious damage is being done.

One of the important advantages of bodyweight calisthenics training is that there are limits to the weight you are lifting; you increase the workload mostly by increasing reps and sets, and not by adding 20 lb weights to a barbell, for example.

Shoulders

One well-known area of injury from resistance exercises (or any heavy lifting) are the shoulders. The group of muscles that control shoulder movements are known as the rotator cuff, and once you've done hard damage here, you can be in for a long rehabilitation. Be especially careful not to push your shoulders beyond their limit. Pay attention to any warning signs or extreme pain and ratchet back the tension when it starts to really hurt.

Exercises to watch out for when it comes to possible shoulder injuries are pull-ups, chin-ups, and push-ups, which nonetheless are great for building your shoulders. Also, when performing side planks, your shoulder will be working hard, especially as you push your hips off the floor to rise to the holding position, so pay close attention here as well.

Another cause of rotator cuff injury is not from damage caused by pulling or lifting too much weight but from excessive or repetitive use. You may be aware of baseball pitchers being sidelined for extended rehabilitation exercises or, worse, rotator cuff surgery. Consider that pitching seven innings can involve seven sets of 24 reps (or more) of maximum exertion (throwing the ball at 90 miles per hour with additional arm and shoulder twists to create curves and screwballs). Your 21-day plans will take into account the need to avoid excessive repetition of certain muscle groups.

Lower Back

The lower back, or lumbar region of the spine, is another area of your body that is susceptible to strain and injury. Avoid arching your back during calisthenic movements. For example, don't let your back sag during push-ups; instead, keep your back straight throughout the pushing up and down and during the pause at the top of the movement.

Be careful, too, when performing the Superman exercise, because it does involve a slight arching of the back. Keep the emphasis on raising arms, shoulders, and legs while keeping lower back arching to a minimum. When doing leg raises, be sure to place a folded towel or your hands under your butt to take the strain off the lower back.

Knees

Your knees are a complicated assembly of muscles, tendons, ligaments, and, of course, your kneecaps. Your quadriceps muscle helps hold the kneecap in place as it swivels and adjusts to everything from walking to squatting. The knee is susceptible to *pattern overload repeat injury,* including torn muscles, pulled ligaments, and the erosion of the lubricating cartilage under the kneecap (ask a marathon runner about "runner's knee" symptoms).

The one exercise of the nine you'll be starting with that could aggravate or injure your knees are squats.

Do not squat deeper than is comfortable, and do not let your knees extend forward past your toes.

But generally, if you follow the gradual building up of resistance and increased repetitions that your 21-day plans will prescribe, you should build muscle bulk and strength gradually and safely. Resistance training, when done correctly, can create the right conditions for muscle building adaptations to take place in the body as you pressure the muscles to overcome the resistance, force, and the new stress being applied.

Positivity and Motivation

Your attitude is as important as the exercises you will be performing. Having the goal of a stronger, more muscular body and a healthier, more robust persona is the starting point. Yet, the next step is having the self-discipline and tenacity to achieve and sustain your goals.

To sum it up succinctly: "Ya gotta believe," as New York Mets player Tug McGraw famously exhorted his teammates when trying to boost their confidence so that they could make it to the World Series (yes, they made it). You need to believe that your bodyweight calisthenics training program is working, building strength, and adding bulk at the molecular and muscular fiber level every day. And that it is happening as a direct result of the time and effort you put into faithfully and correctly performing the exercises.

Experience shows that, for most people, it's hard to start a fitness program, whether it's calisthenics, traditional resistance with weights, or a cardiovascular routine. Experience also shows that starting the program does not ensure continuing with it. How many people do we know who joined a fitness center only to show up once or twice and then stop? You know the excuses, the most common being, "I don't have the time." Really? Someone who wants to get into shape doesn't have 30 to 45 minutes to spare? It's hard to believe that the great feeling of a workout and the benefits of building muscle and getting stronger are not worth that little bit of time.

No, it's not about time; it's about motivation. People who aspire to shape up, get strong, and get fit but don't commit to the routine just don't have the resolve to get started or to keep it going.

How can you ensure that you are motivated to become an acolyte of bodybuilding and overall physical fitness? How can you be confident you will follow the 21-day plans that will get you started easily and take you gradually to higher and higher levels of strength and musculature?

It goes back to "Ya gotta believe." You need to believe deeply that this really works, and you will get out of it exactly what you put into it.

Have you heard of *The Power of Positive Thinking*? It became a bestselling book when Dr. Norman Vincent Peale published it back in the 1950s, and it still influences millions around the world. The concept is simple and applicable to your fitness goals.

You must:

1. **Visualize yourself succeeding.** See yourself with the physique you aspire to and make it a reality in your mind. Imagine yourself performing each bodyweight calisthenics exercise and feel your muscles bulging and firming.

2. **Think positively** about who you are and what you can do. Tell yourself repeatedly that you are on your way to the musculature you dream of. Do not allow negative thoughts or fear of failure affect you.

3. **Minimize any obstacles** that might interfere with your scheduled exercises. Treat your workout time as sacrosanct, inviolable, and untouchable. Dismiss possible obstacles in your workout with the positive affirmation of "I've got this."

Pre-Planning Principles

While the fundamentals of bodybuilding are similar between bodyweight calisthenics and weightlifting, there is a big difference when it comes to increasing the tension so that you can progress to challenging the muscles more. With weightlifting, you simply increase the amount of weight being lifted. There's no need to change the numbers of reps or sets, change the timing of the movements, or change the rest and recovery times. But with calisthenics, your weight remains about the same. So with a pull-up, for example, you can only pull-up your weight, no more and no less. The same goes for chin-ups, push-ups, dips, squats, and calf raises. If you weigh 165 lbs, you can only pull or push 165 lbs.

Therefore, different variables need to come into play to increase the challenge to the muscles when you are doing bodyweight calisthenics. Just as weights can be added to increase resistance, with calisthenics we can adjust the exercise movements in terms of positions, angles, and range of motions to work the muscles harder.

First, just to be clear on the terminology:

1. A **rep** (repetition) is one full cycle of an exercise. For instance, the one up-and-down movement of a push-up. To start, you'll probably be doing six to 12 reps for most of the exercises.

2. A **set** is the group of reps you perform in one sequence. So, your six reps of push-ups, for example, make one set of push-ups. You'll be doing about three to five sets at first.

3. **Rest** refers to the interval between sets, which is 30 to 90 seconds.

4. **Recovery** means the number of days between workouts for a body group. For

example, recovering for two days between upper body exercises and working out different body groups during those two days.

Okay, here's what you can do to raise the intensity and muscular stress of the exercises without changing your own weight:

1. You can **increase** the numbers of reps and number of sets. For example, increasing from six to 10 reps to 12 reps. Or, increasing from three to five sets to six sets.

2. You can **shorten** the rest time between sets. For example, instead of a 90-second rest, you take a 60- or 30-second rest.

3. You can perform the movements **more slowly,** which increases the tension. For example, when performing push-ups, taking ten seconds to lower and ten seconds to push back up (try it; it's impressive).

You can also add in some of the variants we discussed earlier. For example, as you advance, you can make a push-up more difficult by placing your hands closer together or very far apart. You could also alter the body angle to perform a pike push-up, which increases the intensity and tension on the shoulders and upper chest. Or, there the more challenging archer pull-ups, Korean dips, one-arm push-ups, and one-arm pull-ups. You will have the option in the advanced plan to try these or stick with the more basic exercises where you increase reps and sets while slowing the movements.

There is also the option of adding weight to your body. For example, wearing a weighted vest to add 20 pounds while you are doing push-ups, pull-ups, chin-ups, and most of the other exercises. This is an accepted practice among some calisthenics enthusiasts, but to others, it violates the principle of using only your own bodyweight for resistance.

The one variable you will *not be changing* is the recovery period. A full two days (in most cases) is required so that the necessary protein-based repairs to muscles can be made. This is especially needed as the movements become more challenging.

Your objective is to build tension throughout all of the muscles of your body, integrating many different body parts during the bodyweight-challenging movements. This is why calisthenics are more beneficial than the more isolated movements performed with weights and the pushing and pulling of machine training.

Beginning with the Basics

Each of the 21-day plans will be working the three main muscle groups: the upper body (the arms and the shoulders), the core (the abdominals, back muscles, and side muscles), and the lower body (the quadriceps, the hamstrings, the calves, and the hip flexors). The plans include the nine exercises that you have become familiar with, and each can be modified as you progress with variations in form, procedure, and timing.

The order of each exercise within your plan is based on spacing out similar muscle groups. You wouldn't want to immediately follow three sets of pull-ups with three sets of chin-ups or follow squats with leg raises. However, you are free to vary the order to suit your preferences, as long as you perform the recommended number of reps and sets for the specified cycle times.

You may conduct your bodyweight calisthenics workout sessions two or three days per week or more often, such as five or six days per week. The difference between these two extremes is important.

1. **Two or three** bodyweight calisthenics workouts per week means you will perform all nine exercises for the required reps, sets, cycle times, and set intervals just two or three days per week. In other words, you will have fewer workout training sessions but they will be longer, more intensive workouts. The two or three workouts per week total seven intense workout days during the 21-day schedule.

2. **Four or five** workout days per week may be preferred by those who like almost daily calisthenics sessions. For that option, the plan alternates between two exercise groups: Group 1 with five exercises and Group 2 with four exercises. This option results in four or five

calisthenics workouts per week or 14 workout days during the 21-day schedule.

21-Day Plan: Four or Five Exercises Per Session

This 21-day plan divides the nine exercises into two groups of four or five exercises per session.

Movement	Muscle Groups	Reps	Sets	Cycle Time *	Between Sets	21-Day Schedule
Group 1						
PullUps	Upper Body	6	3	3-4 seconds	90 seconds	1 - 4 - 7 - 10 - 13 - 16 - 19
Leg Raises	Core Lower Body	6	3	5 seconds	90 seconds	1 - 4 - 7 - 10 - 13 - 16 - 19
Superman	Core Upper Body	6	3	3 seconds	60 seconds	1 - 4 - 7 - 10 - 13 - 16 -19

Dips	Upper Body	6	3	4 seconds	90 seconds	1 - 4 - 7 - 10 - 13 - 16 - 19
Squats	Lower Body	6	3	4 seconds	60 seconds	1 - 4 - 7 - 10 - 13 - 16 - 19
Group 2						
Push Ups	Upper Body Core	8	3	4 seconds	90 seconds	3 - 6 - 9 - 12 - 15 - 18 - 21
Calf Raises	Lower Body	14	3	8 seconds	30 seconds	3 - 6 - 9 - 12 - 15 - 18 - 21
Side Planks	Upper Body Core	1 each side	3	30 seconds	90 seconds	3 - 6 - 9 - 12 - 15 - 18 - 21
Chin Ups	Upper Body	6	3	3-4 seconds	90 seconds	3 - 6 - 9 - 12 - 15 - 18 - 21

*One cycle is the time it takes to complete the movement in seconds. For example, one pull-up cycle includes the pulling up and lowering down movement, while one Superman cycle includes holding the position.

The below chart shows how the two groups will be performed over the 21-day schedule. This plan provides 14 workout days and seven rest/recovery days. The groups are performed on consecutive days, followed by one rest/recovery day, which means each group is separated by two days.

Day / Acti on	Mon	Tue	Wed	Thu	Fri	Sat	Sun
Days 1 to 7	1	22	3	4	5	6	7
Acti on	Group 1	Rest	Group 2	Group 1	Rest	Group2	Group1
Days 8 to 14	8	9	10	11	12	13	14
Acti on	Rest	Group 2	Group1	Rest	Group 2	Group 1	Rest
Days 15 to 21	15	16	17	18	19	20	21
Acti on	Group 2	Group 1	Rest	Group 2	Group 1	Rest	Group 2

21-Day Plan: Nine Exercises Per Session

This is the one-day-on/two-days-off pattern with all nine exercises performed during one session.

Moveme nt	Musc le Grou ps	Re ps	Set s	Cycle Time	Betwe en Sets	21-Day Sched ule
Pull Ups	Uppe r Body	6	3	3-4 secon ds	90 second s	1 - 4 - 7 – 10 – 13 – 16 - 19
Leg Raises	Core Lowe r Body	6	3	5 secon ds	90 second s	1 - 4 - 7 - 10 – 13 - 16 - 19
Superma n	Core Uppe r Body Lowe r Body	6	3	3 secon ds	60 second s	1 - 4 - 7 - 10 - 13 - 16 - 19

Dips	Upper Body	6	3	4 seconds	90 seconds	1 - 4 - 7 - 10 - 13 - 16 - 19
Squats	Lower Body	6	3	4 seconds	60 seconds	1 - 4 - 7 - 10 - 13 - 16 - 19
Push Ups	Upper Body Core	8	3	4 seconds	90 seconds	1 - 4 - 7 - 10 - 13 – 16 - 19
Calf Raises	Lower Body	14	3	8 seconds	30 seconds	1 - 4 - 7 - 10 - 13 - 16 - 19
Side Planks	Upper Body Core	1 each side	3	30 seconds	90 seconds	1 - 4 - 7 - 10 - 13 - 16 - 19
Chin Ups	Upper Body	6	3	3-4 seconds	90 seconds	1 - 4 - 7 - 10 - 13 - 16 - 19

The below chart shows how the nine exercises will be performed over the 21-day schedule. As noted, this plan provides seven workout days and 14 rest/recovery days during the 21-day schedule.

Day	Mon	Tue	Wed	Thu	Fri	Sat	Sun
1 to 7	1	2	3	4	5	6	7
Action	All 9	Rest	Rest	All 9	Rest	Rest	All 9
8 to 14	8	9	10	11	12	13	14
Action	Rest	Rest	All 9	Rest	Rest	All 9	Rest
15 to 21	15	16	17	18	19	20	21
Action	Rest	All 9	Rest	Rest	All 9	Rest	Rest

Your Initial Progress

You are now ready to get started. Your first decision should be whether you prefer the plan with four to five workouts per week or the alternative of limiting the number of days you exercise. You certainly have the option of trying each schedule to see how they work or don't work for you. Be sure you are getting sufficient rest and recovery between workouts no matter which plan you choose.

Next, you should try to follow the recommended reps, sets, and timing. But since no two of us are equal, you might find *fewer is better* for you in the early days of your training. Or, you may find that you can easily do more. If you can do more reps at a slower pace, with shorter rests between sets, and without strain, by all means, push yourself forward.

As for your initial progress, you're starting on an ambitious bodyweight calisthenics program with high expectations and are hoping you won't be disappointed. Don't worry, you won't be let down. That is, as long as you remember the importance of commitment and dedicate yourself to your bodybuilding goals.

To ensure that you stick with your plan, first and foremost, make some decisions that will ease into your workouts and keep them going on schedule for the first 21-day plan.

Here are some key issues to consider as you embark on your chosen 21-day plan:

1. **Where?**

Ideally, the best location for your exercise routine is a room or place in your home that has the space you need and the features or fixtures that can be of help.

Consider: Does the room have carpeting that will cushion you during Superman, and leg raises, and side planks? If not, do you have a yoga mat or a blanket you can fold into a cushion? What about privacy? It's better to avoid distractions so you can focus on your movements and feel your muscles working. You may be more comfortable not having others watch your workout or make comments.

While your home may have the space you need, it may be necessary to go elsewhere to find a bar for pull-ups and chin-ups; although, it would be great to have your own chinning bar. One of these will be safe to use, and most models can be put up and taken down quickly so you can avoid trouble with roommates, friends, spouses, and partners. There are lots of chinning bar options available online. All you have to do is search the keywords "chinning bar doorway" on Google.

You're not limited to your home; a nearby playground or park may have a bar or equipment, like monkey bars, that you can use. Same goes for structures that you can use for dip exercises.

2. **When?**

The time of day and the days you select to exercise can have a very strong influence, positively or negatively, on whether you stick with your bodybuilding calisthenics program or not. Think through the issue of timing and then be decisive. You need to select one time of day and stick with it.

For example, it's best to work out early morning and before breakfast or, if your schedule allows it, before lunch. If you are a slow starter and pre-breakfast or pre-lunch workouts won't work for you, try before dinner. But don't workout out late, before bed, or after a meal.

Whatever time works for you, commit to it. It will be a mistake to tell yourself you'll work out early in the day, for example, and then decide you'll "get to it later." Chances are, you won't. Consistency and commitment are essential components of achieving your fitness goals.

The same goes for the days you select to exercise. The 21-day schedules can start on any day (no need to wait for Monday), but once you start, it's important to respect the "on" workout days and the "off" rest and recovery days. Of course, things can come up, but if you miss a day, get back to the schedule the next day. As we've emphasized, rest is very important, so an extra recovery day is okay, but don't let it turn into a series of missed days or the progress you've made can start to diminish.

3. **Being Inclusive**

The nine exercises that will be your initial routine have been selected with careful consideration to ensure that your entire body will be challenged, developed, and built-up, so it is important to perform all of these exercises, not just some.

Do not be tempted to concentrate exclusively on your upper body, for example, so you just have impressive biceps, triceps, and shoulders. Give your entire core your equal attention; the same goes for the lower body.

There is a synergistic effect when all nine exercises are performed with equal attention, because your muscles form an interactive network. Every exercise affects multiple regions and muscle groups. Your pull-ups and chin-ups may be very focused on arms and shoulders, but there are tensions extending through your chest, abdominals, and upper back, for example.

4. **Form and Intensity**

Be sure to follow the instructions provided in chapters 4 and 5 about how to perform the nine exercises. These instructions were developed with the objective of helping you perform them fully and correctly. Also, be sure to watch the demo videos. Further, feel free to do your own research, since there are many other demonstrations that you can find online (although, what has been provided here is comprehensive and complete).

You want to perform each exercise correctly and fully; no cheating or shortcuts. When doing push-ups, it's all the way down and all the way back up with a straight back and a momentary pause at the top and bottom positions. You want to ensure you are doing it right. The same goes for pull-ups and push-ups. Half measures will reduce the effectiveness of the movement and diminish the muscle-building effects.

No racing through it, either. Watch your speed and do the movements slower rather than faster, which will ensure the correct amount of tension is being experienced. As you progress in the coming weeks and months, slowing down the movements will be one of the more effective ways to make the exercises more challenging without having to add extra weight. But even at the beginning levels, take it easy.

Feel the tension as you lower and raise back up, pull up and lower down, or sink into each squat. By going slowly, you should be assured that your muscles are receiving sufficient intensity to experience hypertrophy.

Cardiovascular Conditioning

Raising your heartbeat and keeping it elevated for a sustained period is the fundamental objective of aerobics, or cardiovascular conditioning. You're certainly aware of it, seeing joggers everywhere, people walking or running on treadmills, people using ellipticals, people pedaling and spinning on bicycles, and swimmers doing laps. Widespread interest in cardio began in the 1970s when reports began to cite the health benefits of exercise. Before then, you never saw anyone running in the streets, and there were not millions of people of all ages running marathons. Fitness centers were extremely rare, and where they existed, the emphasis was almost exclusively on weightlifting.

Do you have to become a marathoner and train to run 26.2 miles to take advantage of cardiovascular conditioning? No, there are many ways to fulfill your weekly quota of cardio exercise that are far less strenuous and far less time-consuming. You may choose to walk or jog at a good pace outside or on a treadmill, use an elliptical machine or skiing simulator, use an indoor or outdoor bicycle, or swim laps. Just be sure it is a rhythmic exercise that increases your heartbeat, and that you can sustain it for at least 15 or 20 minutes (ideally, though, 30 minutes or more).

Below, we will answer your questions about the benefits of cardio conditioning, and you can learn how to start incorporating an agreeable form of cardio into your regular exercise routine.

1. **What are the health benefits of cardio exercise?**

   The news about the disease preventative potential of cardiovascular exercise is everywhere. You can't miss the countless articles, health reports, and TV programs emphasizing the importance of getting up and getting moving by raising your pulse and breathing deeply for at least 20 minutes.

A continuing stream of new studies and clinical trials cite the role of cardiovascular exercise in helping to prevent heart disease, including slowing the buildup of arterial plaque to reduce the risk of heart attacks and lowering high blood pressure to help prevent strokes. Cardio conditioning is also credited with preventing type 2 diabetes by lowering blood sugar and improving insulin resistance. Further, it may possibly prevent respiratory and digestive disorders and even reduce the risk of some forms of cancer. Aerobics are believed to strengthen the immune system, too.

The onset and progression of cognitive disorders, like dementia and Alzheimer's, are believed to be slowed by sustaining cardiovascular exercise. Even a long-term practice of walking a certain distance at a brisk pace at least three or four times per week is a health benefit.

2. **Does cardio help with weight control?**

One-third of Americans are classified as overweight, and another one-third are obese. These classifications are based on body mass index levels, which take height, weight, and gender into consideration. But, with cardio conditioning, you can get your weight down to a healthier level, since the calories burned during a cardio routine add up.

A robust 30- to 45-minute cardio workout can burn 400 to 500 calories, which helps chip away at excess pounds and keeps them off. Don't worry about burning off protein; your body uses carbohydrates (in the form of glycogen) for energy, and if that runs short (like during a long run), it burns fat.

3. **Does cardio provide psychological benefits?**

Cardio workouts can induce the release of beta-endorphins, the hormone that brings on the famous "runner's high." It's a medically verified effect and can relieve tension and stress, getting rid of both anxiety and depression.

You may now be wondering if a hard calisthenics workout can bring on the release of beta-endorphins. Very possibly, especially if the workout is conducted at a brisk pace. But the sustained intensity of a cardio workout seems to be more effective and consistent in creating the runner's high. When calisthenics and cardio are combined during the same workout period, the psychological and physical benefits are cumulative.

Aerobics are also credited with improving your mood by enlarging the hippocampus, the part of the brain that regulates emotion. It also can help you get a good night's sleep. Aerobics combined with calisthenics can improve brain plasticity to improve learning ability and memory as well.

4. **Will cardiovascular conditioning help you to live longer?**

Since it is credited with preventing or slowing the onset of so many life-threatening diseases and conditions, it is possible that cardio conditioning can help you live longer. But, to be objective, there are no guarantees in life, especially when our genetic profiles have so much influence. The responsible attitude is to do your best to improve the odds and give your body the fighting chance to survive and prosper for as long and as well as possible. Many marathoners believe that keeping in good cardiovascular condition may not necessarily put more years into your life, but it will definitely put more life into your years.

5. **Do you need a doctor's approval?**

It's recommended by medical and fitness professionals that you consult with your doctor before beginning any strenuous activity, especially if you have not had a thorough physical examination within the past year.

It's a good idea to get the heart and circulatory system checked out, and chances are very good that you will be encouraged to begin both calisthenic and cardio training with the advice to start gradually at first, take it easy, and work up to greater intensity over time.

Beware of your body's warnings during cardio workouts, especially pain in your chest, shoulder, or left arm, which could be a signal, like angina, that the blood flow to your heart is being impeded or blocked. Stop exercising if that happens and call your doctor.

6. **How much cardio exercise do you need?**

The current consensus is that at least three days per week of brisk walking or jogging, biking, elliptical, or swimming are sufficient, but four or more days is preferable.

If the pace is moderate, a total of 150 minutes per week is a good base level. If the pace is brisk with deeper breathing and getting the pulse rate up, 75 to 100 minutes per week is a good base. But some fitness enthusiasts push up to 300 minutes per week.

When you are in good condition, the quality of the cardio workout can be enhanced by doing intervals, which are bursts of speed and/or increased incline. The interval should last for 20 to 40 seconds, during which time you are really working hard. After the interval, you slow back down and take two minutes of rest before the next interval. A total of six to eight intervals during the workout will add considerable conditioning benefits.

Since you have now chosen your plan and put together your initial strategy for sticking with that plan, we are ready to advance and discuss progression and how to increase the tension and difficulty of your bodyweight calisthenics exercises.

Chapter 7

Progression

The overall objective of your calisthenics workout plan is to get you started easily and immediately and then to start the transition to more intensive levels. First, you will work through three basic levels, then up to two intermediate levels, and, finally, you'll step up and transition to the first advanced level.

When to progress to a higher level of intensity or a more complex form of an exercise movement depends on you. Factors to consider are your perception of your level of expertise, the ability to perform each exercise correctly (in good form), the ability to complete the recommended number of reps and sets, and the will to follow the recommended timing for each cycle of the movements and rest duration between sets.

You should follow your own sense of progress, but here is a suggested 18-week timeline that covers your first six 21-day cycles. This timeline is based on typical progress and assumes a complete commitment to performing all nine of the exercises correctly and completely and adhering to their workouts schedule.

1st 21 Days			2nd 21 Days			3rd 21 Days		
Week 1	Week 2	Week 3	Week 4	Week 5	Week 6	Week 7	Week 8	Week 9

Basic 1	Basic 1	Basic 1 or 2	Basic 2	Basic 2	Basic 2 or 3	Basic 3	Basic 3	Basic 3
4th 21 Days			5th 21 Days			6th 21 Days		
Week 10	Week 11	Week 12	Week 13	Week 14	Week 15	Week 16	Week 17	Week 18
Inter 1	Inter 1	Inter 1	Inter 2	Inter 2	Inter 2	Advance 1	Advance 1	Advance 1

Mastering the Basic Levels

Basic Level 1

This is where you will begin: Basic Level 1 on Day 1 of Week 1. This is the 21-day plan from the previous chapter that follows the one-day-on/two-days-off pattern where you perform all nine exercises during one session. This plan provides seven workout days and 14 rest/recovery days during each 21-day cycle. Consider this the foundation from which you will advance in the coming weeks and months.

Begins Week 1

Day 1

Movement	Muscle Groups	Reps	Sets	Cycle Time *	Between Sets	21 Day Schedule
Pull Ups	Upper Body	6	3	3-4 seconds	90 seconds	1 - 4 - 7 - 10 - 13 - 16 - 19
Leg Raises	Core Lower Body	6	3	5 seconds	90 seconds	1 - 4 - 7 - 10 – 13 - 16 - 19
Superman	Core, Upper Lower Body	6	3	3 seconds	60 seconds	1 - 4 - 7 - 10 - 13 - 16 - 19
Dips	Upper Body	6	3	4 seconds	90 seconds	1 - 4 - 7 - 10 – 13 – 16 - 19
Squats	Lower Body	6	3	4 seconds	60 seconds	1 - 4 - 7 - 10 - 13 - 16 - 19

Push Ups	Upper Body Core	8	3	4 seconds	90 seconds	1 - 4 - 7 - 10 - 13 - 16 - 19
Calf Raises	Lower Body	14	3	8 seconds	30 seconds	1 - 4 - 7 - 10 - 13 - 16 - 19
Side Planks	Upper Body Core	1 each side	3	30 seconds	90 seconds	1 - 4 - 7 - 10 - 13 - 16 - 19
Chin Ups	Upper Body	6	3	3-4 seconds	90 seconds	1 - 4 - 7 - 10 - 13 - 16 - 19

Basic Level 2

After about two weeks of following Basic Level 1, you should be ready to work a little harder and move onto Basic Level 2. The number of reps increases for most exercises during this level, which begins in either week 3 or week 4, depending on individual progress. Only the side plank remains the same at one rep per side, but the cycle timing is extended. There are no changes in sets or duration of rest time between sets for any of the exercises.

Begins Week 3 or 4

Day 22 or 29

Moveme nt	Muscl e Grou ps	Re ps	Set s	Cycle Time *	Betwe en Sets	21 Day Schedu le
Pull Ups	Upper Body	8	3	3-4 secon ds	90 second s	1 - 4 - 7 - 10 - 13 - 16 - 19
Leg Raises	Core Lower Body	10	3	5 secon ds	90 second s	1 - 4 - 7 – 10 – 13 – 16 - 19
Superm an	Core, Upper Lowe r Body	8	3	3 secon ds	60 second s	1 - 4 - 7 - 10 - 13 - 16 - 19
Dips	Upper Body	8	3	4 second s	90 second s	1 - 4 - 7 - 10 - 13 - 16 - 19
Squats	Lower Body	10	3	4 secon ds	60 second s	1 - 4 - 7 - 10 - 13 - 16 - 19

Push Ups	Uppe r Body Core	10	3	4 seconds	90 seconds	1 - 4 - 7 - 10 - 13 - 16 - 19
Calf Raises	Lower Body	18	3	8 seconds	30 seconds	1 - 4 - 7 - 10 - 13 – 16 - 19
Side Planks	Uppe r Body Core	1 eac h side	3	40 seconds	90 seconds	1 - 4 - 7 - 10 - 13 - 16 - 19
Chin Ups	Upper Body	8	3	3-4 seconds	90 seconds	1 - 4 - 7 - 10 - 13 - 16 - 19

Basic Level 3

Basic Level 3 can begin in either week 6 or week 7, depending on individual progress. The number of reps does not change for any of the exercises, but the cycle time is extended for each exercise. By extending the time it takes to go up and down or down and up each time, the exercise will definitely start to feel harder. There are no changes in sets or rest between sets.

Begins Week 6 or 7

Day 43 or 50

Movement	Muscle Groups	Reps	Sets	Cycle Times *	Between Sets	21 Day Schedule
Pull Ups	Upper Body	8	3	6-8 seconds	90 seconds	1 - 4 - 7 - 10 - 13 - 16 - 19
Leg Raises	Core Lower Body	10	3	8 seconds	90 seconds	1 - 4 - 7 - 10 - 13 - 16 - 19
Superman	Core, Upper Lower Body	8	3	6 seconds	60 seconds	1 - 4 - 7 - 10 - 13 - 16 - 19
Dips	Upper Body	8	3	8 seconds	90 seconds	1 - 4 - 7 - 10 - 13 - 16 - 19
Squats	Lower Body	10	3	10 seconds	60 seconds	1 - 4 - 7 - 10 - 13 - 16 - 19

Push Ups	Uppe r Body Core	10	3	8 seconds	90 seconds	1 - 4 - 7 - 10 - 13 - 16 - 19
Calf Raises	Lower Body	18	3	12-14 seconds	30 seconds	1 - 4 - 7 - 10 - 13 - 16 - 19
Side Planks	Uppe r Body Core	1 eac h side	3	50 seconds	90 seconds	1 - 4 - 7 - 10 - 13 - 16 - 19
Chin Ups	Upper Body	8	3	6-8 seconds	90 seconds	1 - 4 - 7 - 10 - 13 - 16 - 19

Transitioning to Intermediate Level 1

By now, you should have mastered Basic Level 3 and are ready for the transition to Intermediate Level 1, which begins in week 10. The number of reps increases for most exercises here and the rest time between sets is reduced. Side planks remain at one rep per side, but the cycle timing is extended. There are no changes in the cycle time or number of sets.

Begins Week 10

Day 71

Moveme nt	Musc le Grou ps	Re ps	Set s	Cycle Time *	Betwe en Sets	21 Day Schedu le
Pull Ups	Upper Body	12-14	3	6-8 secon ds	60 second s	1 - 4 - 7 - 10 - 13 - 16 - 19
Leg Raises	Core Lowe r Body	18-24	3	8 secon ds	60 second s	1 - 4 - 7 - 10 - 13 - 16 - 19
Superm an	Core, Uppe r Lowe r Body	12-14	3	6 secon ds	50 second s	1 - 4 - 7 - 10 - 13 - 16 - 19
Dips	Upper Body	14-16	3	8 secon ds	60 second s	1 - 4 - 7 - 10 - 13 - 16 - 19
Squats	Lower Body	16-22	3	10 secon ds	50 second s	1 - 4 - 7 - 10 - 13 - 16 - 19

Push Ups	Uppe r Body Core	20-26	3	8 secon ds	60 second s	1 - 4 - 7 - 10 - 13 - 16 - 19
Calf Raises	Lower Body	24-30	3	12-14 secon ds	20 second s	1 - 4 - 7 - 10 - 13 - 16 - 19
Side Planks	Uppe r Body Core	1 each side	3	60 secon ds	60 second s	1 - 4 - 7 - 10 - 13 - 16 - 19
Chin Ups	Upper Body	12-16	3	6-8 secon ds	60 second s	1 - 4 - 7 – 10 – 13 – 16- 19

Intermediate Level 2

Intermediate Level 2 begins in week 13. The number of reps does not change for any of the exercises but the cycle time is extended for some exercise. There are no changes in sets or rest between sets. You should find the longer cycle times having a noticeable effect in making the exercises harder.

Day 92

Moveme nt	Musc le Grou ps	Re ps	Set s	Cycle Time *	Betw een Sets	21 Day Sched ule
Pull Ups	Upper Body	10-12	3	6-8 secon ds	60 secon ds	1 - 4 - 7 - 10 - 13 - 16 - 19
Leg Raises	Core Lower Body	14-20	3	10 secon ds	60 secon ds	1 - 4 - 7 – 10 – 13 – 16 - 19
Superm an	Core, Upper Lowe r Body	10-12	3	10 secon ds	50 secon ds	1 - 4 - 7 - 10 - 13 - 16 - 19
Dips	Upper Body	10-12	3	10 secon ds	60 secon ds	1 - 4 - 7 - 10 - 13 - 16 - 19
Squats	Lower Body	12-16	3	10 secon ds	50 secon d s	1 - 4 - 7 - 10 - 13 - 16 - 19

Push Ups	Upper Body Core	14-18	3	10 seconds	60 seconds	1 - 4 - 7 - 10 - 13 - 16 - 19
Calf Raises	Lower Body	20-24	3	16 seconds	20 seconds	1 - 4 - 7 - 10 - 13 - 16 - 19
Side Planks	Upper Body Core	1 each side	3	60 seconds	60 seconds	1 - 4 - 7 - 10 - 13 - 16 - 19
Chin Ups	Upper Body	10-12	3	6-8 seconds	60 seconds	1 - 4 - 7 - 10 - 13 - 16 - 19

Transitioning to Advanced Level 1

If your workouts have been following the schedule and you have progressed through the Basic and Intermediate Levels, you should be ready to begin Advanced Level 1. If you think you are not yet up to it and need more time at one of the Intermediate Levels, relax and take the time to repeat a cycle. There's no rush, and you should progress at your own speed. Remember, we're all different and no two people will build muscles and strength at the same rate. Advanced Level 1 begins in week 16. The number of reps and the cycle times do not change for any of the exercises, but the number of sets increases from three to four for each exercise. There are no changes in the rest time between sets.

Begins Week 16

Day 113

Moveme nt	Musc le Grou ps	Re ps	Set s	Cycle Time *	Betwe en Sets	21 Day Schedul e
Pull Ups	Upper Body	10-12	4	6-8 secon ds	60 second s	1 - 4 - 7 - 10 - 13 - 16 - 19
Leg Raises	Core Lowe r Body	14-20	4	10 secon ds	60 second s	1 - 4 - 7 - 10 - 13 - 16 - 19
Superm an	Core, Uppe r Lowe r Body	10-12	4	10 secon ds	50 second s	1 - 4 - 7 - 10 - 13 - 16 - 19
Dips	Upper Body	10-12	4	10 secon ds	60 second s	1 - 4 - 7 – 10 – 13 – 16 - 19

Squats	Lower Body	12-16	4	10 seconds	50 seconds	1 - 4 - 7 - 10 - 13 - 16 - 19
Push Ups	Upper Body Core	14-18	4	10 seconds	60 seconds	1 - 4 - 7 - 10 - 13 - 16 - 19
Calf Raises	Lower Body	20-24	4	16 seconds	20 seconds	1 - 4 - 7 - 10 - 13 - 16 - 19
Side Planks	Upper Bod, Core	1 each side	4	60 seconds	60 seconds	1 - 4 - 7 - 10 - 13 - 16 - 19
Chin Ups	Upper Body	10-12	4	6-8 seconds	60 seconds	1 - 4 - 7 - 10 - 13 - 16 - 19

Transitioning to Advanced Level 2 and More Advanced Calisthenics

After completing the Basic Level, Intermediate Level, and Advanced Level 2 18-week schedule, you may feel you are ready to integrate compound versions of the current nine exercises into your routine and/or take on more difficult versions of the exercises. Advanced Level 2 and beyond is where you begin training for maximum results by challenging your body and mind.

Pull-Ups and Chin-Ups with Leg Raises

Fig. 11

Where: Like a regular pull-up or chin-up, for this exercise, you will need a horizontal bar that is at the height of your extended arms.

How: This is a compound exercise, which employs two separate movements to increase the work done within a given time and to engage and challenge multiple muscle groups. If doing pull-ups, grasp the bar with both hands with palms forward and arms shoulder width apart. If doing chin-ups, reverse the grip so your palms face backward. As you pull slowly upward, raise your legs and fully extend them until they are parallel to the ground if possible (or lift as far as you can). When you reach the bar with your head, pause and slowly lower back down while also slowly lowering your legs to the vertical (downward position). Repeat the pull-up or chin and leg raise cycle as many times as you can while doing the exercise correctly and in good form.

The leg raises can be made *easier* by pulling your knees up to your chest (as shown in the image above), instead of extending the legs fully outward. It can be made *harder* by maintaining the legs in the fully raised position (parallel to the ground) as you raise and lower for the required number of cycles.

Link to the video demo:

https://www.youtube.com/watch?v=QyVq5oUBp ss

Result: While this is primarily an upper-body exercise, the leg raises engage the core, the abdominal, the back muscle groups, the hip flexors, and the quadriceps.

Horizontal Rows

Fig. 12

Where: Horizontal rows can be performed at home, using ordinary furniture, using a lowered chinning bar, or simply using a sheet in a doorway (as seen above).

How: One version is to slide under a table and, while facing upward, reach up to the edge of the table and pull upward. Alternatively, you can use a sheet that is held firmly in place in a doorway, as shown in the video demo. You hold onto the sheet while leaning backward, and with arms held apart, lower yourself and raise back up. Do as many cycles of this exercise as you can until fatigued, rest 60 seconds, and perform two more sets.

Link to the video demo:

https://www.youtube.com/watch?v=rloXYB8M3v
U **Result:** Trainers encourage horizontal rows to

improve posture and to strengthen the arms, shoulders, and core for pull-ups and chin-ups.

Reverse Grip Horizontal Row

Fig. 13

Where: At home or in a fitness center where you can hold onto a bar or a set of rings, as you can see in the demo video.

How: There are variations of the grip, including forward (as seen above) or backward. Your hands can also be in both forward and back positions. You will see these reverse and regular grip examples in the demo. You perform the horizontal row by holding onto the ring or bar, leaning back, and pulling yourself upright again.

Link to the video demo:
https://www.youtube.com/watch?v=PGcTxvw6-lo

Results: Reverse and regular horizontal rows build the upper back muscles, especially the rhomboids, lats, traps, rear delts, and the upper arms (notably, the biceps).

Diamond Push Up

Fig. 14

Where: As with regular push-ups, this exercise may be performed indoors or outdoors on a flat, even surface.

How: Assume a normal push-up position, facing downward with your body fully extended and your arms holding you up, but instead of placing your hands under your shoulders, move your hands together so that they form a diamond shape with thumbs and index fingers touching (see above). Shift your weight forward so your hands are beneath your sternum.

Link to the video demo:
https://www.youtube.com/watch?v=ZR5U3sb-KeE

Results: With your hands together and your arms close to your body, the diamond push-up works the triceps, the delts, and other chest muscles.

Handstand Push Up

Fig. 15

Where: The handstand push-up may be performed indoors or out on a flat service or by gripping two parallel bars. It may be advisable to do this exercise close to a wall, which can assist with balance when you are first trying the movement.

How: This is a difficult and challenging exercise, but it can be rewarding if you work through it and progress gradually in stages. As shown in the image and as you will see in the demo video, you may begin with level 1 with your body bent forward and your feet still on the ground. Position yourself so your chest and abdominals will be facing the wall. As your routine progresses through subsequent stages, you will be placing your feet on the wall for support and balance and working your way up to be increasingly vertical. Eventually, your goal will be to push up and lower down in a balanced, vertical position, without touching the wall.

Link to the video demo:

https://www.youtube.com/watch?v=h0HjqYRlXYg

Results: This is one of the most effective exercises to build your triceps, upper arms, and shoulders. Muscle groups throughout the core are engaged, especially the back.

One-Arm Push-Up/Archer Push-Up

Fig. 16

Where: Any floor or flat surface will be satisfactory.

How: Assume the basic starting push-up position but then place your hands a bit closer together to help maintain your balance. Lift one arm and rest in on the hips. Using only the remaining arm, lower yourself and keep your body from sagging or twisting. Control the movements with your arms, shoulders, core, and legs. Do not let your back arch or sway. Don't turn your body or dip your shoulder downward during the descent movement. Keep your body horizontal.

The archer push-up is a variation that uses both arms but keeps most of the tension on one arm. As you will see in the demo, one arm remains vertical, as in the one arm movement, but the other arm is extended to the side with the hand on the floor. The extended arm takes some of the pressure off the vertical arm. This is one way to ease gradually into the full one-arm pull-up.

Link to the video demo:

https://www.youtube.com/watch?v=KIEAbfk4cQU

Results: When you have reached the stage where you can do many repetitions of the basic push-up, the onearm push-up will enable you to have a hard, challenging workout. Among other benefits, performing push-ups unilaterally will reveal if one side is weaker than the other and needs compensatory training. You will achieve the benefits of regular, two-arm push-ups with far fewer repetitions. Shoulders, arms, and all parts of the core will benefit.

Straight Bar Dip and Parallel Bars Dip

Fig. 17

Fig. 18

Where: To perform dips on a bar, a single (straight) bar or double (parallel) bars are needed.

How: The dips are performed by placing hands on the straight bar or by standing between the parallel bars and placing one hand on each bar. Push the weight of your body up until the arms are straight, dip down by bending the arms, pause, and then push back up to complete one cycle. Parallel bar dips are believed to work the muscles, including the triceps, more correctly with a more upright position and a fuller lowering, and they are safer and less likely to lead to injury. Perform eight reps at a slow pace or an amount you can handle without excessive effort or strain.

Link to the video demo:

https://www.youtube.com/watch?v=2IUoEAzjZqY

Benefits: Both straight bar dips and parallel bar dips are beneficial to the arms, the shoulders, and the chest, but compared to parallel bar dips, straight bar dips give you more internal core rotation and put more tension on the pectoral (chest) muscles.

Tucked Planche Progressions

Fig. 19

Where: Like push-ups and other floor-based exercises, the tucked planche may be performed on any flat surface.

How: The tucked planche is often considered difficult, but with the right set-up technique, it can be mastered. It is a great calisthenic exercise and worth learning as part of your advanced levels. Warm-up by stretching the hamstring muscles by bending over and touching the toes or extending one leg and bending toward your knee. Lower yourself to your stomach and rise up on your arms to stretch the core (the yoga cobra pose). Then, sit back on your heels, fold forward, and stretch your arms forward (child's pose) to stretch the lower back. Stand up and then crouch down, knees far apart, lean forward, and place your hands on the floor. Place your elbows inside your knees and roll gently forward until your feet are off the floor and your entire weight is being held up by your arms and shoulders. It will take some practice to achieve the balance you need to hold the position and to make the progressions, which include swinging one knee into the center and to drop one foot one the floor. All aspects of these movements are well presented in the demo video.

Link to the video demo:

https://www.youtube.com/watch?v=iT1q1Ff02mk

Results: The tucked planche is highly beneficial to the core and the shoulders. It also develops the triceps, the chest, and the muscles of the serratus anterior, helping to prevent poor posture.

Lateral Lunge

Fig. 20

Where: Lateral lunges may be performed on a level surface indoors or outside, ensuring there is ample space for you to take long steps sideways.

How: Stand upright with your feet spaced about 18 inches apart. With your left leg, step to the left side, about three feet, and squat down on the right leg. Keep your weight back and toward the glutes. Pause for a second and then push back up to the standing position. Repeat the movement on the left side. Maintain your balance by keeping your body upright throughout the exercise. Perform eight reps to begin and increase to 12 reps as you progress. Perform two or three sets with a 60-second rest interval.

Link to the video demo:

https://www.youtube.com/watch?v=gwWv7aPcD88

Results: The lateral lunge is a simple but effective movement to strengthen the quadriceps, the glutes, and the hip flexors.

With your plan in full movement, you may run into some concerns. So, the following chapter will address some troubleshooting issues and FAQs that may arise as you move through your bodyweight calisthenics program.

Chapter 8

Troubleshooting

In any instructional book, questions may arise that are not addressed in the explanations and instructions, so the objective of this chapter is to anticipate your possible questions and problems and provide answers and solutions. Before getting started, let's remind ourselves of some fundamentals that may head off your concerns.

First, Do No Harm

While bodyweight calisthenics exercises are considered safer and less likely to cause injury compared to weightlifting, do not underestimate the risks of overuse injuries, pulls, tears, and strains. Listen to your body, and don't overdo it. If you are trying to do 12 pushups and are having trouble getting past number eight and your shoulders are crying out, take it easy and don't force yourself to do them in pain. Even if you had done 12 reps a few days ago or during a previous set, this time you may have run out of steam. And that's okay. A few days of rest may be all you need to get back to 12 reps.

Look at it this way: If you work up to a point that it starts to really hurt or you are having difficulty completing the movements in good form, it means your muscles have been pushed far enough for that moment, so back off and let them begin to rest and recover. Pain can also signal a small injury that you might make worse if you continue to challenge the muscles or joints.

It is very important not to push beyond your physical limits, which you can do by performing too many reps, exercising in bad form, not resting between sets, not allowing the full two days to recover between workouts, or assuming a position that puts an unbearable strain on a joint, a ligament, or muscle group.

You Are Unique

No two people have the same DNA (except identical twins), and that means no two people have the same skills, strengths, competencies, and endurance. Everyone has different cognitive and mental capacities as well. So, we should not expect to do exactly what others can do. We based the Basic, Intermediate, and Advanced levels for reps, sets, cycle speeds, and rest time between sets on averages and the experience of countless coaches, trainers, and sports medicine professionals. But they are only estimates meant to guide you and are not hard and fast criteria you must meet.

How you build muscles with bulk and with definition will be unique to your physiology. You should respect your body's particular qualities. Be assured that if you work at this program, you will build muscles, grow stronger, and be more physically fit.

Give Your Muscles Time to Build

The process of working your muscles hard so that cells and fibers are damaged and need to rebuild is a gradual process. While you may feel "pumped up" and muscular immediately after a hard workout, that's the temporary pooling of blood and other fluids; it will subside after a few hours. The real growth of muscle tissue takes place slowly and microscopically, so don't expect your muscles to grow to a bulging size within days. But over weeks and months, the growth of your upper body, core, and lower body muscles will become apparent. Give it time.

Bodyweight Calisthenics Q&As

With that preamble behind us, here are answers to specific questions you may have.

Q: *Are calisthenics a real fitness workout?*

A: Calisthenics comprise a distinct and recognized form of physical training that is meant to build muscles and strength by using one's own bodyweight instead of weights, machines, and other forms of equipment (other than a bar for pull-ups, chin-ups, and rows). Calisthenics can build muscle by adding bulk, strength, and definition. But unlike some other forms of exercise, it also contributes to flexibility and functionality by not making you muscle bound, inflexible and/or tight.

Calisthenics can be easily learned, and the workouts can be performed anywhere. Do not let the simplicity and ease of access to calisthenics cause you to underestimate its potential to create a great physique or underestimate the value of using your own bodyweight. Even if you weigh just 90 pounds, you'll be impressed when your workout has you lifting some or all of that 90 pounds!

Q: *Do I need special preparation to get started with bodyweight calisthenics?*

A: If you are in reasonably good health, you should be able to begin training immediately—today—if you want. The Basic Level plans intentionally start you off with a low level of reps and gradually increases reps and shortens rest times so that you will advance at a reasonable pace.

If you are unsure if your health is up to the challenge, it's advisable to check with your doctor; a physical exam may be appropriate. This is especially important if you are also beginning cardiovascular exercise.

Q: *Can calisthenics really build muscles?*

A: When we're referring to bodyweight calisthenics, as presented in this book, the answer is an unequivocal "yes." Some people associate calisthenics with stretching, jumping jacks, skipping rope, and/or cardio training. But bodyweight calisthenics are a highly effective, cost-free, and safe way to build muscles for added bulk and definition.

Bodyweight resistance creates the process we call hypertrophy: physical tension and metabolic stress that damages muscle fibers and cells, leading to more rebuilt muscle tissue than was lost and creating muscle growth.

Q: *Is bodyweight calisthenics training better than weight training?*

A: No, it is just different. But weight training is not better than calisthenics, either. Both weight lifting and bodyweight calisthenics work to achieve the same primary goals of building muscle and strength. Lifting weights and using resistance equipment are very effective at creating hypertrophy and may bulk you up a little faster. But that is offset by calisthenics being less likely to cause injury and not needing access to a gym or fitness center.

Some advanced calisthenics enthusiasts will bring some weights and resistance machines into their routines. For example, doing squats while holding a pair of dumbbells or a barbell. We recommend you focus exclusively on calisthenics initially, and if you continue to increase reps, slow cycle times, and shorten rest between sets, you will continue to challenge your muscles and grow muscle bulk and strength. You can also graduate to the more advanced calisthenics exercises that are shown in chapter 7.

Q: *How often should I conduct my workouts?*

A: As we discussed in chapters 6 and 7, a top priority is for you to allow adequate time for recovery between workouts, and this was determined to be at least two rest days between workouts. The 21-day plans offer two exercise scheduling options: Performing all nine calisthenics exercises in one session ("nine-in-one") or doing some calisthenics on one day and the remaining group of exercises the next day ("nine-in-two"). In either case, the muscles that are worked are not engaged and challenged again until they have had two days of rest.

For example, with the nine-in-one schedule, if your workout is on Monday, you would rest and do no bodyweight calisthenics on Tuesday or Wednesday and return to all nine exercises on Thursday. If you want to put three days between calisthenics exercises, that's okay. But do not put too much separation between sessions or you will start to lose some strength and it will be more difficult to get back to the exercise. So to sum it up: Each muscle group should be exercised two or three times a week.

Q: *Can I do bodyweight calisthenics and cardiovascular workouts on the same day?*

A: Yes, it is commonly done, especially when both are completed in the same facility like a fitness center or gym. Many people find it convenient and satisfying to "get it all done" in the same extended session. The satisfaction is also due to the increased flow of beta-endorphins. The combination of cardio and resistance exercises is cumulative, or synergistic, meaning the end result is equal to or greater than the sum of the parts.

Most people who are into both forms of exercise prefer to do the cardio workout first, immediately followed by calisthenics. Why? Cardio warms up the entire body by increasing circulation to virtually every cell and muscle in the body, while calisthenics increases circulation to the muscle group being worked. Following cardio with calisthenics ensures that all the muscle groups are already warmed up, making it easier to get going. Conversely, if you exercised your lower body first, you might find it harder to push forward with cardio exercises that are working the quadriceps, the hamstrings, the calves, and the hip flexors.

Q: *Should I do my work out if I am injured or in pain?*

A: Short answer: no. As we said at the beginning of this chapter, "First, do no harm," (which is borrowed from the Hippocratic oath that doctors recite upon receiving their license to practice). But it is worth repeating that there is no advantage to pushing yourself when in real pain, which is a warning that you are injured or soon to be injured. If you feel pain in a muscle or joint, try to work through it slowly, testing it to determine if it's something that you can manage, something that needs rest, or something serious that a healthcare professional should examine.

All the same, it's important to recognize minor discomforts (soreness, stiffness, or the muscle burn of working out) and learn how to work through them. It's natural to have a little soreness left over from the last workout. One of the side effects of post-workout recovery is the buildup of lactate, or lactic acid, in the muscle cells. This is a natural byproduct of muscle work, and until it dissipates, it can cause some stiffness and soreness. It's not harmful, and you just may need to go a little easier when it bothers you. Be sure to allow enough recovery time between workouts, and there is certainly no harm in delaying the workout for another day.

Q: *Will calisthenics help me lose weight?*

A: You can expect to lose weight if the amount of calories you burn is greater than the amount of calories you consume. There is no shortcut or exception to this fundamental rule of science. Your metabolism, which is the rate your body uses energy, is unique to you, which means no two people use up calories at the same rate. So, two people on the identical diet and on the identical workout schedule may vary in their weight gains or losses.

Generally, a good calisthenics workout will burn 200 to 400 calories. If the rest of your physical activities remain the same and you include calisthenics workouts in your routine, then, over a couple of weeks, that can add up to as much as a pound of weight loss. Over a year, it can mean some serious slimming.

But there are some additional factors to consider. More muscle bulk can add more pounds, since muscle is denser than the fat it is replacing. Also, after working out, whether it's with calisthenics or cardio, your metabolism slows down, especially when resting, so the net calorie loss for the day may be less than you think. Reducing the calories in your diet in combination with exercise is the single most effective way to lose weight. Refer to chapter 2's coverage of nutrition and the Mediterranean diet to review the best sources for calories.

Q: *What if I can't do all of the reps in the Basic or Intermediate 21-Day Plans?*

A: As explained, the plans are recommendations based on averages and extensive experience, but you should follow your own abilities and do the number of reps for each exercise that challenges you, but you should know when to stop. Generally, between eight to 12 reps should be the ideal amount with the last two reps feeling really tough but doable without wrecking your form. Bad form includes kicking your way toward the chin-up bar or doing your push-ups without lowering all the way down. Use the "last two" being tough as your guide to when to stop. If you are straining to get rep number eight completed in good form and without doing the movement sloppily, that should be your stopping point.

Be aware of the rest time you are taking between sets as well. If your place in the plan has you resting for 60 seconds, you may need to raise it back to the original 90 seconds or even to two minutes, if it will enable you to complete more reps.

Q: *What if the number of reps in the plans are not enough? Can I do more?*

A: Again, as mentioned in the previous answer, the 21day plans are recommendations, not firm rules, and you should recognize your own abilities. When the number of reps is not enough to cause you to reach the "last two" being tough, you have three options to consider:

Do more reps. Just be sure you are performing all reps correctly with full ups and downs, with a straight back, and with good form and posture. Also, be sure that you are not taking shortcuts.

Shorten the rest time between sets. For example, lower the 60 seconds to 30 seconds of rest between sets. You should find the reps getting harder to do when your rest time between sets is shorter.

Slow the cycle rate of each rep so that each movement takes longer. For example, taking 12 seconds to perform one push-up cycle or slowing down and taking 10 seconds for one complete chin-up or pull-up.

Q: *What if I am not seeing the results I am expecting?*

A: First, refer to the sections at the start of this chapter entitled "You are Unique" and "Give Your Muscles Time to Build." These explain how you develop muscles at a unique pace and why you need to have patience before seeing the results you are hoping for.

But this is not to imply that you should lower your expectations for a good physique and greater strength. The series of 21-day plans will definitely get you there, even if it may take longer than you think. What is most important is that you follow the plans as best as you can, doing the hard work during each calisthenics session and allowing sufficient rest and recovery time between workouts. You also want to ensure that you have enough protein in your diet to fuel the rebuilding of muscle fibers.

If you push through the 21-day plans, do more reps, perform the reps more slowly, add sets, and shorten rest time between sets, you may shorten the time it takes to get bulkier, more cut-looking muscular results.

The harder you work your muscles, the faster they will rebuild larger and stronger. Just pay attention to your physical limits to avoid injury, and be sure to maintain at least two days of recovery between workouts to let the repair and rebuilding process run its full cycle.

Things You Might Be Doing Wrong

There are some other factors that could be slowing you down in reaching your muscle and strength building goals. These include diet, sleep, stress, and both underwork and overwork.

1. **Protein**

    We've mentioned diet in the above section, but let's focus on protein. Are you getting enough? It can be difficult because meat is one of the best sources of protein, yet for cardiovascular health, we are encouraged to limit red meat consumption. But that refers to meat covered with and marbled through with saturated fats.

    Stick with lean, fat-free or low-fat servings of beef, turkey, chicken, and pork. Trim any visible fat before cooking. Fish is an even superior source of quality protein, plus other nutrients and antioxidants, so include fish in your diet at least twice a week.

However, there are other important protein sources apart from meat and fish. Choose vegetables, nuts, whole grains, and beans with high protein content. Also, include eggs and fat free or low -at dairy in your diet. If you like yogurt, choose the Greek or Icelandic versions, which are very high in protein (18 to 19 grams of protein in a ¾ cup serving). If you remember from chapter 2, a normal adult need about 50 grams of protein per day, but as a muscle builder, you need at least 100 grams per day. Some serious calisthenics and weightlifting enthusiasts take in up to 150 grams of protein daily; although, that's a bit excessive for most of us. You need sufficient protein so that your body has enough available to do all the rebuilding your workouts make necessary.

2. **Sleep**

Are you getting enough sleep to enable your body to repair itself?

Everyone needs a good night's sleep. First, our brains need to process all of the day's impressions and inputs by letting our 100 billion neurons readjust their trillions of neural connections and flood the cells and neurons with the cleansing fluids and enzymes that remove potentially toxic wastes and plaques that can mess with cognitive abilities. We dream during sleep and need that time to further clear up and sort thoughts and memories.

Additionally, when we sleep, much of the repairing and rebuilding of our damaged muscles takes place. It's the ideal time since the muscles are inactive and the repair process has minimal interruptions. But if you do not get the requisite amount of sleep every night, the repairs will be interrupted or diminished, which will slow your bodybuilding progress.

This is worth thinking about: All that hard calisthenics exercise and the needed rebuilding is interrupted due to bad sleep habits. See chapter 3's discussion of sleep and remind yourself that eight hours every night is ideal. Take note of the steps that will help you fall asleep and stay asleep. Especially, plan to go to bed at the same time every night and wake at the same time every morning. And leave the digital devices out of the bedroom!

3. **Stress**

Are you experiencing continuing stress or anxiety in your life?

It happens to all of us. Stress is actually a normal reaction to danger or risk, and it's the central nervous system's self-protection mechanism. It activates the sympathetic nervous system's well-known fight-or-flight response, which includes surges of adrenaline and cortisol (the hormones that send glycogen to the muscles for an instant energy boost) that speed up heart and breathing rates and raise blood pressure.

But this response is designed by nature to be a short-term emergency fix. It should fully subside once the danger is passed. But too often stress becomes chronic. Under those conditions, your body's rebuilding process can be diminished or slowed down, and in consequence, your muscle building is slowed or even stopped.

Do not let stress affect your health and quality of life. Fortunately, exercise is an excellent counter to stress and can bring your body back to a state of homeostasis where heart rate, breathing, and other functions are normal. If stress and its partner anxiety try to affect your mind and body between workouts, practice meditation, yoga, and deep breathing.

4. **Too Little or Too Much**

Are you under-exercising or over-exercising?

You may not be achieving your muscular development goals because you are under exercising. The 21-day plans have been designed to work your muscles:

- ➤ in the right frequency (reps)

- ➤ at the right speed (cycles)

- ➤ in the right number of sets

- ➤ with the right amount of rest between sets

- ➤ with the requisite rest and recovery time between workouts

If you are not trying to at least reasonably keep up with the plans, the muscular growth you are hoping for will be slower to occur or may not occur at all. Nowhere in life is this expression more relevant: "You get out of it what you put into it." We all have days when things are slow or we miss an occasional workout, but you have the opportunity to build a great physique, if you are prepared to work at it.

Come on, you've got this.

Over exercising causes problems of its own. Exercising too often and too intensely can damage your muscles in a way where they cannot be repaired with rest and recovery. And instead of building bulk, strength and definition, your muscles can atrophy or reduce in size and strength. Follow the plan, and if there is anything that is at the top of the list, it's the rest and recovery days between workouts. Give your body the rest it needs to rebuild what has been broken down within your muscle fibers. Stay close to the limits of reps, sets, and the speed of cycles recommended in the 21-day plans and don't be tempted to jump ahead to the advanced levels prematurely.

If you do end up overworking or overextending yourself, avoid injury and ensure your recovery with rest. If you are able, perform your calisthenics at a slower pace with fewer reps, fewer sets, more time between sets, and three days to recover between workouts.

Aches and pains can, generally, be managed with NSAIDs, or nonsteroidal anti-inflammatories, better known as aspirin, ibuprofen, and naproxen. Acetaminophen, or Tylenol, can also be used.

Injuries, including sprains and strains, are best treated, according to trainers and orthopedists, with RICE, which stands for Rest, Ice, Compression, and Elevation.

Our last chapter takes a look at some of the myths, mistakes, and misunderstandings associated with calisthenics and bodybuilding.

Chapter 9

Myths and Misconceptions

With all that is published in magazines and on social media, plus what is promised in advertising and what you may hear others saying in gyms and fitness centers, you may not be sure what is true and what is a myth or misconception.

Here are 10 of the most common myths about calisthenics and fitness as well as the facts you need to know to refute them:

Myth 1: The more/harder you train, the bigger the muscles you will build.

It's normal to be excited and anxious. You've started your calisthenics bodybuilding program, and it's going well, so why not ratchet up the intensity and frequency of the workouts for faster, better results? You know the answer from the previous chapters, but just to repeat it: Overuse of your muscles and not allowing enough time for recovery between workouts will not allow your muscles to grow and may even lead to atrophy or muscle tissue loss. Plus, overdoing it can be a recipe for injuries. Stick to the pacing of the 21-day plans and do not punish your muscles with too much work and not enough rest.

Myth 2: You should feel pain every day after each calisthenics workout.

Some day-after-workout pain is normal and is generally not a concern; it may give you a satisfying reminder that you had a good workout the day before. But pain that is intense or discomforting or that lasts for two or three days is a sign that you are working too hard with too many reps or not enough time between sets. As you condition, there should only be muscular pain on occasional days; pain that is not intense or long lasting. Be alert to joint pains, and be sure you are performing each movement correctly.

Myth 3: Your dietary practice is less important than taking supplements.

We humans evolved over many thousands of years by eating a diversity of natural, unprocessed foods, and there is no precedent for us to ignore a good, balanced diet and try to get our nutrients from highly processed and intensely concentrated supplements. A supplement that promises pumped-up, bulkier muscles in a short time is making false and misleading claims. You may consider whey protein supplements, since getting 100 grams of protein from diet alone can be tough, but your priority should be a quality overall diet. There are also food-based shakes and beverages available at supermarkets, which provide 20 to 30 grams of protein. (See chapter 2 for the full rundown on nutrition.)

Myth 4: Once your workouts slow or stop, your muscle turns to fat.

Muscle is composed of protein, which is a complex molecule, constructed from 20 amino acids, including nine we can only get from foods we eat. As we exercise and damage the muscle fibers, they respond by using protein and amino acids to rebuild. If we begin to slow or even stop our workouts, the muscles will slowly reduce in size. It is physically impossible for muscle to turn to fat, which is chemically composed of free fatty acids. But when exercise slows and caloric intake increases, you can gain weight, which is stored in your body as fat.

Myth 5: You can get rid of belly fat by working your core, especially your abdominals.

While it's true that core exercises will harden and define abdominal muscles, it is not possible to "spot reduce" or burn off fat deposits by exercising. There is only one way to get that fat off your gut and reveal that six-pack hiding behind it: lose weight. And the best way to lose weight steadily is to combine your bodyweight calisthenics workouts with a responsible diet that reduces your caloric intake and the amount of food you eat, especially refined carbohydrates. Also, avoid the empty calories of sugar, watch the fats you eat, and add more protein to your diet to build muscle and keep you feeling fuller longer.

Myth 6: Older people should not exercise too hard or too often.

People of all ages benefit from regular exercise, especially as they grow older. Exercise is good for your muscles, and that includes your heart. Getting your heart to pump harder by gradually warming up and then increasing to a steady, rhythmic pace and sustaining it for 20, 30, or more minutes for several days a week (or more) can keep your heart strong and your arteries open. Practicing calisthenics, as prescribed in our 21 day plans, will build and maintain strength, improve flexibility, and help prevent injuries. Cardio training will optimize heart health, too.

Myth 7: Calisthenics can't really build big muscles.

This all depends on what you consider big muscles. If your goal is to look like an Olympic weightlifter, that means you will have to train like an Olympic weightlifter, working with incredibly heavy weights over several years of, frankly, brutal training. But if your goal is to have the well-developed muscle size, definition, and strength of an athlete, then calisthenics is the ideal exercise routine for you. If you want to see where a good calisthenics program can take you, look instead at Olympic gymnasts.

Myth 8: Calisthenics is only good for certain body types.

There is a misconception that calisthenics mostly benefits those with slender physiques and not people with heavier or broader builds. While it is true that physique types respond and build muscle differently, calisthenics can work effectively for all body types.

Lightweight builds seem to achieve the gymnast's physique and good definition faster but don't tend to add much bulk. Heavier builds benefit from their extra body weight providing more resistance, so they bulk up more readily and increase strength faster. Most of us are in-between these extremes and can build both muscle mass and good definition through calisthenics.

Myth 9: The upper body is the area of greatest importance to develop.

We're all impressed when we see big biceps, triceps, shoulders, and, of course, well-developed pectoral muscles of the upper chest. But the core and lower body muscles are of equal or even greater importance, so you need to focus on working the total body. The core muscles include the abdominals, the back, and the lower back muscles. A strong core gives great overall strength and helps prevent injury. You also want to strengthen the hip flexors, the quads, the hamstrings, and the calves, since they hold you up and carry you forward for over 2,000 miles a year on average.

Myth 10: You don't need to do all of the exercises in perfect form to bulk up and get stronger.

It's all up to you: Your results will follow the principle of *getting out of it what you put into it.* So, the better you perform the exercises and complete the routine of the nine calisthenics that are included in the 21-day plans, the more impressive your results will be. The nine exercises were selected to work all of your muscle groups to ensure a complete body workout. Your form and procedure will determine the quality of the calisthenics exercises, so the more fully you perform each exercise, the faster you will see results.

Conclusion

This book was written with the objective of helping anyone at any level achieve the muscular physique and overall physical condition of their dreams. By choosing to read and follow the instructions in this book, you have made a commitment and an investment in yourself, so congratulations for taking this first, important step. Know that:

> ➤ You have committed yourself to finally getting into the shape you have always wanted but just never found the time or had the motivation to accomplish before.

> ➤ You understand that it will take less than an hour for as few as three days a week to achieve your goals.

> ➤ You are ready to take on the challenge.

> ➤ You are making the most important investment of your life, supporting your health, strength, and longevity.

> ➤ You have the right path forward to perform the bodyweight calisthenics that have been carefully chosen for optimal results; just nine exercises in 21-day plans that will take you from basic to advanced, building solid muscle every step of the way.

> ➤ You are aware of the importance of two additional factors that will help you achieve

your strength and fitness goals: choosing a healthy, balanced, natural, and unprocessed diet and avoiding the wrong foods.

➤ You will practice cardiovascular conditioning to keep your heart and circulatory system in good health while keeping your weight down as you trade unwanted body fat for lean muscle mass.

Never underestimate your potential. Despite any doubts or uncertainties, you may have, you are already stronger than you realize. And now, you are on your way to grow stronger with bigger, better-defined muscles and a huge surge in your overall physical ability. You have the undeniable right to grow stronger and look better. You deserve to be healthy and physically fit so that you can build your self-esteem as you become confident in the knowledge that you have the strength to accomplish whatever you set your mind to.

You can look forward to the support and respect of others, who will turn to you for leadership, knowing that you have both the physical strength and stamina of a finely conditioned athlete. You are approaching the day when you can say, whatever the challenge:

"I've got this. I'm in control of the situation. I'll get it done."

Please leave honest feedback about your impressions and thoughts about this book so that we can keep on making improvements to ensure this is the best source of instruction and motivation for all who want to develop bigger muscles and achieve greater strength through bodyweight calisthenics. If this book met or exceeded your expectations, please leave us a top rating so that others will know this is the right book for them.

In wishing your health, success, and personal fulfillment, consider and believe what we know to be unquestionably true:

"You are stronger, fitter, and tougher than when you started, and that is certainly something!"

- Daily Jay

Reference List

Ajani, L. (2020, June 2). How to build muscle at home. *WikiHow.* https://www.wikihow.com/BuildMuscle-at-Home

Antranik. (2017, January 11). How to do horizontal incline rows with minimal equipment. *YouTube.com.* https://www.youtube.com/watch?v=rloXYB8M3vU

Avatar Nutrition (2020). The science behind muscle growth. *Medium.com.* https://medium.com/@avatarnutrition/thescience-behind-muscle-growth-a1b5e9cba225

Bodyweight training and workouts. (2020). School of Calisthenics. Retrieved from https://schoolofcalisthenics.com/

Buff Dude Workouts. (2017, December 7). How to perform chin-ups. *YouTube.com.* https://www.youtube.com/watch?v=brhRXlOhsAM&t=26s

Buff Dudes Workouts. (2017, July 18). How to perform diamond push-ups. *YouTube.com.* https://www.youtube.com/watch?v=ZR5U3sb-KeE

Build insane muscle mass using only your bodyweight. (2020). Bodyweight Training Arena Retrieved from https://bodyweighttrainingarena.com/workouthow-to-build-insane-muscle-mass-just-withbodyweight/

Calisthenic Movement (2016, June 16). The perfect push-up -do it right! YouTube.com.

https://www.youtube.com/watch?v=IODxDx X7oi4&t=48s

Calisthenic Movement (2016, September 8). The perfect pull-up - do it right! YouTube.com. https://www.youtube.com/watch?v=eGo4IYlbE5g

Calisthenics Movement. (2017, August 10). Ultimate push-up can you do it? *YouTube.com.*

https://www.youtube.com/watch?v=K1EAbfk 4cQU

Calculate your basal metabolic rate (BMR) (2020).

Retrieved from

https://www.bodybuilding.com/fun/bmr_calculator.htm

Cardio exercise, Good for more than your heart.

(2020). WebMD. Retrieved from

https://www.webmd.com/fitnessexercise/ss/slideshow-cardio-exercise-good-formore-thanheart?ecd=wnl_spr_091020&ctr=wnl-spr091020_nsl-

Bodymodule_Position6&mb=MukfT6opS3Axb

F5kSEwI0ng0WleHxvIqssh%40W36l9r4%3d

Chertoff, J. (2019, November 12). How to add compound exercises to your workout routine. *Healthline.*

https://www.healthline.com/health/fitnessexercise/compound-exercises

Creveling, M. (2020, April 15). The best bodyweight exercises you can do at home. *Health.*

https://www.health.com/fitness/bodyweightexercises

Davies, D. (2020, July 28). Build serious muscle with these at-home bodyweight exercises and workouts. *Men's Health.*

https://www.menshealth.com/uk/buildingmuscle/a756325/10-best-bodyweight-exercisesfor-men/

Eastman, H. (2018, February 28). The ultimate beginner's guide to calisthenics. *Bodybuilding.com.* https://www.bodybuilding.com/content/theultimate-beginners-guide-to-calisthenics.html

FitnessFAQs. (2017, November 23). Straight vs. parallel bar dips | which is better? *YouTube.com.* https://www.youtube.com/watch?v=2IUoEAzjZqY

FitnessFAQs: (2017, October 12). The worst ab training mistakes. *YouTube.com.* https://www.youtube.com/watch?v=QyVq5o UBpss

Gunnars, K. (2019, June 13). 50 foods that are super healthy. *Healthline.*

https://www.healthline.com/nutrition/50super-healthy-foods

Gunnars, K. (2018, May 7). 5 simple rules for amazing health. *Healthline.*

https://www.healthline.com/nutrition/5simple-rules-for-amazinghealth?slot_pos=article_1&utm_source=Sailthru%20Email&utm_medium=Email&utm_campaign=generalhealth&utm_content=2020-09-10&apid=25264436

Herring, R. (2019, April 8). Recuperation and muscular growth! *Bodybuilding.com.*

https://www.bodybuilding.com/content/recuperation-and-muscular-growth.html

Holland, T. (2016, August 31). How-to | squats for beginners. *Bowflex/YouTube.com.* https://www.youtube.com/watch?v=aclHkVak_u9U

Hybrid Athlete. (2012, August 31). Lateral lunge. *YouTube.com.* https://www.youtube.com/watch?v=gwWv7aPcD88

Jackson, D. (2020). Building muscle with calisthenics. *School of Calisthenics.*

https://schoolofcalisthenics.com/2019/08/12/building-muscle-with-calisthenics/

Kamb, S. (2020, March 17). The 42 best bodyweight exercises. *Nerd Fitness.*

https://www.nerdfitness.com/blog/the-42best-bodyweight-exercises-the-ultimate-guidefor-working-out-anywhere/

Kavadlo, D. (2017, June 6). How to build a calisthenics body. *BodyBuilding.*

https://www.bodybuilding.com/content/howto-build-a-calisthenics-body.html

Keet, L. (2020, September 5). Calisthenics training mistakes with Lee Downing Keet. *Red Delta Project.*
https://reddeltaproject.com/calisthenicstraining-mistakes-w-lee-downing-keet/

Kerksick, C., Wilborn, C., et al. (2018, August 1) ISSN exercise and sports nutrition review update: research and recommendations.

Journal of the International Society of Sports Nutrition.

https://jissn.biomedcentral.com/articles/10.1186/s12970-018-0242-y

Kravitz, L., Kwon, Y.S. (2004). How do muscles grow?

University of New Mexico.

https://www.unm.edu/~lkravitz/Article%20folder/musclesgrowLK.html

Leech, J. (2018, September 14). 11 proven benefits of olive oil. *Healthline.*

https://www.healthline.com/nutrition/11prove
n-benefits-of-olive-oil

Legumes and pulses. (2020). Harvard T.H. Chan
School of Public Health. Retrieved from
https://www.hsph.harvard.edu/nutritionsourc
e/legumes-pulses/

Leonard, J. (2018, September 18). What are the benefits
of protein powder? *Medical News Today.*
https://www.medicalnewstoday.com/articles/3
23093

Lewis, A. (2020, September 27). 3 muscle mass building
myths destroyed. *New Motivation Coaching.*
https://newmotivationcoaching.com/workouts
/3-muscle-mass-building-myths-destroyed/

Lieberman, B., Tucker, A. (2017, October 3). 53
bodyweight exercises you can do at home. *Self.*

https://www.self.com/gallery/bodyweightexerc
ises-you-can-do-at-home

Lumsden, B. (2019, August 26). Importance of sleep for
muscle growth. *Relentless Gains.*

https://relentlessgains.com/importance-
ofsleep-for-muscle-growth/

Merrick, T. (2018, May 6). Bodyweight row tutorial.

YouTube.com.

https://www.youtube.com/watch?v=PGcTxvw
6-lo

Michael, Yannick. (2020, August 3). Calisthenics pull
workout routine. *Calisthenics Family.*

https://calisthenics-family.com/articles/calisthenics-pull-workoutroutine/

Nunez, K. (2019, June 24). The best core exercises for all fitness levels. *Healthline*.

https://www.healthline.com/health/best-coreexercises

Peale, N.V. (1955). The power of positive thinking. *Good Reads*.

https://www.goodreads.com/work/quotes/11 21350-the-power-of-positive-thinking

Petra, A. (2019, April 8). 13 habits linked to a long life (backed by science. *Healthline*.

https://www.healthline.com/nutrition/13habits-linked-to-a-long-life

Pigmie. (2017, September 24). Tucked planche positions fix. *YouTube.com*.
https://www.youtube.com/watch?v=iT1q1Ff0 2mk

Quinn, E. (2020, August 29). Scientific rules that lead to physical fitness. *Very Well Fit*.

https://www.verywellfit.com/the-6-scientificrules-you-must-follow-to-get-fit-3120111

Quinn, E. (2020, March 25). Signs and symptoms of overtraining syndrome in athletes. *Very Well Fit*.

https://www.verywellfit.com/overtrainingsyndrome-and-athletes-3119386

Quinn, E. (2020, February 13). Importance of rest and recovery after your exercise. *Very Well Fit.* https://www.verywellfit.com/the-benefitsof-rest-and-recovery-after-exercise-3120575

Reed, K. (June 18, 2018). How do muscles grow: the science of muscle growth explained. *Positive Health Wellness.*

https://www.positivehealthwellness.com/fitness/how-do-muscles-grow-the-science-of-musclegrowth-explained/

Rizzo, J. (2012, June 12), How to do a leg raise | Ab workout. *Howcast/YouTube.com.*

https://www.youtube.com/watch?v=l4kQd9eWclE

Rizzo, J. (2012, June 11), How to do a side plank | Ab workout. *Howcast/YouTube.com.* https://www.youtube.com/watch?v=NXr4Fw8q60o

Robson, D. (2020, July 8). The importance of sleep.

Bodybuilder.com.

https://www.bodybuilding.com/content/theimportance-of-sleep.html

Rogers, P. (2020, August 3). The best lower body strength exercises. *Very Well Fit.*

https://www.verywellfit.com/best-lowerbody-weighttraining-exercises-3498517

Salyer, J. (2016, December 19). 5 Examples of isometric exercises for static strength training. *Healthline.* https://www.healthline.com/health/fitnessexercise/isometric-exercises

Singh, E. (2019, May 20). Beginner advice from 5 calisthenics experts. *Warrior Academy.* https://warrioracademyhk.com/beginneradvice-from-5-calisthenics-experts-includes-alkavadlo/

Teagarden, C. (2020, July 12). How to do dips at home (without a dip bar). *YouTube.com.* https://www.youtube.com/watch?v=isikOOF0W3k

Tober, J. (2016, November 12) Calf raises - the easiest way to instantly get better athletically.

YouTube.com. https://www.youtube.com/watch?v=TZrBb5M1CdM

TPindell Fitness. (2015, September 28). How to do Superman exercises. *YouTube.com.* https://www.youtube.com/watch?v=VUT1RHyMEuc

The 30 best bodyweight exercises for men. (n.d). Men's Journal. Retrieved from

https://www.mensjournal.com/healthfitness/the-30-best-bodyweight-exercises-formen/

Ultimate list of compound exercises - 104+ exercises. (2020). Bodyweight Tribe. Retrieved from

https://bodyweighttribe.com/list-ofcompound-exercises/

Weiner, Z. (2020, June 2). Trainers say the Superman exercise is the best way to work your obliques. *Well and Good.*

https://www.wellandgood.com/supermanexercises/

What is a serving? (2020). Retrieved from *Heart.org.* https://www.heart.org/en/healthtopics/caregiver-support/what-is-a-serving

Wilson, K.L. (2018, December 12). How much carbs, fat and protein should you eat daily to lose weight? *SFGate.*

https://healthyeating.sfgate.com/much-carbsfat-protein-should-eat-daily-lose-weight-6278.html

Yetman, D. (2020, May 28). What muscle groups are best to workout together? *Healthline.* https://www.healthline.com/health/exercisefitness/muscle-groups-to-workout-together

Image Sources

Fig.   1   (2020). Retrieved   from
https://pixabay.com/images/search/push%20up/

Fig.   2   (2016). Retrieved   from
https://www.youtube.com/watch?v=eGo4IYlbE5
g. Screenshot by author.

Fig.   3   (2017). Retrieved   from
https://www.youtube.com/watch?v=brhRXlOhsA
M/. Screenshot by author.

Fig.   4   (2016). Retrieved   from
https://www.youtube.com/watch?v=IODxDx
X7oi4&feature=youtu.be. Screenshot by author.

Fig.   5   (2020). Retrieved   from
https://www.youtube.com/watch?v=isikOOF0W3
k. Screenshot by author.

Fig.   6   (2012). Retrieved   from
https://www.youtube.com/watch?v=l4kQd9e
WclE. Screenshot by author.

Fig.   7   (2012).
https://www.youtube.com/watch?v=NXr4Fw8
q60o. Screenshot by author.

Fig.   8   (2015). Retrieved   from

https://www.youtube.com/watch?v=VUT1RH
yMEuc. Screenshot by author.

Fig. 9 (2016). Retrieved from
https://www.youtube.com/watch?v=aclHkVak
u9U. Screenshot by author.

Fig. 10 (2016). Retrieved from
https://www.youtube.com/watch?v=TZrBb5
M1CdM. Screenshot by author.

Fig. 11 (2017). Retrieved from
https://www.youtube.com/watch?v=QyVq5o
UBpss. Screenshot by author.

Fig. 12 (2017). Retrieved from
https://www.youtube.com/watch?v=rloXYB8
M3vU. Screenshot by author.

Fig. 13 (2018). Retrieved from
https://www.youtube.com/watch?v=PGcTxvw
6-lo. Screenshot by author.

Fig. 14 (2017). Retrieved from
https://www.youtube.com/watch?v=ZR5U3sb -
KeE. Screenshot by author.

Fig. 15 (2016). Retrieved from
https://www.youtube.com/watch?v=h0HjqYRl
XYg. Screenshot by author.

Fig. 16 (2017). Retrieved from

https://www.youtube.com/watch?v=KIEAbfk4cQU. Screenshot by author.

Fig. 17 (2017). Retrieved from https://www.youtube.com/watch?v=2IUoEAzjZqY. Screenshot by author.

Fig. 18 (2017). Retrieved from https://www.youtube.com/watch?v=2IUoEAzjZqY. Screenshot by author.

Fig. 19 (2017). Retrieved from https://www.youtube.com/watch?v=iT1q1Ff02mk. Screenshot by author.

Fig. 20 (2012). Retrieved from https://www.youtube.com/watch?v=gwWv7aPcD88. Screenshot by author.

Book 3

BEASTMODE CALISTHENICS

A Simple and Effective Guide
to Get Ripped with
Bodyweight Training

INTRODUCTION

Earlier this week, I was speaking with a friend of mine about our respective workout habits. This is a subject we had discussed many times before, but today I decided to ask a very specific question.

"Why did you start doing calisthenics?"

In our previous conversations we had talked about increasing flexibility, variations in squat positions, and appropriate set repetitions; and yet I had never asked that simple, fundamental question. Even though working out had created a great deal of positive change in my life, somehow, I had overlooked that inquiry.

Despite the amount of experience, I had in this particular area, my friend's purpose for it had slipped my mind. It was a question I had been asked many times when starting with a new trainer. However, it had somehow gone overlooked in my personal life. His response proved that it was a much bigger subject than I once thought.

"Six months ago, I didn't want to live anymore." Honestly, I

expected to hear something similar to the other reasons I had heard over the years—increasing strength, becoming more attractive, or a variety of more surface-level issues. This was something much deeper. It was something that even I, who placed so much value and weight in working out, had not seen.

I put so much of myself into working out, but all of it had been from *my* perspective and not trying to see through the eyes of others. By listening and expanding my thought process, I was able to learn so much more about a subject I considered myself fully learned in.

My friend explained that he had been experiencing a very low point in his life for several reasons, ranging from family to work. He tried to use his usual methods of coping but it merely put off the problem without repairing or bettering a thing. One day, he walked into a fitness center, took the time to sit down with a trainer, and began what he so poignantly referred to as his *journey*—the journey of calisthenics.

Maybe you aren't struggling with life in the ways my friend was, but you are reading this book to find a solution to some issue within yourself. It could be something simple and short-term, or perhaps it is a life change that will take a true journey to accomplish; either way, you are looking to calisthenics as a catalyst and guide to that change.

Or perhaps you are like myself and were unaware of how deep this lifestyle can become. It isn't easy, of course, but the changes are lasting and the scope of life-altering moments are for the better. You may have stumbled into this simply looking for your usual, small-thought workouts. Those are more of a one-dimensional approach to life's issues; a single solution for a single issue solved through one action alone. For certain personality types, or for a smaller impact, those routines work just fine. For a true change in your life, for

better health and a broader mind, and for more trust in and with yourself; for all this, you need a workout that is different.

Together, we will learn new and better habits, in both your life and your workout routine. Through these proven steps, you will establish a solid baseline and discover how to build upon it for an altered, healthier life. There are likely some areas in your life that got the spotlight, as you have been reading. It is very common and can be extremely helpful to recognize this early on. Your mind and body are aware of what is needed for true repair of self, but people rarely take the time to listen hard enough. This may seem like an attack, but it is simply an observation. Because the majority of workout programs I have experienced or studied seemed to lack a multi-subject approach—as well as giving proper focus to the honesty within yourself—something jumps out when you feel heard. You may not have considered these parts of your life to need improvement, but noticing patterns that can be changed for the better is not a bad thing! It is the first part of understanding the necessary steps to alter your life for the better!

I believe it is always best to set out from a place of positivity; so let's celebrate the beginning and the journey that is about to start!

CHAPTER ONE:

STARTING YOUR JOURNEY

There are many reasons why people would choose this book; and they are often very personal, as you may already know. What I mean by that is there are arcs of thought that tend to cover most workouts—devote time, work out, get better. There is too much focus on a singular area for the routine to give attention to every part that needs bettering. You had reasons before you opened the book, and I am sure you have even more by now.

As you make your way through the steps and workouts, taking the time to appreciate the achievements along the way, you will discover and fulfill your promise to yourself. It is important that there be no judgement at any point throughout this process. It will be difficult at first, but you need to be able to recognize your problem areas without allowing the degrading power (that part of you that is much too hard on yourself) to emerge. By removing judgement from the equation, you don't waste time being down on yourself and can instead focus on the solutions! Every *journey* has ups and downs, but they do not take away from both the results and the willpower gained by following through.

You've probably been here before and you may feel a bit of déjà vu. The positivity, the layout, even the wording may already have you on edge. For most people, there is a long list of workout routines that never panned out, and that is nothing to get down on yourself about! You are probably feeling that same skepticism starting up again.

Breathe. Now breathe again. One more time. Three breaths —good, solid breaths—create an excellent reset point.

Your doubt is real and should be recognized, because the promises that other programs offered you in the past fell short. Now, there will be many, many times throughout this program when you will be asked to be very honest with yourself. This may not be something you are used to, nor are comfortable with. That is also understandable. This, however, is a give and take between the reader and the program. A true relationship is one cultivated in trust and faith for the things to come; this should operate no differently! I have faith in you! Within you is a desire to better yourself in a way you haven't considered before. There is something to be said for comfort; but if the other programs were also from a source of comfort, it sounds like you need something new!

In order to get the most out of this experience, it is vital that both openness and honesty are present. To begin, be honest with yourself—what are your reasons? They have begun to show themselves in ways you probably weren't even expecting. There are no wrong answers to this question. You may have one main purpose for beginning this journey or several that combined to bring you to this point; the reasons do not matter, so long as they are important and personal to you!

The most common reason, I have found, is weight loss.

This can come in many different forms and goals that range from a slight change to a complete life change. Your journey is your own and you need to be bonded with the foundational reasons behind it. If you only have a general idea, rather than a specific goal, that is perfectly fine! You will have plenty of time and will be given plenty of tools to identify and implement the changes you want to bring about. Consider from what angle you want to attack this weight loss; muscle endurance, mass, strength, or simple toning? By developing a strategy, you will be prepared once the action is needed.

For most people who choose this approach, they have most likely tried to attack the problem from only one angle, or the life changes weren't customized for them. That is where you will see the differences here! A multi-aspect approach to a common problem will give you the tools to not only complete and maintain the program, but to carry more confidence and ability onward throughout your life! The desired results may vary, but the drive remains the same. Even though this is common, it is unique to you and that cannot be forgotten!

There will be variations that work a wide range of muscle groups and offer different scales of impact. This will enable you to personalize the experience even more! There are alterations to focus on muscle mass and others for endurance. If you have a specific problem area you want to improve, each workout will explain the muscle groups they target. Every portion is designed to ensure that *your* journey is the best for *your* life.

Perhaps, rather than weight loss, you simply cannot find the time in your schedule to properly devote to a workout regiment. As we will touch on consistently, life does not come to a halt when a new event occurs. This program functions as an incorporation into your life rather than something piled on top of it. You'll find a better system for scheduling, a way to track the details of problem areas, and the power to overcome disruptions to that schedule. Your time is precious and important; your commitments should be as well.

Many times the scheduling isn't your issue, but rather finding a space in which to do the actual working out becomes the problem. This is no small issue, as many people continuously put off beginning a routine—or maintaining one—due to a lack of space. Having the right environment to nurture that motivation is a key tool to fighting off those distractions. Think on this as we move forward—what kind of space do *you* want? You are aware of the past attempts and where they fell short, so avoid the same missteps you made then. Don't try to make a space that you think you *should* want, and instead make one you actually *do* want. Never underestimate the impact of a safe, nurturing workout space.

All of these reasons are legitimate and, up to this point, have been stumbling blocks along the way. At no point should you feel judged. Every point brought up is designed to relate to issues you and many others have had, and still have. The important thing to remember is that no problem will be introduced or brought up without a solution being offered. You deserve to better your life and all the past reasons for not following through are going to be directly addressed and repaired!

Once you have done some inward searching, we must establish what factors led you here. By creating bonds between this experience and your personal reasons, you can build a strong foundation for the coming months. Let's break down how we can attack these "speed bumps" and turn them into motivation!

By facing these "speed bumps" head-on, you begin the process of giving the power back to yourself. Every time these "bumps" derailed a promising series of workouts or somehow lessened your drive, the power was given away. At the time, it probably did not seem as dire as I make it out to be; but the compilation of these excuses, regardless of their legitimacy, built up these "bumps" until they seemed insurmountable. Over time the mere idea of starting that regiment, because of that build-up, brings anxiety or an overwhelming feeling. In my experience, most workouts do not address these issues and instead plow forward haphazardly. This undoubtedly leads to more failures than successes and can put a bad taste in your mouth for future endeavors.

You may have noticed that a consistent tool offered in these regiments is the idea of taking time to review, preview, and list different variables. It is important that these are taken for what they are: chances to slow the speed and really get a chance to analyze. Make a conscious effort to not skip over these opportunities. Allow yourself that time to think over a situation; it could make all the difference.

Rather than using the tried-and-failed routines, together we can create an environment that renews your drive, pushes you positively towards the set goals, and finally helps you achieve the kind of lifestyle that has evaded you in the past. Remember that honesty is paramount in this journey in order to get the most out of the regiment. By attacking the root of these issues, you are empowered to push through when the days are tough. Life does not stop because you made this commitment. In fact, there will be times when life itself is enough to derail this effort. Do not be discouraged; you are more ready for this than you realize!

Let's stay in that place of positivity and take a deeper look at the life choices, or "speed bumps", that brought about this desire for change. Rather than thinking from a negative viewpoint about those reasons, let's celebrate the want to better yourself and, in turn, those around you.

Weight Loss

This is the most common reason for beginning a workout routine, although I have found it is not enough to simply want to lose weight. Usually when that is the specific purpose and goal, the problem is not a new one. Most likely, it is one that has caused you to begin many times but not truly follow through. Now look at that desire with positivity and see it for what it truly is—a selfless decision that will bring about a chain reaction of betterment in your life. This is not a singular action you are undertaking; rather, it is a series of good choices followed by even more of the same. Every single act will bring progress, and being able to fully embrace that will strengthen your base for those difficult times. Celebrate your choice here and now!

Lack Of Time/Scheduling

As I said before, life will not come to a stop when you begin this process. It is very important for you to fully understand that you are adding something to what is most likely an already busy life. That brings with it some challenges from the get-go; so start combatting those challenges with facts and logic. The best weapon is that this routine will only take 30-45 minutes from your day. If you just rolled your eyes, that is to be expected. There isn't a workout that exists without that lofty, quick-fix promise. Rather than simply throwing flashy times out there, let's take a look at what 30-45 minutes entails.

This program is time-sensitive because your time is worthwhile. Most days begin with light running—either in place or your best option—which takes around 5 minutes. From there you will go into four different exercises of varying muscle groups. Each one takes around 5 minutes as well. Only taking into account the *actual* physical actions, you've used 25 minutes. In between, it is crucial to give your body rest periods to hydrate and control your breathing; these normally take between 1-3 minutes, depending on the exercise intensity. By allowing yourself those moments, you have been working out for approximately 35 minutes. Every person is different, so there is room for extra time if needed, but that is a usual session.

When you break it down like that, it seems much more doable! Details can make a big difference as well as perspective. By focusing on the progress and actual actions, you can see exactly where your valuable time is going. In Chapter 6, we will go into even more detail to allow your scheduling complete accuracy!

Rarely are there blocks of time that go unassigned when scheduling, and that is the key roadblock for you personally. By undertaking this journey, you must accept the *addition* to that schedule. By utilizing foresight and adjusting accordingly, you can avoid any major disruptions to your daily life. Most problems when dealing specifically with time management arise because these realities were not fully understood. It is going to take some shifting and flexibility from you at the beginning in order to allow the workout it's full efficiency. You are most definitely up for this challenge! Scheduling is your strength—just look at your busy life and how you handle the day-to-day difficulties. By seeing this as a welcome addition to your life rather than an extra part that needs to fit, the positivity is sown while accepting the reality of the situation. No doubt you are already formulating times in your head, so take a breath and sketch something out. Use those gifts of time management and positively implement them now!

Finding Workout Space

I have found that this reason goes hand-in-hand with the previous one. When you cannot find the space and a gym is not an option for you, the issue of time comes into play as well. Usually, there just isn't room in the home unless it was built in or included; and if you are having trouble finding the time to work out, then the thought of any construction or redesign is daunting to say the least. This all adds up into the overwhelming feeling that tends to result in failure to follow through.

Earlier, you were asked to think about the past workout spaces you have had and how you can make better choices this time around. What were those errors? It could be something as small as not taking sound into account and discovering that your space is less noise-proof than you thought. In the past, you may have shrugged it off and pushed forward; but this time you can act with more change! You have control of this aspect and it is important for you to feel comfortable within that workout space. Everything can impact it, and the distractions should not be shrugged off; they rarely go away and usually end up returning with a vengeance later on. Now is a good time to remember that there is no judgement here; just like you will make that space for yourself physically, ease up on yourself mentally and emotionally. The answer lies in the simplicity of our regiment. You only need one thing to truly begin, and it has nothing to do with equipment or barbells. Your own body weight is your gym and wherever it goes, so does your ability to get that workout time in. There are varying degrees of each specific exercise which we will cover in-depth as we progress.

The important thing in this moment is to eliminate those roadblocks and excuses. Take pride in the fact that you are all you need to begin. The looming thought of investing in equipment or the fine print within a gym membership can put off even the strongest of wills; but when viewed in our positive light, it is an answer instead of a hindrance. We take small steps in the beginning to enable the sprint that will come!

There is a distinct possibility that neither of these have caused you problems in your past workouts. For some people, there is an intimidation factor in the thought of a workout program. The idea creeps in that being of a lower experience level will cause a natural halt in either motivation or ability in general. Despite previous tries, that looming sense still follows and robs you of joy and possibility in this area. For you, the key lies in adhering to the honesty within this program. Every system within this machinery was created with the intent to give accountability back to you! At the end of the day, you face yourself; so there is no better person to be your motivator on this journey! You will be empowered and built up through a natural, progressing incline. As the weeks pass, your ability will rise with it, enabling you to buy into the confidence you have been searching for.

Always remember that there is no one more capable for this than you!

These are some of the more common roadblocks that I have encountered in my experience. Yours may be different completely or a variation on what we discussed. Remember not to ignore the feelings you have during these preparedness chapters. Stay alert and confront them when they arise. Your mind and body want to have a say in this matter, and it is important to listen. Whatever brought you to this moment is a real and deep part of you that wants to change. The ability to maintain that honesty with yourself and with the steps in this book will pave the way for concrete success. Do not be deterred from your goal! If your specific roadblock was not covered, let's take some time and look inward.

The reasons behind your desire to make a change are unique and important—not just to you personally, but to the entire process. You are beginning to see the reason, or multitude of reasons, and uncovering them. Addressing them and utilizing them in a positive manner is also something you can fully achieve. The key is to not shrink away from the change you see. When a disruption rears, the natural response is to halt and worry. You will hone skills throughout this process that will enable you to focus, confront, and identify these disruptions without worry.

Depending on your past experience, the positivity that is woven into this program may be off-putting for a multitude of reasons. Whatever they may be it exists for a purpose, although it is understandable why that would be a cause for skepticism. What I have usually found is that when a program preaches a message of positivity, that is all it is built upon. Without other foundational keys, positive thinking is simply masking a form of denial.

Instead, we pair that positivity with accompanying tools that help focus that thinking into action. Rather than blindly moving forward in a bright, sunny mood, you will be instilled with real confidence. There is no rock unturned when it comes to both your physical and mental preparation, and that is where the positive thinking comes from—not a hope that things are good, but instead a knowledge that you are more than capable. From that mindset will come lasting results. That is true positivity—one that comes from a real place and is backed up with pertinent information and solutions!

Your knee-jerk reaction may be to set aside this book, but don't. Instead, use this as another chance for positivity. Discovery of self is vital—not just in this particular process, but throughout life in general. Perhaps other approaches to calisthenics haven't been as in-depth, or it is something you are not completely comfortable with. That is okay. This is not one of the "other approaches", nor will it be a comfortable journey. The design is to alter parts of yourself in such a way that habits are formed in a deep, lasting manner.

In the next chapter, you will be introduced to the program, we will go deeper into the problems you are looking to solve through this process, and we will discuss what issues with other programs led to this point as well.

The more honesty you bring to the table, the stronger your resolution will be to complete the regiment. Not only should you strive for that, but you will leave with a sense of awareness, a positive view of both yourself and the process as a whole, and, in a very real way, a life refreshed!

Chapter Summary

- How can this calisthenics workout regiment change my life?
- What brought about this desired change?
- Weight loss?
- Lifestyle change?
- Why have your past attempts not been followed through on?
- Lack of time?
- Lack of space to conduct the workout?
- Not a "gym person"?
- Honesty with yourself and the program is vital! Take the time to discover your personal "roadblocks".

CHAPTER TWO

MONTHS 1-3

As you begin each chapter—each forward step—it gives you a chance to reset and check that light of positivity. By now, you have given yourself permission to be honest and have discovered the reasons behind your journey. These are not surface-level variables and should be treated with respect and importance. Each step is a reminder for yourself— your reasons are real and vital to this journey. As many times as you need to hear it, repeat it one more time for luck.

Before you jump into some early looks at the physical aspect of the program, you have the chance to alter another perspective. Up to now, you have probably looked back on your past experiences quite a bit. It may be difficult at times to do this without feeling the need to be harsh. It is an understandable view— you may see your past self as someone who put you in this position and didn't follow through. More often than not, it is an overhanging sense of failure. That is a very damaging place to draw motivation from. I have rarely seen any positive results from people who work out solely from a place of avoiding failure. That perspective is incredibly effective in jumpstarting the beginning of a routine, but it burns bright, hot, and fast, leaving you burned out and more frustrated than before. This can easily become a toxic cycle of quick starts and frayed nerves.

By avoiding that label of failure, you end one cycle and begin another. Just like this program is a long-term commitment, changing a perspective—especially one with a lengthy past behind it—can prove to also be a lengthy process, but one that is incredibly worthwhile.

Now that the foundation has been laid, we can begin going into more detail regarding the actual workout. Each day along the way is another chance to take power back from those roadblocks. Just like honesty was vital in discovering your personal reasons for choosing this workout, patience is needed for every step moving forward. This is not a short event in your life; it is a vigorous, six-month routine that is designed to truly alter your life.

The more you understand the span of the program, the better prepared you will be for the marathon. You have no doubt noticed that, through repetition, you retain much more information and form habits faster. It may seem monotonous, but keep your focus on the purpose behind it. These are not just words and the exercises are not simply actions; these are methods that are all working towards a massively positive end! Your focus and effort are beginning to pay off already! Your understanding is growing and so is your appreciation for the program as a whole.

Hopefully by now you have a much wider view of your entire workout history—the times it worked, the times it didn't, and everything in-between. You will add to this more and more as you continue to learn the proper tools. In whatever method you desire, ensure that these discoveries are noted so you can refer back during this journey.

No one likes to read the instructions when they get something new; but the more time you spend on the inner workings, the better understanding you gain. The same can be said for the Ultimate Calisthenics Workout Plan. There is no lock and key preventing you from skipping ahead and simply completing the actions required. You can see some results from this method, but the truth of the matter remains—the only way to get the full impact of this process is to believe in the journey itself. As in life, without making that trek—your journey—you won't fully understand what to do with the results you gain. It seems harsh, but instant gratification rarely breeds excellence and good habits.

You know the basics and how to follow images and graphs, but when you have the backing of a deeper self, that is when the once momentary results become lasting. Rather than seeing a picture explaining the exercise, following it, and repeating, you will be able to see the workout and think back on other times you tried it as well as ways to avoid the same pitfalls this time around. You will make connections between your past self and who you are becoming now, enabling you to problem solve with a much deeper sense of change. The potential lies entirely inside you and cannot wait to begin!

Month 1

In the first month of the program, it is absolutely imperative that we lay groundwork. It may seem slow or redundant, but the actual progress you make will speak for itself. Remember, patience will be needed from the first day to the last. As with anything that requires commitment, the effort will be worth it!

Coming from a place of positivity, there has to be a focus on the environment in which you will be working out. There are many schools of thought when it comes to the actual layout of a workout area, but there is one encompassing similarity: cleanliness. Keeping a nice and tidy area is a huge step in creating the proper atmosphere for motivation! If you are of the personality type where the act of cleaning is calming, consider taking a minute at the beginning and end of each session to focus solely on cleaning. Even if that isn't something that eases anxiety, following a consistent routine in all aspects will go a long way in forming the correct habits. There is something to be said for a place where, no matter the chaos that surrounds your day and/or your physical space, peace can be found. There is control and organization that you nurture, and that is a powerful thing to have.

You will be starting with a four-day action week. This simply means that four days will be spent working out, and three days will be spent recovering. Intersperse these accordingly while making sure you try to have a rest day between action days. The start

393

day really does not matter, although I would recommend using your usual schedule to dictate how the Ultimate Workout will be conducted. The extent to which you make these alterations are up to you. I have known people to completely scrap their usual schedule and build a new one entirely centered around their program. For the minimalist, a simple tweak here and there is all you need to allow the incorporation to occur. Keep in mind that you are not *adding* this workout program to your schedule, you are *incorporating* it. Seeing this as a priority and an organic part of your daily life will help build those foundational habits swiftly and efficiently.

In my experience, there is rarely one schedule that fits all walks of life—retail, service industry, teachers, and so on.

Even if you tend to keep a "regular" schedule—Monday through Friday, 9 AM to 5 PM—using this format still might not be the most efficient. This idea may seem daunting at first. For the most part, there is a tendency for people to stick to one main schedule and to work everything else around that. The idea of something as intensive as this workout being brought in *and* altering a schedule that has been a mainstay is intimidating, for certain. But remember, you take your power back by acknowledging the reality rather than shirking from it.

From that place of power, you can then begin the changes to your schedule. The important thing to remember is that a flexible, open mind is less prone to frustration. You will be able to see more chances for productivity if you aren't locked in to one singular method. As you make your way through the schedule, be ready to recognize any stress triggers. These can occur when you suddenly realize that you didn't include an event to the calendar and have to alter it. Don't stress over the time because you are most likely seeing it as a loss. You have lost nothing; rather, you have given yourself another opportunity to conduct the proper change. Breathe and begin the solution right away! The longer you allow that issue to remain unaddressed, the more power you grant it.

We'll break it down in a less-complex way so you can apply it to whatever schedule you may keep:

- Day 1: Full Body 101

- Day 2: Rest

- Day 3: Full Body 101

- Day 4: Rest

- Day 5: Full Body 101

- Day 6: Rest

- Day 7: Full Body 101

Muscles worked out in Month 1: Full leg muscles, glutes, abdominals, pectorals, upper arms, and shoulders

Now that you have something more concrete to consider, take a moment to plan out your first month accordingly. Be honest with yourself. Nothing is gained from overreaching, so there is no need to rush this process. You should always feel free to set this book aside and take the time to map things out. Other than your Workout Journal, keep another pad to jot down improvements or thoughts you have while reading. Some people don't mind writing directly on the page while others consider that idea quite horrific, or you may be reading this on a tablet/phone. However you keep track of these details, ensure that somehow you do. A fleeting thought mid-paragraph can easily be lost, so keep that pad handy and allow the thoughts to flow throughout the process!

Remember that the way we phrase a situation has a direct effect. This is your *journey*. This is the time to organically add this to your life. It should fit in a way that is easy to maintain without disruption. Don't give yourself a reason to back out by skimming over something this important.

Before we begin previewing the upcoming months and the exciting possibilities, it is imperative that you understand the importance of the rest periods between workout sets. Later on, we'll go into more detail on just how you can get the most recovery from those periods. For now, we can focus on the basics:

- Ease into the rest period. Avoid sudden stops in transition.

- Controlled breathing will help maintain your heart rate during the rest

- Avoid sitting or becoming motionless

You are going to be using a four-week format for each month of the program. For the more detail-oriented reader, don't place too much focus on the date, but rather the day of the week. This is a space you are crafting that will alleviate stress and promote motivation, so use a method that is comfortable for you! There will be many times during this program where you will feel uncomfortable and will be pushed, so find ways to keep some form of recuperation in that comfort. It could be something as simple as using an unorthodox ink color (or multiple colors) to track your workouts, or something more complex like an entire Excel worksheet dedicated to getting every detail you can. Make it your own!

The first month will be very generalized in regards to muscle focus. Each workout is considered Full Body and is vital in building the core for the future. Even though we are starting from a low-impact place, use this time to solidify how you see and contextualize your workouts. Don't let the rest days be considered a "day off". Focus instead on the rest and allow your body time to revitalize. If you are using a specialized diet along with this program, then these rest days are a chance to meal plan or fill in your workout journal, which we will discuss in detail later.

As we will go into more in Chapter 4, this is one of the more important stretches of time in the program. You will be building bonds with your foundation, learning a new routine, adjusting to whatever alterations you have made to your schedule, and balancing a new physical stress. It isn't a small undertaking, but that fact makes it all the more impressive!

Your mantra is this: patience. It is worth repeating. You will not see any real results until you hit that 30-day mark. Remind yourself of this often, because there *will* be moments during this first month where you get discouraged. You will be putting in a great deal of effort, and the feeling that nothing is changing can be the number one reason for ending a program prematurely. The more prepared you are for the reality of a long-term workout such as this, the more motivation ammunition you give yourself! Invest in this knowledge now and, as you progress, you will be at ease and fully ready to face each day and session! Focus instead on the other positive effects by asking a few honest questions.

How do you feel throughout the day?

Just like you will be documenting the changes in yourself during this program, note how you feel before. Take that moment and analyze your morning, midday, and night moods and general health. If there are other people in your household, check in with them and see what changes they have noticed. It can help to have multiple sets of eyes to catch every detail. Being able to plainly see different aspects of your life improving in front of you thanks to all your hard work can be very interesting and rewarding!

Are there better ways to rest yourself to avoid injury?

This doesn't just mean your Rest Days and resting times during a workout. Are you aware of your sleeping positions? What soreness do you experience right out of the gate in the morning? These can be clues to help avoid injury down the line. Your body is going to be tested more than it is used to, and there will be nights and following days that bring aches and groans. By taking notice of your physical habits, you can be better informed on where the adjustments need to be made!

Are you sleeping better?

After the first few days of working out, you can start to make this a focus as well. We will get more into the importance of sleep later, but for now simply notice what your sleep habits were and how they begin to change. There may be times when your sleep suffers, and you will need to address that as well. No matter the direction your sleep goes, you can ensure you will be prepared for it!

These are just a few self-check questions that can help chart your progress in more than a visual way.

Month 2

The second month of the program is going to keep the same four-day workout, three-day rest cycle as Month 1. The variations are in the form of different workouts and increased impact and repetitions. You will not see a large amount of difference from the types of exercises; however, the way you go about doing them will start to change. In this way, calisthenics are very much like mathematics—you build on what you learned before in order to accomplish the current task. By taking your time in the first four weeks, you will have given yourself that foundation to properly build upon.

Your muscle group focus is going to stay very general. Consider this a step up from the first set. If Month 1 covered Full Body 101, then we are moving to Full Body 102 for Month 2. The exact workouts and details are further explained in Chapter 6, but we are creating that base for the moment. As before, map out the second month the same way you did the first. You should have an idea of how things will fit into your life and what pitfalls to avoid from the first month of scheduling.

- <u>Day 1</u>: Full Body 102

- <u>Day 2</u>: Rest

- <u>Day 3</u>: Full Body 102

- <u>Day 4</u>: Rest

- **Day 5**: Full Body 102

- **Day 6**: Rest

- **Day 7**: Full Body 102

Muscles worked out in Month 2: Full leg muscles, glutes, pectorals, abdominals, biceps, and backs

As we remember to move forward in positivity, this is another chance to celebrate a milestone! Two months of hard work and planning have gotten you to this point! With each day and workout, you are presented with a new opportunity to solidify your foundation.

As you make you way further into the program, you will have already encountered a good variety of exercises. The entire workout follows an upward incline in intensity and impact, but the difficulty will consistently remain at a steady, even pace. This is not a situation where you will ever feel left behind! During the detailed workouts further in the book, you will be given images and explanations to guide you along and make the process smooth. Frustration only leads to improper form and stilted breathing, neither of which helps to cultivate a positive atmosphere.

As we take a moment to look back on the progress thus far, a new roadblock may be forming or has already begun to take ground: boredom.

It seems odd when looking at it from the beginning, but by the time you reach this two-month, milestone there is a good chance that you have felt the twinge of monotony. No doubt there have been days that didn't pan out according to your calendar and times when you simply didn't feel like working out. Despite beginning and continuing from a place of positive thinking, there is no shame in understanding why you are feeling bored. It is a strange place, that plateau of eight weeks. You haven't reached the halfway point and the visual results may not be showing— the reasons to let that doubt creep in will begin to present themselves. This is not to be taken lightly. Remember, taking back power is a very large component of your journey. Don't shy away from facing this directly; you owe that to yourself.

When times like this arise, it is imperative that we use our tools of self-awareness. You know yourself very well, and this program has helped you discover foundational issues along the way.

Perhaps the details are overwhelming and you need to take a step back. View the program in its entirety rather than seeing every moment. By seeing it from that perspective, you can map out other times you felt distraught or less than inspired. Those were key moments, and I am sure you can recall the inner struggle that you went through to regain power. From the start, you have been asked to use your past as a tool for discovering present solutions, and this will be no different. It is a skill that is continuously sharpened, and for good reason.

With each moment you turn from a low point to a teachable one invests in your confidence—not just now, but for life continuing after. You are building a foundation that will be lasting and stronger than you had previously thought. That is well worth the effort! That same fire and fight can be put to work in any future situation as well. Reminding yourself that this isn't something new and that you overcame it before can be that spark you need to get you through.

Some people, instead, need the details to understand the purpose of the journey. Seeing the forest doesn't ignite anything, and instead brings a haze. By focusing on the individual workouts and days—seeing how you plotted your course—you can navigate your doubt. Break everything down to the core components and lay it out. You can see the magnitude of what you have already accomplished in plain text. Read back over your previous entries you made in the Workout Journal—again, we will cover this in detail later. The key is giving yourself detailed reminders, in detail of times you pushed through.

Both schools of thought will accomplish the same goal so long as they are applied correctly. Again, we revisit that core principle of honesty with yourself. You know the inspirations that got you to this point and as long as you follow that same path of honesty, you will have many more milestones to celebrate!

Month 3

The third month is where we introduce the first big change to your routine. The foundation is set, and I know all the work you have put in so far will begin paying off! Again, as we do to remind ourselves, begin this month with a fresh mind and preparedness. You have your schedule at the ready with pencil in hand—or pen, if you're feeling adventurous! You deserve a moment to recognize what you have achieved to this point. Plan out some extra time for this recognition! Like you did at the end of four weeks, this is your chance for a little applause. You have charted your progress and by making it this far you have started to feel and live better. There has been a commitment to honesty throughout this process, and that will continue now.

With twice the knowledge since you began this journey, you are beginning to see the patterns that your workouts are taking. You have a better sense of the pitfalls and times that strain you more than others. This is another chance to better yourself. Going into the third month, are there any tweaks you need to make? Is the schedule you have set still the best way to proceed? Taking the time to properly ask and subsequently answer these questions will increase your already impressive preparedness. You have put the work in, both physically and mentally. Be proud of yourself!

The third month of our program has two possible choices for you depending on where you find yourself. Again, being honest with yourself is paramount. By transparently evaluating yourself and your progress, you know best what level of intensity will fit. Don't be afraid to tinker with the schedule if needed. You may find that staying at the lower level isn't as challenging as you thought and you need to increase the impact. No problem! The same can be said for the reverse; if you find the higher intensity too much, ease up and find that level where progress is made without risk of injury. Remember, no judgement!

It is important to remember as you make this decision that there is also a system for adding intensity and impact to a routine through increased sets and repetitions. This program sees the third month as the vital launching point for the second half of the workouts. Because of this, it is the only month that gives you a guideline for a higher impact schedule. Before you commit to either one, review the other options for increasing the workout overall, as described in Chapter 7. The customization of the routines are foundational in creating an open and flexible environment.

The next step in this process is considered Intermediate 101. You will find a higher degree of difficulty while still building our foundation. The options will differ in your workout days and rest days, depending on what you decide. If you want to remain at a lower intensity and the challenges have progressed correctly thus far, you will follow the Low-Impact schedule. However, if you need added intensity and your schedule can avoid disruption, proceed to the High-Impact schedule.

The High Impact schedule will substitute a "Light Running" day for a Rest day to push you that extra bit. On the Light Running days, you should jog for 20-30 consecutive minutes, be it in place, on a treadmill, or outside in the beauty of nature. Whichever you choose, you will feel the added impact; but make sure you adhere to the *Light* aspect and make that simply a more active Rest day, if you will.

Remember that in order to honestly evaluate yourself, you have to come from a place without judgement, as you have throughout the journey. It may seem repetitive, but there is nothing more valuable to the success of this program than the accountability you build with yourself. It enables you to relate to each session on a very personal level.

Low-Impact Schedule:

- Day 1: Intermediate 101

- Day 2: Rest

- Day 3: Intermediate 101

- Day 4: Rest

- Day 5: Intermediate 101

- Day 6: Rest

- Day 7: Intermediate 101

<u>Muscles worked out in Month 3</u>: Full leg muscles, glutes, pectorals, and back

When you are planning out your third month, you must place additional focus on your rest days. These are incredibly important to you achieving your goals, and how you schedule and utilize them has a direct impact, especially if you have chosen the High-Impact schedule.

Take the time now to review the schedules you have put together so far. You have a better understanding of what each session and cycle will entail, so you can take note of alterations that are needed. Specifically, regarding Rest Days, here are a few useful tips and questions that will help you notice patterns that signify a change is needed:

- Are there any personal events that happen in the first three months that will require more rest after, or that will have a large impact on your sleep schedule?

- Take special note of the Rest Days that follow back-to-back workouts to avoid disruptions from soreness or exhaustion.

- Are you comparing your current schedule to your previous workout attempts? Are any old patterns emerging that could derail your progress?

- If you chose the High-Impact schedule, do you need to do an honesty check to ensure that you will still have the proper recovery time?

Celebrate! You have reached the critical halfway point of this program! I am sure the going has been tough at times, but I know that a sense of pride accompanies this moment. You adapted and adjusted events in your life, and I know you are seeing these sacrifices paying off. By now, you should be feeling a multitude of effects across your life—physical, emotional, social, and so on. You implemented very important tools into your life and it is necessary to take a moment and consider how they have helped you outside of the workout space. You are crafting and nurturing a lifestyle that will have positive ripples long after the last page of this book.

The next three months will bring a variety of new exercises as well as bringing some old ones back! No matter if you are doing an exercise for the first time or the fiftieth time, your form is where all the efficiency is! By remaining self-aware, you will be more cognitive of slips in breathing or movements. You have quite the collection of useful tools that will no doubt lead to continued success long after this program has ended!

Chapter Summary

- A breakdown of the first three months of the
- Ultimate Calisthenics Workout

- Month 1

- How to schedule Workout Days and Rest Days

- Brief explanation of muscle focus

- Month 1 workout schedule

- What muscles are worked out this month?

- Month 2

- Full Body 101

- High and Low Impact schedules

- Light Running days Importance of Rest Days Patience!

- Month 2 workout schedule

- What muscles are worked out this month?

- Month 3

- How to combat boredom

- Intermediate 101

- Difference in Month 3 workout options

- Break down of Low Impact/High Impact schedule

- Month 3 Low Impact workout schedule Month 3 High Impact workout schedule

- What muscles are worked out this month?

- 3-month summary

- What to ask yourself now...

- What tools have you used to avoid skipping ahead or cutting corners?

- What day will start your Workout Schedule?

- Why that day?

- During the first 30 days...

- How do you feel throughout the day? Are there better ways to rest yourself to avoid injury?

- Are you sleeping better?

- What steps are you taking to combat boredom/monotony?

- Are you taking the workout changes in Month 3 into account?

- Do you need to adjust your Workout Schedule?

In the next chapter, you will be introduced to the second three-month cycle of the workout regiment. This will include simplified schedules for each four-week period.

CHAPTER THREE

MONTHS 4-6

As you begin this next part of the journey, it is important to restate that this is a celebratory moment. Just as you made it a point to recognize completing the first three months of the program, taking the time to celebrate beginning the next cycle is vital as well. Every recognition moment is a chance for you to refocus on a place of positivity —to notice when a breath and a cheer is needed.

It is no small feat, reaching this point. The time spent building a solid foundation, as you have, creates an atmosphere of growth. You have faced difficulties and you overcame them in every instance— scheduling, keeping reliable journal entries, and managing a non-stop life all the while. The next three months will not be easy; but because of the efforts you put in before now, you will certainly rise to each challenge!

Month 4

The next four-week cycle, Month 4, is a higher-impact focus on the muscle groups. The routine returns to a simplified schedule—as shown below— but the exercises themselves are more advanced. Remember to not feel defeated or disheartened! You have earned these challenges and are more than capable of handling them!

In Chapter 6, when we get into the detailed workouts and their respective diagrams, there will be several options when executing the routines. Not only are there ways to increase the impact of an exercise, but there are ways to lessen it as well without removing sets or reps. These options are not designed to be a permanent substitute for the original routines; but in the case of struggling or pain, you will be able to lessen the strain for the moment.

The aim of this program is simplicity and user friendliness. It's just like when you operate a computer—the screen can be fancy and sleek, but unless the user can fully operate it with confidence and ease, none of that matters. Your results are not purely aesthetic and the more effort and time spent on the foundational ideals discussed, the deeper the impact.

Some of the exercises, as shown in Chapter 6, are normally executed using a bar or similar equipment. It is not necessary to complete the program and great care has been taken to replace complex gym maneuvers with easy-to-follow actions to get the best results for the session!

Muscle Impact 101 Schedule:

- <u>Day 1</u>: Muscle Impact 101

- <u>Day 2</u>: Rest

- **Day 3**: Muscle Impact 101

- **Day 4**: Rest

- **Day 5**: Muscle Impact 101

- **Day 6**: Rest

- **Day 7**: Light Running

Muscles worked out in Month 4: Full leg muscles, glutes, abdominals, full arm muscles, shoulders, and back

Remember when you schedule this cycle to take into account the rise in intensity. You may need to change the start day to allow for a more natural integration. By taking the time to properly chart this out now, you will eliminate one task when you reach the actual workout section. Use this formula as we move forward. Each cycle increases in difficulty and intensity, and it is necessary to schedule accordingly.

By this point, you are well-versed in mapping out the month's routines. Simply by reaching this part of the program, you have shown that your life and the Ultimate Calisthenics Workout are symbiotic. Not only have you turned a new addition to your life into a welcome habit, but I am sure you have a list of the ways you feel better. With that in mind, now is perfect to take a moment and create that very list! Celebrating your personal accomplishments are a vital part of your mental workouts, and seeing them laid out before you makes the gravity of your success all the more real! Do a quick self-check using the handy questions we provided earlier:

- How do you feel throughout the day? Are there better ways to rest yourself to avoid injury?

- Are you sleeping better?

In fact, this is another perfect moment to recognize you!

Take some time and allow yourself to breathe. As you do, list the changes you have noticed in your life. List the different ways you have gained more energy! How are you being more active? By speaking these out loud or writing them down, you are making an extra effort for yourself. It is something you deserve; after all, you have put in months of hard work!

With a mere two months remaining in our time together, make sure you look back as much as you look forward, as we always have. In the early part of this book, we stated that this was not a race—you are not in competition. Allow me to alter that slightly now. You are in competition, but it is only with the past version of yourself. No one else can know the true depth of the changes like you can. Utilize this self-awareness! Enable yourself to see this from two simultaneous perspectives, if you will. The first being one of eventual completion—the program is winding down and the end is in sight. The second, and just as important, is that there isn't much time left!

Now, I don't mean that in a panic-inducing way. That is contradictory to the entire purpose. Instead, use the second point of view as a chance to appreciate where you've come from and the progress along the way! It has already been quite a journey for you and there is a great deal of pride in that.

By combining these two views, you will have a much better grasp on the final two months. Just as with every cycle and statement before, make sure you see from that light of positivity. Your time is precious and the devotion you've shown is certainly something to think about.

Month 5

The fifth month, our second-to-last, begins to combine earlier sessions into newer ones to create a more customized routine. When you are actually executing these exercises, you can refer to the provided diagrams in Chapter 6 at any time.

As with Month 4, if an exercise has the option of equipment, it is not necessary to get the most out of the actions. You will always be given the best versions of the exercise even without equipment. This is to make sure your schedule and setup are best utilized.

Muscle Impact 102 Schedule:

- <u>Day 1</u>: Muscle Impact 102

- <u>Day 2</u>: Intermediate 101

- **Day 3**: Rest

- **Day 4**: Muscle Impact 102

- **Day 5**: Intermediate 101

- **Day 6**: Rest

- **Day 7**: Light Running

Muscles worked out in Month 5: Full leg muscles, glutes, biceps, and back

Don't put any pressure on yourself in regards to scheduling. Throughout the program, you have found the correct times and days in which to create a productive environment; and you've done it well! Apply the same focus to Muscle Impact 102. Refer back to your workout journal entries for Month 3 (Intermediate 101) and take them into account. Keep in mind that you have been judgement-free up until now, and there is no reason to halt that streak! Adjustments are perfectly fine and sometimes necessary to create that atmosphere. You are the subject and the focus! Your commitment has been followed through and I know the same will continue!

Month 6

Take a deep breath; you have reached the final month!

As you enter this state of finality—and a well-deserved one, at that—use the tools you picked up along the way to properly celebrate this milestone!

From a blank slate to this moment, you have persevered! By this point, you have a full grasp of the exercises, scheduling, and everything in between. This will all be needed for the final month.

Thanks to all the knowledge you have in your possession, we can go straight into the final routine. As before, we will be combining previous routines to form a comprehensive and completed cycle. Month 6, known as The Ultimate Calisthenics Workout, will test all of the factors you have built up. You know your limits and how to properly rest and recover, so keep them in mind when you are scheduling this month. There is no need to rush through this. I know you can see the finish line, but there is more to be run yet.

The Ultimate Calisthenics Workout:

- Day 1: Muscle Impact 101

- Day 2: Muscle Impact 102

- Day 3: Rest

- Day 4: Muscle Impact 102

- Day 5: Light Running

- Day 6: The Ultimate Calisthenics Workout

- Day 7: Rest

Muscles worked out in Month 6: Full body workout

By keeping to the schedules you make and believing in yourself, you've made it through the program! Use this chapter as a reference while you move forward. Your journey is personal and unique to you. This is quite the accomplishment!

As you continue onward, you will find the answers to common troubles that arise along the way, in-depth focus on the first 30-day period, and the full, diagramed Ultimate Calisthenics Workout. Every chapter is a new tool that will help you maintain and follow through like you were never able to before! Stick to the foundational basics and you can't go wrong: honesty, efficiency, and honesty again!

I celebrate you as this journey continues to better your life!

Chapter Summary

- Have you taken the time to celebrate getting to the halfway point?

- **Month 4**

- Review Muscle Impact 101

- Have you reviewed the upcoming changes in your workouts?

- As with Month 3, do you need to adjust your schedule?

- Will you be using a bar/equipment or is that not possible/preferred?

- Make sure you have the correct routines according to your preferences

- What muscles are worked out this month?

- **Month 5**

- Were you able to complete Month 4 without disruption? If not, how did you correct the situation?

- Do you have more energy?

- Are you more active?

- Review Muscle Impact 102

- Are you rushing your sets/reps or letting posture slip?

- Are you keeping up with your Workout Journal?

- What muscles are worked out this month?

- **Month 6**

- Have you celebrated reaching the final month? Review any problem areas you have encountered in the last 5 months

- Is your schedule prepared for the final month?

- Review The Ultimate Calisthenics Workout

- Review all diagrams associated with The Ultimate Calisthenics Workout to ensure familiarity and efficiency

- What muscles are worked out this month?

In the next chapter, we will focus specifically on the first 30 days of this process, the importance of using that time to form the correct habits with confidence, and a deeper look at the importance of a Workout Journal.

CHAPTER FOUR

THE FIRST 30 DAYS

It is a well-known piece of trivia that it takes thirty days to form a habit. This was taken into consideration as our workout routine was created. The first thirty days are crucial to any action plan, and this is no different for one as intensive as the Ultimate Calisthenics Workout. In the previous chapter, we examined the different pitfalls during this experience, but now we can go into more detail in regards to that foundational starting period.

Why is thirty days important? Not only are these the formative days that will have a direct impact on the following five months, but the most common period of time to drop a workout routine is within those first four weeks. It makes sense when you think about it—the habits haven't formed yet, the commitment is new, and to be honest, the investment is still low. The approach to this program took that fully into account as well. By the time you make that first movement in your first session, you will have made a solid investment in yourself already! You will have spent some real time learning about yourself and creating bonds and trust in the new choices you are making.

Every milestone and moment during your journey is important; but by focusing on the first cycle, it gives the chance to build a foundational habit. Taking every day as it comes and allowing yourself to absorb as much information as possible is a direct investment into yourself and the results you know will come! Every skill and tool you obtain during this time will be put to use in every following cycle. Remember, you are the focus!

It is within this time period that you will experience a higher chance for roadblocks.

Some days, the workout can feel like an intrusion on your usual schedule; that is a direct chance to alter your perspective. By taking action immediately, you are laying important groundwork! When you experience these moments, take the extra time to journal them. You know yourself the best! Utilize your workout journal in a way that is the most efficient *for you*!

As the program progresses, the focus will shift from foundational to the application of that knowledge. Without the proper time given early in the workouts, you will find more difficulty further down the road. With all of this in mind, the key to not only completing the first month, but getting the most out of it, is accountability. That is, without a doubt, imperative to your success!

You and yourself—that is who this contract is between. Some people have workout partners, gym buddies, and the like. This is a personal event for you and should be treated as such. We discussed the importance of honesty with yourself, and that ties directly into accountability. You have to be firm and stick to the commitments your scheduling creates. Don't overreach! You are yourself and any attempt to create a workout that doesn't fit you will result in more difficulty than is necessary.

Take some time to look over the detailed workouts for the first month in Chapter 6. Note that they are not advanced in nature. Sometimes not knowing what one is getting into can cause undue stress; so, educate yourself fully on what this beginning cycle entails. The focus should be correct form and adherence to repetitions—the glitz and glamor will come later. As you learn to use your workout journal to its fullest capacity, you can jot down notes to ensure you get the most out of each session. Imagine yourself in the middle of Month 5 and you are finding a specific position more difficult than usual. Take a moment and look back on your entries from when you were learning that position. Thanks to your efforts, you can see differences in how to correctly execute the position! No more unnecessary pain, plus you get the full impact of the workout!

Without taking the time to make that first month as comprehensive as possible, you rob yourself of knowledge in the future. If it helps, continue envisioning your future self and what would best help them through. As long as you and your betterment are the focus, you are on the right path!

Looking back can often help improve the forward progress! As we previously discussed, this is most likely not your first attempt at maintaining a workout regiment. Before you go to a place of judgement—which we never do—remember that by being able to see your past mistakes or pitfalls you will be empowering for you this time around!

Take some time and list every past attempt you remember. Try to be as detailed as you can—the more you can understand about those experiences, the more you can fix! As you go through the list, you will start to see patterns emerge that will tell a clearer story about your workout history. Is there a specific place in the routine that tends to burn you out? Maybe you found that you were trying too much too soon and caused injuries. These may be difficult questions, considering that the case study is you, but that just gives you a special perspective on the matter.

As you go through your list of workouts you may find times when you want to be less than honest with yourself. This is incredibly common. After all, it is just between you and yourself. The accountability falls solely to you.

Now, take a moment and breathe...

That was an intense statement, and it is important to take it all in. While a variety of patterns cause a slowing and eventual halting of the workout itself, there tends to be a common denominator: lack of accountability. It can take many forms—letting slips in schedules go, "there wasn't enough time", "life happened", and so forth. These are all real and viable occurrences and in no way should the impact be lessened. That being said, a workout is like any other commitment in your life—it takes time, effort, and then more time again. It is for these reasons that we spent so much time on scheduling.

Your life is important, and the activities and events that fill it are just as important. When you set out on this journey, a vital part of the preparation was to be honest about if this was something that could viably be assimilated into your daily life. Considering we find ourselves here, I can assume that you did indeed make that commitment to yourself. *This* is important to you too. If it wasn't, you wouldn't be pushing yourself and making life a little uncomfortable for the sake of personal growth!

You are more than capable of accomplishing all this and more! There is no doubting yourself here!

While you are using these first thirty days to perfect habits that will lead to success, it is just as important to shift some focus to the tracking throughout. Depending on your personal preferences, the idea of keeping a detailed account of your workouts can be quite daunting. It may seem like just another added pressure to an already stressful situation. If this is the case and the subject brings about anxiety, there are several ways to combat it. Remember, the pressure you feel is real and you shouldn't feel any shame from it. By admitting that it does cause an issue, you are giving yourself the chance to solve a life problem!

Maybe you've never really been the type to keep a journal of any kind. I had a friend when I was younger who tried and tried to keep a journal just like many of us did at that age. Every single time it was the same result—a new, blank book that was filled with potential! After a few entries, the well of motivation dried up, and a few months later it was simply forgotten. It may have seemed like a small thing—a quirk rather than a real issue—but it was not something my friend was willing to let go. Rather than get frustrated time and time again, he was able to step back and see the patterns he had developed. He recognized that there was a sense of motivation inside him; it just seemed to dim as he pushed at it. When he was able to be more honest with himself, he said that he was never a big fan of a physical, written journal. It was the common choice and what our friends were able to do, so he never considered a different method to accomplish the same goal. He did *want* to keep a journal; he just needed a different medium. To this day he still uses a small, handheld voice recorder to keep his audio journal; and to this day, the lesson of that situation has stuck with me.

The overall school of thought that keeping this account of your workouts is an incredibly positive factor, for the experience allows for many forms of actually doing it. There are digital versions for those who prefer a screen, there are helpful fill-in-the-blank workbooks to accompany a routine, and then there is the classic blank notebook method. The choice of which is yours and it should be one influenced by *you alone*!

To start from the beginning, why is a Workout Journal so important? Not only is that an excellent question, but it has to be one that you answer. Just as the first thirty days will build physical habits within your workouts, this practice of tracking your progress and noting any issues will solidify habits of organization! There are many unknowns when you are undertaking something like this program, but one absolute is that you will want something to reference down the road. As you read in Chapters 2 and 3, you will be building on previous knowledge as you move through the specific workouts. More often than not, in my experience, there will come a time when an issue will arise or some stumbling block that begins to disrupt a session or more. Rather than having to start without any prior information, you will have at the ready a detailed solution guide; and it's one that you've written yourself!

Now that we've established how vital the Workout Journal will be to this process, we'll break down the different elements that make up something of such importance. We'll focus on the specific details that you will be tracking and different formats that may be helpful.

While every individual has their own preferences when it comes to the actual layout, ensure that you are meticulous in these areas:

- Accurate date/times
- Current weight

- Specific exercise

- Sets

- Repetitions

- Problem/Success notes

These variables will provide a clear and efficient account that you can, and will need to, look back on during this program. Take some time and consider how you want to proceed with the actual journaling portion. When I was making my first functional Workout Journal, I looked over some old work, essays, and such to see if I had a comfortable way to document data. I also spoke with an old friend, the same one from the Introduction, to get another perspective on journaling.

Now, it is important to remember that these are simply examples of formats that worked in certain scenarios, and they may not fit your lifestyle or schedule. That is perfectly okay! If you haven't already, take some time now to at least skim over any of your old documents to get an idea of your specific patterns. The main purpose for the examples is to get you thinking outside the box a little. Once you have a general process in mind, use the next examples to expand your thinking to see if there are any areas of improvement.

When I went through my old journal attempts, I saw a pretty basic layout with a primary focus on the changes from week to week. I was consistently thorough when it came to those details and the data was impressive. Despite that, every journal ended the same way—a slow tapering off until it just stopped. Rather than turning to a place of judgement, I took a breath and used it as a glaring error in my process that I had the opportunity to repair.

I began putting a more even focus across the board, and I realized that my notes were more spread out among the data fields. Before, I simply had a block of text below the numbers that, in all honesty, became daunting. I didn't feel like reading paragraphs to find out information and I used that negativity to justify my deteriorating motivation. I wasn't being realistic or self-aware in those moments. I am a fast paced person and I was not taking that into account. When I altered that and began jotting short, concise notes in all the data fields, it made for a quick reference guide! I had been mimicking methods that had been successful for others, but it did not translate correctly to myself. Once I was able to be honest with myself, using my past patterns as an example, the corrections were much easier to identify and implement.

My friend, however, found an entirely different set of struggles. He tried a multitude of ways to keep a Workout Journal on his own and nothing seemed to stick. Some methods had more longevity than others, but nothing foundational enough to sustain an entire program or even enough time to form any solid habits. He told me that it took a large toll on his emotional energy when it came to exercising, which was understandable considering the frustrations. As we learned earlier, you won't be fully and personally prepared for the journey unless every aspect of the program is taken into account. Maintaining the Workout Journal is just as imperative to your success as the workouts themselves! This was obvious when it came to my friend and his struggles. When he finally took the time to sit down and hold himself fully accountable, he was able to take that important breath and analyze the situation. His frustration was real, but when it became his focus there was no forward motion—no progress. Taking the time, he also reviewed old methods; even going back to his college coursework. What he discovered was that his best work and results came when he had more guidance throughout the process. That presented a large issue, as he was doing the workout individually due to scheduling and distance, so guidance was difficult to have consistently present. He considered using videos and webcam meetings to keep an outside form of guidance going, but he mentioned that he felt less motivated than ever.

This went on for several weeks and, through a few conversations, I was beginning to feel my friend's frustration. He had a tendency to take a classic approach to most things and it had usually worked out—no pun intended—but in this situation, I suggested taking a different angle to it. First, as with the entire program, it was vital that he was completely honest with himself. He always had willpower, and it was displayed in other aspects of his life. However, when it came to keeping a journal, there was difficulty. Then it was important to make sure to approach the solution from a place without judgement. He was feeling like he failed and that sense of failure was overwhelming. When there is so much negativity, it becomes increasingly difficult to overcome it when you are addressing it with the same approach. By taking a different perspective and applying new methods to the issue, you are expanding the possibility of a solution!

After a few days, my friend called me saying that he had indeed found a way that seemed to work. Intrigued, I asked what methods he ended up going with. He had gone to a local bookstore and found several journal-like guides to working out that gave him the parameters to measure ahead of time. He had never considered anything with a fill-in-theblank theme for several reasons—he admitted it just seemed juvenile, he didn't put much stock in that style to help him, and that pride had held him back from expanding his thought process to include all methods. Within a day of having this guide, he felt energized and motivated to start the routines again! Not only did this book aid him during the program, but he was able to think outside his usual parameters. He has said that now, since that experience, he approaches his life with a different attitude—one of open thought and no judgement.

That has made all the difference!

With your Workout Journal in hand, you are one step closer to being completely prepared for this incredible journey! Celebrate another milestone in this process!

Chapter Summary

- Why are the first 30 days important?

- Forms correct habits

- A chance to identify problem areas early on This is a contract between you and yourself Why are the first 30 days important **to you**? Do not try and force yourself into the wrong workout

- The workout must fit you!

- Have you reviewed Chapter 6 for details on the upcoming workouts?

- List your past workout attempts

- Why didn't you follow through on those? What patterns do you see in relation to them ending?

- Are you being truly honest with yourself?

- Have you kept a Workout Journal before?

- Did it help with the process?

- Why or why not?

- Why is a Workout Journal important?

- What kind of Workout Journal is going to be most effective **for you**?

CHAPTER FIVE

DIET AND AVOIDING PITFALLS

Shortcuts are everywhere in life and they are becoming increasingly easy to find. The unfortunate reality is that the result has become exponentially more important than the journey. We want the finish line and when opportunities arise that promise us that sooner than others—or even just sooner than our previous time—it is incredibly tempting to jump at that chance.

We previously discussed both honesty and accountability with yourself and, as with your workouts themselves, we built upon previous knowledge to enhance the current task. Without the tools you've either discovered or honed, this moment will provide much more difficulty than necessary. Some of these "easy ways to win" are built on the assumption that you are not dedicated to the *journey* and would rather get to the end. This may have been the case in the past, but I know you are committed to your workout path and not just the desire to skip ahead! You have bettered yourself and it is going to pay off!

I have always been a firm believer in education for every single situation. The more you know, the more ready you are when that part of life occurs. With this in mind, it is also important that you educate yourself on the kinds of shortcuts that could be temptations along the way.

Rather than tiptoe around an issue, I've always believed that meeting it directly is a much more effective choice. At no point in this journey should chemical alterations be brought into the mix! While for many this seems fairly obvious, there are times when a quick fix is enticing. The commercializing and ease of availability creates many problems when dealing with steroids and hormone treatments.

Despite the well-known downsides and potentially deadly side-effects of using these methods, the injuries, deaths, and various handicaps still happen because that end result takes up the entire view. The bottom line is straight-forward and should be adhered to: never use either!

During this process, as we've said before, you may decide to include a diet as well. While we do not provide one, finding a diet to fit the changes you are looking for is an excellent addition to your journey. That, and two other foundational variables will help you not only get the most out of this program, but form habits that will last!

Rest

The importance of rest cannot be overstated! In our fast paced lifestyle, there is barely a moment to take three deep breaths, let alone get as much sleep as we need. You know the facts and you've known them for most of your life: 7-8 hours of sleep! The first thoughts you just had were most likely a list of reasons why that amount of sleep is rarely possible, if ever! That is a viable and real reason—life does not stop when you begin a program or make a change. Just like we made sure the importance of proper scheduling was stated, it is just as vital that you see proper sleep as an absolute as well.

By following the program, you will be taking time and effort to schedule your workouts to not only fit into your life, but improve it as well. This same method *must* be applied to your sleep schedule. You most likely have not made major alterations to your schedule in order to accommodate sleep; or if you have, they have been minimal. This time around, the changes will be real and lasting! Take some time now to go over the potential schedule you've been creating for the coming months and jot down how much sleep you think you will get each night. Remember, be honest! It does no good to make it look impressive on paper when you know the reality is not. Once you have seen the sleep you assume you will get laid out, begin finding adjustments you can make to add more sleep each night. There will not be a sudden opening that magically gives the time to keep your schedule as it is; there *will be* changes made!

Before moving on to the next foundational aspect, continue focusing on your sleep schedule. It is going to take some tinkering, so it is perfectly fine to bookmark this spot and finish before continuing.

Eating Habits

Just like every person will have a different approach to working out, the same applies to your eating habits during the program. Adapting to a new diet can require just as much effort as the workout regiment, but will also yield wonderful results. It is up to you how much you plan to alter your current diet and it largely depends on, again, your ability to be honest and direct with yourself. Take into consideration your current diet and general food habits when making this decision.

There are different approaches to creating a diet depending on the results you are looking for. Some people are looking to bulk up while they go through the program, while others prefer a more balanced approach across a larger range of varieties. The world of food and exercise are directly linked, and we'll cover the basics regarding the do's and don't's of a calisthenics diet. To help you create your own custom plan based around what works best for your schedule and budget, we'll cover two possible, specific diets—one for bulk and one based around calisthenics in general. You should feel free to consider this a buffet of knowledge. Pick through, find the things that will fit your journey, and commit to those changes!

One of the best things about calisthenics and its relationship to food is that it isn't complicated to follow! While there are detailed diets that relate very well to workouts—and we'll go over some of them—when you break it down, there are a few simple rules to follow; but the first and most important is that common sense will solve most questions you have. You already know most of what you need to know! It seems too easy, doesn't it?

One of the most common pitfalls people encounter when they begin creating a diet plan is that they have to relearn everything. This just isn't true! While there are some complexities that we will also cover, what you have learned about basic health and what foods are "good and bad" for you translate directly to this process! You have the control and are more than capable of creating a working diet for this journey!

Here are a few tips to get the ideas flowing! Take some time to review these before you start creating the actual plan.

- Take the time to get a better idea about where your current diet is. Over the course of a week—or whatever time frame will give you an idea of your patterns—keep track of your diet. Be as detailed as you would like. Remember, all of this information is for *your benefit!*

- Make notes where you see areas of improvement. After you have collected that data, review it to give yourself a wider view of your possible problem areas.

- Again, because it cannot be overstated, the more honest you are with yourself, the better chance you have to make real progress!

- *"In everything, moderation."* By keeping this mantra in mind, you will already have an excellent guide to beginning the alterations to your diet. This simple rule applies to every part of life, but is especially true in regards to what you eat and drink. When you identify your problem areas in regards to food, moderate where you see excess. The most common excess is sugar, for example, in the daily lives of the average adult. By taking the correct steps early in the process, you will magnify your results and solidify those good habits!

- I really do not like when a program or diet refuses to take budget into account. It is a reality of life and should be taken seriously. While an ideal diet would consist almost entirely of organic foods, that is not always a possibility. Instead, find a few foods you enjoy that you can replace with an organic substitute—a few small changes will go a long way!

- A great place to start is with your fruit and vegetables. Find a local farmers' market or produce shop where you can discuss organic options with the growers themselves!

- When it comes to nutrition for a workout, nothing is more useful than protein! No matter what changes you make in your diet, it is imperative that the addition or increase of protein be top of the list. You can't replace or substitute for protein, especially when undertaking a program such as this. Depending on your personal preferences, you can supplement this with meat or another choice of yours.

- If you are including meat in your diet, to the best of your ability, focus on grass-fed animals and wildcaught fish products. You may experience the same budgetary restrictions when doing this; so again, focus on altering what you are able to. It is recommended to include between 0.6 grams to 1 gram of protein for every pound of body weight. As long as you are getting the necessary protein you are making the correct decisions!

- If you prefer not to include meat or fish, there are still plenty of sources to get that all-important protein from—tofu, edamame, chickpeas, lentils, hempseed, quinoa, or soy milk, just to name a few. By adding or increasing your intake of these products you will be taking the right steps towards your goal of betterment.

A vital part of the diet that isn't always addressed in these sections is the importance of hydration. This may seem redundant and unnecessary since everyone knows to drink water, right? That is partly true. Every person may *know* to drink water and properly hydrate, and yet we all know that few people actually follow through. It could be a matter of personal preference or just something you never really thought about. There are many times that common sense subjects such as this are incredibly interesting, considering the assumptions behind it. If everyone knows how to stay hydrated then everyone must be doing it, right? Wrong again, unfortunately.

Hydration is absolutely something you should include as part of your diet. Don't assume that you will just fall in line along the way and become a master of hydration; this simply isn't realistic. However, by putting that effort in and changing it from an assumed subject to a discussed subject, you give yourself all the power and possibility!

Do some research into the subject. What kind of hydration is recommended? Is water the only suitable choice? Are the water-energy additives harmful? These are exactly the kinds of questions you should be asking. Don't remove your personal preferences from the equation, as it is important to enjoy as much as you can. There are many more options than ever before to allow hydration to take a form you are more familiar with.

There are actually other ways than simply water to ensure you are properly hydrated. Did you know that?

Adding oatmeal to your diet will actually provide a great source of electrolytes and help aid your natural hydration!

If you are going for a diet that includes pasta, possibly consider replacing your usual pasta with a zucchini noodle. The zucchini noodle can be over 90% water and an incredibly fulfilling addition to any diet.

Choosing a low-sugar fruit smoothie option for a small snack can add that midday burst of energy you needed. Fruit smoothies, when the sugar isn't the main ingredient, are an excellent source of water and allow you that fun side as well.

Do you have frozen fruit? While fruit in general provides excellent hydration, freezing them can, once thawed, create even more chances to increase your health and continue bettering your life!

Be flexible in all your thinking, even on how to get the right amount of water. You'll probably be surprised by the options available to you with just a little research!

These two foundational parts—proper sleep and diet—of the workout journey will be invaluable tools as you move forward! They are more than just variables in the process. By maintaining the habits you are learning here, you will have gained invaluable knowledge and trust between yourself and the depth of this program. There is a third and final foundational principle before you get to The Ultimate Calisthenics Workout in the next chapter.

The Workout

We have covered a wide array of tools, techniques, and troubleshooting that will be vital during the program—the Workout Journal, self-awareness, honesty, and accountability of self, to name a few. While these are all important, we broke it down into three key factors that, when customized to your schedule and adhered to, will be foundational paths to success! We reviewed both proper sleep habits and diet, but the third is one that you have actually been learning along the way this entire time: the workout itself!

There is no middle ground for this subject. As we discussed earlier, many workout routines have a singular approach; and even if they touch on a variety of areas, it is from a surface perspective and rarely offers in-depth solutions or tools to better oneself. When considering the possible variables that would help build this program, it became apparent very early on that by only adhering to one or two of the three keys, you create a problem area rather than solving one. The design includes all three in order to ensure the changes are lasting and the altered life you have formed will not falter.

This cannot be overemphasized! While other sections are more of a buffet-style that allows you to pick and choose, this requires a stricter adherence. You *must* give the same focus to sleep, diet, and workout. An imbalance will prove incredibly disruptive down the line, even if you don't see it right now. By taking the time early into the program and solidifying the perspectives you will be coming from, you are making that all-important investment in yourself. That's one that will certainly pay huge dividends! By beginning from a place of detail and focusing on changing your habits, you have readied yourself for the challenges ahead. To truly bring about change—*real change*—in your life, it takes all three factors! If you allow that honesty to yourself, then it has become apparent why past attempts had faltered and burned out. We've been able to look at these reasons not as failures, but as chances to get better and learn where our life alterations needed to happen.

Most programs have a tendency to put a disproportionate focus on the workouts and leave the other two factors on the backburner. By doing this, the habits you develop are lopsided. You'll find yourself trying to address proper rest when you're halfway through the second month, or you'll become stressed by struggling to alter your diet without putting the proper time and thought into it before reaching the halfway point. It's harder to change the rules when you're in the middle of the game. This just means to build those habits the correct, balanced way. Empower yourself for those difficult moments down the road—ones you probably haven't even considered! The first two keys give you the extra energy and time to give your effort where it should be: your workouts.

Every day of the program—and maintaining it afterwards— is built on reminding yourself of those three factors. This can be made easier by putting it into the form of three questions that are part of beginning your day:

1. Do I feel rested?

2. Will my diet for today help me succeed?

3. Have I familiarized myself with my workouts for today?

Everyone knows that starting your day correctly will help create a more balanced and aware daily life. These three baseline questions to yourself will give you a readiness right out of the gate! Also, take this chance to customize your *Readiness Questions* so you feel motivated and excited about the new day before you! I speak out loud when I ask myself these questions in the morning, others have a motivational reminder beside the bed or in the bathroom, and some find entirely new ways of going about it. The bottom line is that up to now you have found ways to make this journey truly yours—a custom path that does not disrupt your life, but rather flows through and enriches it. Do the same here.

That was a large and important section to cover there. Do you feel like you absorbed it all? There is a massive amount of information in this program, and each piece is designed to bring the best out of you. If there is ever a time you seem confused or less than sure of why or how to implement one of these betterment chances, take the time to keep investing in yourself. Reread sections if needed, or sometimes hearing a section out loud alters the way you take in that information. The bottom line is to not worry about changing things up. Flexibility where it can be utilized will make the entire experience all the more personal.

When dealing with the possible problems and pitfalls that come with a workout commitment, there is still one important thing to cover: where you went wrong before.

Take that all-important breath and return to that judgement free place. There are no attacks here, simply direct confrontations. You've taken time in previous sections to think upon and even list your past workout attempts in order to identify problem patterns. We were able to skim and collect data that has proved invaluable! In the best method for your productivity, single out the specific problem areas you encountered in the past and this time don't avoid detail. These pinpointed problem areas will lead to what we call your *Problem Journey*. Just as this process is a journey of betterment, the past times it just didn't work ended up creating a journey as well—one of negativity and a lack of confidence. You have probably been harder on yourself than you needed to be; and as that compiled, it weighed you down more and more until the mere idea of starting a routine up again carries no motivation. It simply brings back memories of not following through.

Here is a vital place in your journey where you can alter the perspective you naturally take. As you go over the list you made and map out the ways you hit the road blocks and difficulties, be sure to notice why you ended up stopping altogether. Now compare that to the ongoing notes you've kept in regards to the positive steps you recognized during this time around. You'll find that, more often than not, you are solving old issues you have had without even realizing it.

Many people starting out include others in their routines. Really take a look and see if this occurred and did it bring about distraction or worse? That is not a judgement on yourself or the partner(s) you chose for that workout. Some people work better when the accountability is with them and another person, but this system is designed to nurture honesty with yourself.

Perhaps you let early schedule disruptions fill you with a feeling of being overwhelmed. You may see now that you've managed to take the disruptions in stride and alter your schedule to smoothly keep your responsibilities and still work out.

On the other hand, maybe your issue was pushing way too hard in the beginning and you strained yourself, gave yourself extended time to recover, and just never started up again. Well, this time you were able to be honest with yourself and crafted a schedule with your physical limits in mind.

Another possible reason is what I call "the allure of equipment"! The amount of unused exercise equipment sitting in rooms across the country is staggering. If every person who bought a treadmill or stationary bike followed through on those commitments, there would be no health issues regarding working out! Unfortunately, this is far from the case. The promise that tends to come with these machines is usually overstated and comes with a slew of fine print; and nothing good ever comes filled with fine print! As you learned prior, you will be relying on you and your bodyweight to be all the equipment you need. A little imagination, and suddenly you don't need some elaborate mechanism to inspire you—you have become your own muse!

No matter what the problem is, you will keep finding solutions to issues and pitfalls you had encountered previously as you continue through the program! These are just the beginnings to the positive changes you are well on your way to bringing about!

Chapter Summary

- Are you focused on the results or the journey?

- Avoid bringing chemicals into the mix?

- Hormones and steroids are harmful and will not create a positive result

- How much sleep do you get per night?

- Do you feel rested or energized?

- Does your schedule reflect a balanced focus on sleep as well?

- Are you still being honest with yourself?

- What changes need to be made to your diet? Will you be using a specific diet in collaboration with the program?

- Is your diet currently where you want it to be? Have you taken your budget into account when planning your dietary changes?

- Are you starting your day with the three *Readiness Questions*?

- Do I feel rested?

- Will my diet for today help me succeed? Have I familiarized myself with my workouts for today?

- Are you holding yourself accountable daily?

CHAPTER SIX

THE ULTIMATE CALISTHENICS WORKOUT

As you've no doubt noticed, there is a great deal of focus on celebrating moments and goals in this program. This is a big one! You have gone through some very honest times to get to this point, and for that you should be incredibly proud of yourself! There were moments in which you were asked to be very direct and self-aware, all of which you took on and not only utilized, but have now truly prepared you for the rest of this journey!

The key to your progress up to now has been preparedness in all aspects. By taking the time to increase your self-awareness, you have built an armory of knowledge all before even lifting a finger! You should be familiar with the upcoming workouts in a general sense; and thanks to your adherence to scheduling, you enter this phase without the worry of the unknown.

These are the last few moments before the actual physical portion will begin; so take the time, as we do, to review your preparedness to this point.

In Chapters 1 and 2 we gave you a brief overview of what you could expect from the workout routines and the schedule you would be keeping. Now the program will be fleshed out and you will be able to start this incredible journey!

Before you move ahead and begin the actual routines, take some time and review the tips and foundational keys for your workouts. When you start that first exercise it should be from a place of peace and preparedness. Any feelings of being unsure should not be ignored. By now, you have become pretty comfortable with self-honesty, so do a self-review now to see if anything seems off or is a lingering bother. Maybe there was one day in your schedule that just seemed overly stressful to maintain, or you need to do a check on groceries to ensure you can follow your chosen diet without distress. As discussed, these are all real and important aspects of this journey and should be recognized and fixed.

There is no need to rush through these last self checks. It is much more beneficial to address any possible pitfalls now rather than attempting to adjust when it could have been prevented.

You know yourself, so don't over-analyze the situation. If you feel comfortable and ready, which you certainly are, then you are welcomed to The Ultimate Calisthenics Workout!

Month 1 - Full Body 101

Here are the exercises, form, and methods you will be doing during the first four-week cycle:

Running In Place [Works the quads, calf muscles, hamstrings, glutes, and hip flexors]: Use a steady pace. Knees maintain a smooth motion. This is an excellent warmup. Control your breathing, avoiding sharp breaths or halting breathing. Try to avoid jarring motions when your feet strike the floor. Keep the movements smooth to avoid undue pressure on your joints.

Squats [Works the abdominals, calves, glutes, quads, and hamstrings]: Use your legs, not your back. Feet slider wider than your hips. As you go into the squat position, work your hips backwards into the sit. Keep both of your entire feet on the ground. To stand, push from your heels and straighten your legs. Avoid jerking motions; instead aim for smooth movement.

Push Ups [Works the pectorals, shoulders, triceps, and abdominals]: For an effective push up, your form is much more important than speed or quantity. View your body as a plank—unbending from heel to head. Hands shoulder-width apart. As you begin the push up, keep your elbows at a 45 degree angle from your body. Adjust for comfort. Lower to about an inch from the ground and, in a smooth motion, extend your elbows to push back to the starting position.

Knee Raises [Works the hamstrings, quads, glutes, and calves]: Lay flat on your back with your arms to your side and your legs straightened and together. In one smooth motion, pull both knees from the floor towards your chest. Exhale as you let your legs straighten back to lying straight.

Chair Dips [Works the triceps]: The preferred method is to use a **solid** chair for this exercise, but a bottom stair or a raised, level area will work just as well. So long as you ensure your form and motions are correct, you will get the most out of this exercise!

Sit normally on a **sturdy** chair (or desired option). Grip the front of the chair on either outer side of your legs. Shift yourself up onto your hands and shift your body forward. Your feet can scoot forward to help you, knees bent. When you are hovering, lower yourself by bending your elbows, breathing in. Exhale as you push yourself back up. If you feel uneasy, go back to sitting position and try a better angle.

Follow this guide for sets and repetitions:

- **Running In Place:** 3 minutes

- **Squats:** 2 sets of 10

- **Push Ups:** 3 sets of 5

- **Knee Raises:** 3 sets of 5

- **Chair Dips:** 3 sets of 5

If you find that you need more of a challenge—give yourself at least one session before deciding—you can add a set to each routine. Track how you feel from this increase and ensure that you are not pushing yourself too hard. As this is the first month, avoid putting unneeded stress on yourself. You are laying a foundation here and by expecting a journey rather than a sprint, you can better prepare yourself for the basics you have learned here.

This is the first month and your focus needs to be on correct form and following the guide laid out in Chapter 4. As a reminder, here is your schedule guideline for **Full Body 101**:

- Day 1: Full Body 101
- Day 2: Rest
- Day 3: Full Body 101
- Day 4: Rest
- Day 5: Full Body 101
- Day 6: Rest
- Day 7: Full Body 101

Month 2 - Full Body 102

This month will give focus to a wider range of muscle groups. Month 1 began giving you the tools to create a solid foundation; and in this month, you will be building upwards and adding in more impact on core muscle groups.

Here are the exercises you will be doing during this four-week cycle:

Running In Place [Works the quads, calf muscles, hamstrings, glutes, and hip flexors]: See **Full Body 101 Lunges [Works the hamstrings, glutes, and quads]:** Stand feet shoulder-width apart. Taking a large step forward, ensure your heel lands first. Lower your body until your lower knee barely touches the ground. Push back from the heel to go back into standing form.

Decline Push Ups [Works the upper chest, pectorals]: For this exercise, the best method is to use a low stool or bottom step. Use the same proper push up form that you learned in **Full Body 101** but with your feet up on the raised surface. Lower yourself in push up form, straightening your elbows to rise back up.

Standing Leg Raises [Works the abdominals and hip flexors]: Standing feet shoulder-width apart, lift one leg straight forward and up in a slow, direct motion. Hold for a 2-count, exhale while lowering the leg to the ground. Avoid bending your knee at any time during the exercise.

Reverse Row [Works the trapezius, biceps, and back]: This is an exercise that will be modified later on, so ensure your basic form is correct.

For this exercise the best way is to be underneath a **sturdy** table. The height should be 6-10 inches from the tips of your fingers, lying underneath, arm pointed upwards. Once you have a **strong** table or similar surface, position yourself underneath shoulders aligned with the table edge above you.

Raise your arms and bend at the waist upwards until you can firmly grip the edge of the table. Using a surface with a low slip-possibility is best. Your body is your counterweight as you bend your elbows, pulling yourself up towards the table. Breathe in while going up, exhaling while straightening your elbows back to original form. Be cautious not to drop yourself to avoid injury!

Follow this guide for sets and repetitions:

- **Running In Place:** 5 minutes

- **Lunges:** 2 sets of 10

- **Decline Push Ups:** 3 sets of 5

- **Standing Leg Raises:** 3 sets of 10

- **Reverse Row:** 3 sets of 5

If you find that you need more of a challenge—give yourself at least one session before deciding—you can add a set to each routine. Track how you feel from this increase and ensure you are not pushing yourself too hard.

For the second month you will be following this schedule guideline:

- <u>Day 1</u>: Full Body 102
- <u>Day 2</u>: Rest
- <u>Day 3</u>: Full Body 102
- <u>Day 4</u>: Rest
- <u>Day 5</u>: Full Body 102
- <u>Day 6</u>: Rest
- <u>Day 7</u>: Full Body 102

Month 3 - Intermediate 101

As you progress further into the program, take note of any tightness or strain into pain that you have felt. You may need to incorporate a minute or two of stretching to help with those more complex routines. If you do feel that pull of tightness, do not try and push past it. You may hyperextend or tear a muscle. Avoid injury at all costs. Stretching is an easy way to avoid these pitfalls.

Here are the exercises you will be doing for the next four-week cycle:

Running In Place [Works the quads, calf muscles, hamstrings, glutes, and hip flexors]: See **Full Body 101**

Duck Walk [Works the thighs, lower legs, and glutes]: Stand feet shoulder-width apart. Lower yourself into a squat and then lower your buttocks so your knees are bent in front of you. Keep your feet flat on the ground. If you are having balance problems, use your arms to the sides and front to help. Staying as low as you can—avoid overextending your knees and lower back—step forward, and in a waddle-like motion, step with the other foot.

Calf Raises [Works the hamstrings and calves]: On a step or raised area, stand with your heels off the edge of the step (or desired option) and the rest of your feet flat on the step. Inhaling, raise your heels up until you are on, or as close to as is comfortable, your tiptoes. Exhale as you lower your heels down until your feet are back to the flat, original form.

Be aware of your surroundings when doing this exercise as you will be facing up the stairs, if that is your desired option. Avoid injury!

Higher Decline Push Ups [Works the upper chest, pectorals]: You will be using the same push up form that you have learned to this point. Use a raised area that is higher than the one used in **Decline Push Ups**. Perform the correct form for a push up to complete the sets.

Back-Bridge Push Ups [Works the hip abductors, glutes, hamstrings, and erector spinae (length of the spinal cord)]: Unlike most of the other exercises you have done to this point, there is extra caution to be taken when approaching this particular one. Your flexibility has most likely improved by this point in the program, but this specific angle and form may be stretching in a way you are not used to. Because of this, take time to build up to full form. Do not be discouraged if your initial, and even first few, attempts are not as refined or with the same ease that you have with the other exercises.

To start, lie flat on the ground and stretch your arms and legs away from your body. You should feel the stretch in your joints. Now with your torso still flat, shift your legs until your knees are pointing up and your feet are flat on the ground. Do the same with your arms—elbows pointing up, palms as flat as possible.

Again, this seems extremely complex; but after a few times, the form will be more understood and your muscles will loosen.

From that position, push from your palms and feet, arching your back in the air. Do not push yourself past a point of pain. It should burn, not hurt. Once you reach your apex, exhale as you lower your torso back to the ground in a smooth motion.

Follow this guide for sets and repetitions:

- **Running In Place:** 5 minutes
- **Duck Walk:** Forward 10 steps, backwards 10 steps.
- 2 reps
- **Calf Raises:** 3 sets of 5
- **High Decline Push Ups:** 3 sets of 5
- **Back-Bridge Push Ups:** 2 sets of 5

If you find that you need more of a challenge—give yourself at least one session before deciding—you can add a set to each routine. Track how you feel from this increase and ensure you are not pushing yourself too hard.

Here is your schedule guideline for the third month:

Low-Impact Schedule:

- Day 1: Intermediate 101

- <u>Day 2</u>: Rest

- <u>Day 3</u>: Intermediate 101

- <u>Day 4</u>: Rest

- <u>Day 5</u>: Intermediate 101

- <u>Day 6</u>: Rest

- <u>Day 7</u>: Intermediate 101

High-Impact Schedule:

- <u>Day 1</u>: Intermediate 101

- <u>Day 2</u>: Rest

- <u>Day 3</u>: Intermediate 101

- <u>Day 4</u>: Light Running

- <u>Day 5</u>: Intermediate 101

- <u>Day 6</u>: Light Running

- <u>Day 7</u>: Rest

DUCK WALKS

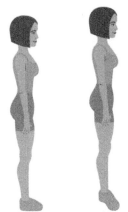

CALF RAISES

Month 4 - Muscle Impact 101

For the next four-week cycle, here are the exercises you will be doing:

Running In Place [Works the quads, calf muscles, hamstrings, glutes, and hip flexors]: See **Full Body 101**

Horizontal Jump [Works the hip flexors, glutes, quads, abs, calves, and hamstrings]: Stand feet shoulder-width apart. With your arms up, stretched, rise onto the balls of your feet. As you bring your arms behind you, rock slightly forward, then raise your arms as you stand. Repeat several times to prepare. Arms, behind, rock slightly, then drive your feet down and push to jump, your arms moving forward. Make sure to land flat-footed in a smooth motion.

Mountain Climbers [Works the glutes, shoulders, triceps, full legs, and abdominals]: Use the plank-like form to begin —back straight. Bend one knee inwards, towards your front. In a smooth motion, bring the leg back and return to original form. Bend the other knee inwards, and in the same smooth motion, return to form.

Reverse Row Dips [Works the trapezius, biceps, and back]: Using the same method in form you used for **Reverse Row**. This time reverse the form so your head is the only thing under the table, your legs and torso out from underneath. Reach up and reverse grip the table edge. Bend at the waist until you have a firm hold. Like a pull-up, keep your body straight as you pull yourself up (inhaling) and lower yourself (exhaling) in a smooth motion. Take caution to not drop yourself to avoid injury!

Reverse Row Leg Raises [Works the trapezius, biceps, hamstrings, glutes, and back]: Use the same reverse form from **Reverse Row Dips**. Rather than lifting yourself, grip the edge of the table, focusing on your abs and core, raise one straight leg and hold for a 5-count. Release and lower your leg in a smooth motion.

Follow this guide for sets and repetitions:

Running In Place: 5 minutes

Horizontal Jump: 3 sets of 5

Mountain Climbers: 3 minutes

Reverse Row Dips: 3 sets of 5

Reverse Row Leg Raises: 3 sets of 5, alternating legs, 3 sets per leg

If you find that you need more of a challenge—give yourself at least one session before deciding—you can add a set to each routine. Track how you feel from this increase and ensure you are not pushing yourself too hard. Here is your schedule guideline for the fourth month:

- <u>Day 1</u>: Muscle Impact 101
- <u>Day 2</u>: Rest
- <u>Day 3</u>: Muscle Impact 101
- <u>Day 4</u>: Rest
- <u>Day 5</u>: Muscle Impact 101
- <u>Day 6</u>: Rest
- <u>Day 7</u>: Light Running

Month 5 - Muscle Impact 102

For this month, you will begin interspersing previous routines into your schedule. While you *will* be learning new exercises, we will be referring to older routines to help continue your amazing forward progress! Make sure to take the time and review the exercises and form you used for the routines we are doing again. You have kept excellent notes and this is exactly why!

For the fifth month four-week cycle here are the exercises, you will be doing:

Running In Place [Works the quads, calf muscles, hamstrings, glutes, and hip flexors]: See **Full Body 101**

Jumping Jacks [Works the calves, glutes, and thighs]: You are probably familiar with this exercise. Rather than just trying to get through it, focus on the form and the smooth motions. As a child, there was probably flailing involved, so let's get it right this time around!

Vertical Jump [Works the hamstrings, quads, calves, and glutes]: Start from a standing position, legs shoulder-width apart. Stretch slightly by lowering yourself slowly into a squat, then back to standing. After repeating this a few times, you are ready for the jump. Lower yourself from the standing position a level slightly lower than a typical squat. You should feel the stretch in your thighs. Pressing from the balls of your feet, spring upwards, pointing your toes as you jump. Keep a smooth motion, avoid locking your knees, and avoid any jerking motion. You may also want to draw shorter breaths— avoid this by breathing fully during stretches.

Reverse Row Leg Raises [Works the trapezius, biceps, hamstrings, glutes, and back]: See **Muscle Impact 101**

Chin Hold Reverse Row [Works the trapezius, biceps, and back]: For this exercise, you will be using the same, under the-table form from **Reverse Rows**. This is an advanced version of that routine, so ensure that your grip is non-slip and you are using extreme caution to avoid injury!

With your shoulders and head out from under the table, your torso and legs underneath, bend at the waist until you can firmly grip the edge of the table. Like in **Reverse Rows**, you will pull yourself upwards; but the goal with this exercise is to get your chin above the table edge. Do not push yourself past pain or if you feel unsure! Work your way until you find that level of comfort. Once you reach the apex, hold for 2-3 seconds, then exhale as you lower yourself to the ground.

Follow this guide for sets and repetitions:

- **Running In Place:** 5 minutes

- **Jumping Jacks:** 3 minutes

- **Vertical Jump:** 3 sets of 5

- **Reverse Row Leg Raises:** 3 sets of 5, alternating legs, 3 sets per leg

- **Chin Hold Reverse Row:** 3 sets of 5

If you find that you need more of a challenge—give yourself at least one session before deciding—you can add a set to each routine. Track how you feel from this increase and ensure you are not pushing yourself too hard.

Here is your schedule guideline for the fifth month:

- <u>Day 1</u>: Muscle Impact 102

- <u>Day 2</u>: Intermediate 101

- <u>Day 3</u>: Rest

- <u>Day 4</u>: Muscle Impact 102

- <u>Day 5</u>: Intermediate 101

- <u>Day 6</u>: Rest

- <u>Day 7</u>: Light Running

Jumping Jacks

Month 6 - The Ultimate Calisthenics Workout

Here we are—the last month in the program! You should be both ecstatic and incredibly proud of yourself! Not only did you accomplish physical goals, but you have learned invaluable tools that are sure to stay with you long after you complete the final month!

Before you begin this last four-week cycle, take the time to do what we do best: review! By going back and seeing the progress you've made, you will get a broader, fuller understanding of just how much your journey has changed. You will be referring back to various routines that have made up your schedule to this point, as well as adding one day of high intensity!

The main addition to this final month is The Ultimate Calisthenics workout. This is a compilation of various muscle impact exercises that will give you that big push. You are more than ready and capable for this next step!

For the sixth month, here are the exercises you will be doing:

The Ultimate Calisthenics Workout

- 5 minutes Running In Place

- **[Works the quads, calf muscles, hamstrings, glutes, and hip flexors]** 5 Reverse Row Leg Raises

- **[Works the trapezius, biceps, hamstrings, glutes, and back]** 10 Reverse Rows

- **[Works the trapezius, biceps, and back]** 15 Push Ups

- **[Works the pectorals, shoulders, triceps, and abdominals]** 15 Decline Push Ups

- **[Works the upper chest, pectorals]**

- 10 Squats

- **[Works the abdominals, calves, glutes, quads, and hamstrings]**

- 3 minutes Running in Place

The first time you go through this workout, take some extra time to ensure you do not rush! The combination of these workouts bring about the best results, so the more detailed you are in form and movement the better! Be patient with yourself and focus on the individual sets rather than the entire routine.

As with **Muscle Impact 102**, you will be using previous routines blended into your schedule. It is a higher impact schedule than the previous five months, so if at any time you need to take a moment, do that! You need to feel comfortable with the motions, and you have given yourself all the tools to succeed. Because many of these exercises are ones you have done in past months, you can refer back to your Workout Journal at any time to ensure you get the most efficiency out of every movement.

Here is your schedule guideline for the sixth, and final, month:

- <u>Day 1</u>: Muscle Impact 101
- <u>Day 2</u>: Muscle Impact 102
- <u>Day 3</u>: Rest
- <u>Day 4</u>: Muscle Impact 102
- <u>Day 5</u>: Light Running
- <u>Day 6</u>: The Ultimate Calisthenics Workout

- <u>Day 7</u>: Rest

At this moment you should be basking in exhilaration! What you just accomplished is something that should be celebrated continuously and is a goal you've had in sight for six months! You took on a commitment and, for maybe the first time in your life, you have followed through on a workout routine. Say that out loud to yourself, even if it is just once:

"I have successfully completed a workout routine!"

The first time I got to say that felt incredible! There is something to be said about the power behind vocalizing a moment. As you finished your last rep and tidied up your area, it may not have hit you. Even when you turned out the light and walked away, it still might have barely registered. For me, it hit when I sat down to fill in my workout summary for the day and I saw the date and the schedule; and for the first time, there wasn't a next page. That is a big moment.

You may feel intimidated by that last statement, and it is a scary moment as well. There is no next page. It holds such a sense of finality that I am sure you feel the need to shift that perspective. Yes, something has finished and it *should* be recognized. However, it is not as much a closed door as you entering an entirely new hallway with a brand new set of doors. By completing this program and gaining the knowledge and ability that you have, life itself has actually been altered for you as well. Six months ago, your mindset and thought process were drastically different than the positive, confident, healthier you that exists now.

Before you completely move forward and begin the cool down portion of the program you, should take another moment. Thank your past self. I always prefer these moments to be vocal—it's between you and you after all—but your methods have worked for you to this point, so do not begin doubting them now. However you go about it, just thank that past version of yourself. It is easy to be hard on that person because you have the hindsight and experience to recognize the issues that need to be bettered, but you were not less of a person! In fact, you were an incredibly strong version of yourself because, despite being on that side of the spectrum, you took the step and began the process! There was no absolute assurance or magic ball to see what the future held; but you trusted and kept faith throughout! That, in a time in history where speed and results are the sole focus, you were patient and let the journey create growth. It is because of all this that your past self deserves your thanks and appreciation. From this point forward, because of that decision, you are better and shall continue to progress to heights that you can't even imagine yet.

"Thank you, past self."

Chapter Summary

- Have you taken the time and reviewed the tips and foundational keys for success?

- What day is going to begin your workout schedule?

- What muscle groups will be worked on in Month 1?

- Month 1 - Full Body 101

- Running In Place - 3 minutes

- Squats - 2 sets of 10

- Push Ups - 3 sets of 5

- Knee Raises - 3 sets of 5

- Chair Dips - 3 sets of 5

- Review your schedule for Full Body 101

- What muscle groups will be worked on in Month 2?

- Month 2 - Full Body 102

- Running In Place - 5 minutes

- Lunges - 2 sets of 10

- Decline Push Ups - 3 sets of 5

- Standing Leg Raises - 3 sets of 10

- Reverse Row - 3 sets of 5

- Review your schedule for Full Body 102

- What muscle groups will be worked on in Month 3?

- Month 3 - Intermediate 101

- Running In Place - 5 minutes

- Duck Walk - Forward 10 steps, backwards 10 steps,

- 2 reps

- Calf Raises - 3 sets of 5

- Higher Decline Push Ups - 3 sets of 5

- Back-Bridge Push Ups - 2 sets of 5 Review your schedule for Intermediate 101 Did you choose High or Low Impact? Review the first 3 months of progress What changes can you see so far?

- How has your sleep improved?

- What aspect of your personal life has improved the most?

- What muscle groups will be worked on in Month 4?

- Month 4 - Muscle Impact 101

- Running In Place - 5 minutes

- Horizontal Jump - 3 sets of 5

- Mountain Climbers - 3 minutes

- Reverse Row Dips - 3 sets of 5

- Reverse Row Leg Raises - 3 sets of 5, alternating legs, 3 sets per leg

- Review your schedule for Muscle Impact 101 Have you previewed the changes from last month into Month 5?

- Are there any schedule changes you are uneasy about?

- What actions are you taking to rectify those issues?

- What muscle groups will be worked on in Month 5?

- Month 5 - Muscle Impact 102

- Running In Place - 5 minutes

- Jumping Jacks - 3 minutes

- Vertical Jump - 3 sets of 5

- Reverse Row Leg Raises - 3 sets of 5, alternating legs, 3 sets per leg

- Chin Hold Reverse Row - 3 sets of 5

- Preview the final month to recognize and address any uneasiness

- All muscle groups will be worked in Month 6

- Month 6 - The Ultimate Calisthenics Workout

- Running In Place - 5 minutes

- 5 Reverse Row Leg Raises

- 10 Reverse Rows

- 15 Push Ups

- 15 Decline Push Ups

- 10 Squats

- Running In Place - 3 minutes

- Are you rushing through The Ultimate Calisthenics Workout?

- Are you maintaining focus on your form despite the increase in intensity and impact?

CHAPTER SEVEN

WHEN PROBLEMS ARISE

As much as we would like a perfect world, the reality is that life becomes difficult sometimes. Unexpected events can disrupt any routine or commitment and it is not just an excuse, but a valid reason for that disruption. It may seem like a harsh word, but it describes what occurs quite perfectly—it is a hiccup, those roadblocks we have been discussing. An issue or scheduling problem can easily become a distraction, and from there it can take hold and begin throwing off your daily life and the new changes that come with it and become a disruption. It is vital to address these issues as they arise because, faster than you think, a disruption will lead to a complete derailment of the entire program.

Issue into distraction, distraction into disruption, disruption leads to derailment. The ability to repair these lies with you!

This journey that you have undertaken will be no different and, as such, is subject to possible distraction that creates the potential for disruption. Rather than press onward without truly taking that into consideration, let's take a moment and discuss the possible upcoming issues.

You have created a welcoming environment that is founded in honesty. There has been much asked of you and you have not only risen to the challenges, but excelled. Because of this, you have a distinct advantage when approaching problems in this program. When an issue comes about, rather than imploding or reacting with sudden impulse, you can breathe and know that this is not unexpected. These difficulties that derailed your past attempts are now dwarfed by perspective and trust. That is a valuable weapon against doubt! You wield personal experience and a plethora of knowledge at the ready and you enter each day and each session with readiness.

First and foremost, you must approach this section with the same lack of judgement that you have kept thus far. The subject of troubleshooting can bring up complications in that area, but know that you have a full handle on this! You've picked up tools that you can put to use whenever these road bumps occur. You have thanked your past self and from that you can continue to pull away from seeing that past in a negative light. The lack of judgement doesn't just apply to the present, but rather it extends backwards and forwards. Forgive yourself for the errors and derailments in the past, and trust that you will continue forward in that same vein of thought.

Scheduling

The most common instance where distraction can be planted and grow into the routine withering away is scheduling. By this point, you should be fairly protective of your schedule. We spent a considerable amount of time making sure the importance of proper scheduling is given to this commitment, and it was for a very good reason. Armed with a well thought out and functional schedule, one that incorporates and promotes fluidity in the face of adversity, you are multiple steps ahead of every situation. Each time you move forward in the same spirit you strengthen that resolve!

Your life is a daily whirl of activity and events, so timing and properly blocking out days plays a huge role in ensuring you can succeed! You put considerable effort into creating a functional schedule for this workout program and it is worth standing up for!

When an issue does arise, the first thing you should do is be honest about the priority of the disruption to the schedule. It could be absolutely legitimate and is a responsibility that is yours alone, and for that you must put the same effort into altering your schedule. It is incredibly easy to shrug off a workout day as a knee-jerk response, but that becomes dangerously easier the more it occurs. See every moment as an individual event and give it the focus that deserves. You know your commitments that existed prior to beginning this journey, and those do not fade away or become less of a priority because you took on this program. You know from how life works that commitments are going to arise that were not planned for whatsoever. Luckily, you have already given yourself the solutions.

You did this and it is not a small thing. Just as you shouldn't compare your workouts to anyone else's, forming, keeping, and adjusting the type of schedule you have is an accomplishment that cannot be taken from you. You didn't back down from that challenge. Instead, you made lasting changes that incorporated the routines instead of just adding them. You already know how to best do this to suit your lifestyle! You have already created the guideline with your original method of scheduling!

It sounds simplistic, but it really is the best approach. Scheduling conflicts *will occur* because life didn't stop, but your ability to be flexible in the face of that didn't stop either. Seeing your workouts as important and deserving priority will give a more balanced perspective. Most of the time, when schedule conflicts derails a program, it is because almost everything that came up immediately became more important than your commitment to working out. By adjusting that mindset, you will find yourself more prepared and rarely caught off guard.

Overexertion

Another common and quite broad subject that may occur during this journey is overexerting yourself. This can take many forms, but it usually leads to injury and eventually becomes a complete disruption to the process. You will certainly be asked to push yourself during the routines, but the absolute rule is that there is a massive difference between the burn of a good muscle stretch and a painful movement. The key, as discussed before, is moderation.

There may be times when you feel that you are not being challenged and you need to add onto the routine. This is a very normal occurrence, and there is a guide in each section of the program to adding sets or reps to your session. Not only is this common, but it is recommended if you are not getting enough of that routine. You should feel challenged and pushed throughout the program, but your safety and health should be foremost in your mind.

This is where your time away from the workout environment is still linked directly to the program. Everything from your sleep patterns, sleeping positions, posture, times spent looking at screens, to the endless other person reasons will have a correlation to your growth and success. You wouldn't be able to conduct the workout and then begin to drink heavily and slouch in front of a TV for six hours the moment you leave. That is an extreme example, but the premise remains true—the way you act in your life is an extension of the way you work out, and vice versa. The two are not possible to separate and they really shouldn't be separate.

There is a danger in creating too much of a barrier between your workout routine and the remainder of your life. A jarring transition will occur every time you go from life to working out and then back. The difference would be so drastic that you run a high risk of developing anxiety about exercising or of having problems applying the lessons of the program to anything outside the workout area.

There are two ways to help avoid injury and still challenge yourself the correct way: resting correctly, and knowing how to increase impact during a session.

Your schedule has Rest Days to ensure your body recovers, but just as important is your resting time between sets. You have been taking breaks to breathe or hydrate in between your sets, but are you doing it the right way? Depending on the type of exercise, you'll need to rest differently as well:

- After running you should hydrate and rest for between 2-4 minutes. Avoid resting too long before the next exercise.

- To help build endurance you lower the rest periods to 30-60 seconds. Do this sparingly as it is an easy way to cause injury or cramping.

- Maintain focus during your rests. Control your breathing and avoid staying stationary.

Once you have ensured your rest periods are being used correctly, the next step is learning the proper method to add to an exercise to increase the impact and challenge. One way to increase a set's impact is to include a *Power Set*.

A Power Set has no specific amount of reps, instead it finishes when you have reached a limit. For example, if you are doing push-ups and following a 5-rep, 3-set session, you will begin a fourth set and continue doing push-ups until you cannot maintain correct form. As always, notice the difference between reaching that limit and pushing yourself past a healthy point! You can sporadically add Power Sets to your routine, but avoid overexerting and causing an avoidable injury.

Then there is the option of creating a *Superset*. A Superset is made when a series of workouts focus on the same muscle area and has similar forms. Remove the rest periods in between the sets and instead make a fluid transition from one exercise into the other. Doing this creates more isolation on a muscle group and causes more fatigue, leading to hypertrophy and the opportunity to build those specific muscles.

If this is your desired option, you must take into account that your rest period following a Superset is a particular event. Do not make a sudden stop; instead, ease into the rest by staying in motion. Control your breathing and avoid sitting or remaining motionless.

A third option if you are looking to add to a set is a Cluster Set. This is only to be used if the entire workout, all reps and sets within, are minimally challenging. Once you complete the sets in an exercise, take a full rest period and then repeat the entire exercise again. This doesn't give the intensity or impact of the previous options, but increases the strength training within the workout.

A Cluster Set is a rare choice and needs to be observed carefully. Note in your journal how you feel after the first time you complete a Cluster Set directly after, later that day, and the next day. You must ensure that there is no negative fallout. Your health is the ultimate goal!

Boredom

Six months is not a small length of time, and your commitment to it is commendable! That being said, when dealing with that extent of time, you encounter the possibility that boredom occurs. Do not be disheartened or stray from that place of no judgement. That perspective got you to this point, and it is going to keep you going! A basic but effective key to remember right away is to put away the massive, overhanging stigma related to boredom. Especially in regards to a workout routine, the idea of boredom can be catastrophic. It has most likely signalled the beginning of the end in some of the past attempts you had, so it carries that weight forward until the proper actions are taken.

There is a power in recognizing what something truly is and pulling away the curtain. Most fears are as scary as they are because of lingering, attached memories and feelings. This is no different and should be approached the same. The more you learn about a subject, the more power you have over it in regards to changing a perspective. Boredom is in the same class as laziness and tends to function in the same way as well. The fear of laziness tends to bring on anxiety as well. That usually leads to overthinking the problem which, over time, will cause the image and impact of that fear to magnify exponentially! Before you know it, time has passed and you actually fell into the trap of laziness while still being afraid of being lazy.

When you fear boredom and your thought process becomes focused on making sure you aren't bored, you create a fastpaced, uninterested theme. The retention of interest wanes quicker and the desire to do something becomes a lack of action in anything. The cycle of boredom restarts and the rut continues. Instead, confront it directly. You will still feel that initial fear at first, but the more times you recognize the pattern and identify the trigger, you have already removed much of the power. By taking action on that trigger, you take further steps. With a positive spin now, before you know it you have conquered that moment, moved past it, and are ready to continue in growth.

This program is designed to not only provide physical growth, but also mental stimulation. Every month provides a wide variety of workouts that also vary from one session to the next. Despite this consistent variety, there is a good chance that you will feel a sense of monotony at some point in this process. Do not try and simply ignore those feelings of boredom; that solves nothing and will allow it to fester until it becomes a complete lack of motivation. Instead, confront it directly as you have done with road bumps and pitfalls along the way!

Don't be afraid to note when you get a wave of that boredom. Instead, see if you can pinpoint what brought it on. Perhaps a certain exercise tends to drag for you and takes you out of the moment, or you notice that certain days tend to drain you and create a sense of exhaustion that carries into the next workout or, worse, carries into your personal life.

Another option you shouldn't shy away from is changing up your atmosphere. Maybe adding music on certain days or only for specific workouts would add a motivational theme to a difficult day? These are the types of questions you must explore as you combat monotony. Honesty and accountability with yourself has been foundational in getting you here, so trust that and trust yourself to make positive changes when these unmotivated moments hit.

As you make your way through the program and you encounter any of these problem areas we discussed, you should feel empowered to handle them! Recognizing patterns and confronting them will result in huge positive changes! You are worth that effort and you have given yourself so much strength that will carry forward long after you complete the workouts. Celebrate that and yourself!

The basics of troubleshooting really comes down to understanding the possible problems. Knowledge is power, and the goal is to empower yourself with as much preparedness as possible! While a large amount of information was covered there is a beauty in simplicity—you have all the ability! In breaking down each problem rather than letting it overwhelm you, the solution presents itself and also gives you a guide for future problems.

Even if you find an issue arises that wasn't specifically covered, you are sure to navigate those unsure times by simply utilizing the tools you've already learned! Be honest with yourself about the problem, review your notes or think of a time when you encountered a similar issue, and finally find a way to positively repair the situation.

Chapter Summary

- Are you approaching this chapter from a place free of judgement?

- What distractions have you encountered so far?

- Have you taken steps to alter those moments?

- If there are still areas of distraction, make a list that you can refer to as a chapter progresses Which problem area relates to you the most?

- Scheduling?

- Overexertion?

- Boredom?

- Are you giving the proper focus to your Rest Days? Are you giving your rest periods between sets the same focus?

- Have you familiarized yourself with the three options for adding intensity and impact to a workout?

- Power Set?

- Superset?

- Cluster Set?

- Have you been feeling bored or have a sense of monotony?

- If so, have you taken steps to recognize what brings it on or is causing it to linger?

CHAPTER EIGHT

THE COOL DOWN

Throughout this entire experience, there has been one absolute that you should walk away with: positivity!

The amount of effort and time put into this program is an exemplary accomplishment and you deserved those positive changes! I know there have been times when even the most meticulously planned schedule hits speed bumps and gets disrupted, and yet you pushed forward!

You've been honest with yourself since the first day and you deserve the same honesty in return: a great deal was asked of you. That is the simple truth. Changes are never easy and you did it while applying important life lessons along the way. At no point should this be a small event in your mind; it is worth joy and celebration!

You were asked to alter your diet, adjust your sleep patterns, push yourself physically, fine-tune yourself mentally, and all the while maintaining a space free from judgement. Perhaps while you were in the midst of the journey, you didn't see the list of goals you were checking off; but having them laid out in front of you now should elicit pride!

Actually, take a moment, as we have many times before, and think of those moments that you weren't sure you were going to continue. I know there were days where time dragged, where an exercise felt like a bored motion, and still you persevered! By going back in your mind, you will get a better view of all the times you overcame! Little by little, you built yourself up and trusted the tools we gave you to find success.

Now it is up to you! There is no reason why you should stop now! You've created a new, healthy, positive lifestyle and that is worth hanging on to. You've used ingenuity to customize in many areas that were presented to you, and there is no doubt you will maintain from here on out!

Create your own routines and process to make sure this change is one of permanence. You have all the capability in the world, and you have proved it time and time again! You've gotten very good at taking the time to review your Journal and recognize patterns, so now you can keep putting that into action!

Whatever methods you determine will work best to help you keep this change in your life, move forward in it with the same lack of judgement you used and have grown within. Your honesty served you well and gave you a better understanding of what works and does not work in different aspects of your life. These accomplishments are no small feat and will continue to prove invaluable!

Again, congratulations, because you have truly bettered yourself! Let's take this last time to celebrate together and recognize your milestone! You are strong and you are better than when you started, and that is certainly something!

Final Words

This has been quite the journey!

During this process, a bond developed that created the trust between the reader and the program! This is not by accident, and your success was the goal of every action you took!

If this was the sort of journey you would want to explore more of, then there is a community ready to help!

The Daily Jay group on Facebook is a group of experts in their fields working together to provide the most immersive, life-impacting workouts that are possible! With a wide range of subjects at the ready and tips for a continued betterment of your life, this is a safe space for discovering more in this new world of positive health.

Our page and community are not only focused on Calisthenics, but anything fitness and health related! A wide range of subjects and people to help with all your questions, or if you simply want to learn!

If this was an experience that bettered you, which I am sure it did considering all the effort you put forth, then please stop by and see if we can help you!

ACKNOWLEDGMENTS

Image Credit: Shutterstock.com

THE END

Made in the USA
Monee, IL
07 January 2025

75937064R10275